EDGAR: THE INVESTOR'S GUIDE TO MAKING BETTER INVESTMENTS

Gene Walden

McGraw-Hill

New York   Chicago   San Francisco   Lisbon
London   Madrid   Mexico City   Milan
New Delhi   San Juan   Seoul   Singapore
Sydney   Toronto

The *McGraw·Hill* Companies

1 2 3 4 5 6 7 8 9 0   AGM/AGM   0 9 8 7 6 5 4 3

ISBN 0-07-141038-4

This publication is designed to provide accurate and authoritative information in regard to the subject matter covered. It is sold with the understanding that neither the author nor the publisher is engaged in rendering legal, accounting, or other professional service. If legal advice or other expert assistance is required, the services of a competent professional person should be sought.

> *—From a Declaration of Principles jointly adopted by a Committee of the American Bar Association and a Committee of Publishers.*

McGraw-Hill books are available at special quantity discounts to use as premiums and sales promotions, or for use in corporate training programs. For more information, please write to the Director of Special Sales, McGraw-Hill, Two Penn Plaza, New York, NY 10121-2298. Or contact your local bookstore.

 This book is printed on recycled, acid-free paper containing a minimum of 50% recycled, de-inked fiber.

Library of Congress Cataloging-in-Publication Data

Walden, Gene.
    Edgar: the investor's guide to making better investments / by
Gene Walden.
        p.   cm.
    ISBN 0-07-141038-4 (hard cover : alk. paper)
    1. EDGAR (information retrieval system).   2. Information storage and
retrieval systems-Securities. I. Title.
  HG4010.W258   2003
  332.63'2042—dc21   2002152450
                                             CIP

Dedication

To the Gingerys

Contents

Acknowledgments

I'd like to thank several people who were major contributors to the success of this book, including my editor, Stephen Isaacs, and our copy editor, Sally Glover, as well as Kathy Welton, who helped develop the concept for the book. I also wish to thank my literary agent, Carol Mann.

Introduction

In many ways, buying stocks is really no different than buying a car, a computer, or a cup of cappuccino—the more you know about the product, the better your chances of making the right decision.

Fortunately for investors, reams of detailed information are available at your fingertips, absolutely *free*, on each of the thousands of stocks that trade on American exchanges. You can probe the inner chasms of each company's operations, unlock the hidden tunnels in its corporate underbelly, and pore over balance sheets, inventories, management compensation, pending suits, offshore operations, and hundreds of other details of the company's business.

And you can do it all at one Web site provided for free by the United States Securities and Exchange Commission (SEC). The site, called EDGAR (Electronic Data Gathering Analysis and Retrieval) can be reached through *www.sec.gov*.

If you're an investor, an analyst, or just a student of the market, EDGAR should become one of your very closest friends.

In fact, professional stock analysts from the top brokerage firms on Wall Street use EDGAR constantly to analyze companies and generate research reports. It's not unusual to see entire pages of information in analysts' reports that were lifted word-for-word from the company's own 10-K reports. With EDGAR, you have free and open access to that very same database, giving you the ability to research and analyze stocks the way the professionals on Wall Street do.

Understanding EDGAR and the forms and financial numbers available at your fingertips will help you sift the wheat from the shaft and make informed decisions about the stocks you may be interested in buying. It will also help you cut through the overhyped spin that many companies and their public relations people try to hoist on unsuspecting investors. PR flacks with a velvet touch can make almost any company sound promising—as the Internet bubble demonstrated. With EDGAR, you can find the facts behind the fluff.

For instance, I recently heard a spokesperson for an online broker mention that his company was "one of the most profitable firms in the industry." I found the comment a little suspicious, considering the market was in a slump and the company was in the process of being acquired. So I checked some facts on the company at EDGAR. Indeed the company showed a nice profit for the most recent period, but the facts behind the numbers told a different story. The company's net revenue had dropped 44 percent from 2000 to 2001 and another 23 percent in the first quarter of 2002. Average daily trades for the brokerage had dropped 30 percent from May of 2001 to May of 2002. Net income dropped 35 percent from 2000 to 2001. And while the company did show a gain in net income growth, it came as a result of a 54-percent cut in marketing and advertising expenditures—a $19 million cut in all, which dwarfed the company's total net income for the period, of just $7.1 million. The brokerage's new funded accounts had also dropped about 40 percent year to year. Yes, the company showed a profit, but the business was clearly heading south.

Once you know EDGAR, the well-chosen words of corporate spin-masters will no longer taint your investment decision-making process. You'll make your decisions based on facts.

That's not to say, however, that you won't ever be fooled. Virtually the entire brokerage industry overestimated the potential of the tech stock market. And scores of analysts and money managers failed to recognize a trace of trouble in Enron's corporate books before the energy giant collapsed into bankruptcy. But then, Enron simply lied—with its auditor's endorsement—so its early numbers would not have revealed impending doom. But there were other signs that might have raised the suspicions of shrewd investors long before Enron's final demise.

In this book, you'll learn why you might have dumped Enron's stock (or declined to invest at all) long before the majority of shareholders discovered that the company was a house of cards in mid collapse. You'll learn how to assess a company's operations and its financial position from top to bottom.

The wave of corporate scandals makes it all the more essential that you do your best to scrutinize a stock thoroughly before you invest. Enron, World-Com, Tyco, Global Crossing, and Xerox are among the many recent examples of corporations that have been accused of intentionally distorting their financial statements to inflate the stock prices and enrich the top executives. That's why it's important to look beyond the balance sheet to see the real essence of a company. The vast library of information at EDGAR on every publicly traded company in America is your window into the operations, management, growth prospects, and financial performance of those companies.

But first you must learn to navigate the maze of nonrecurring charges, depreciation, amortization, and inventory write-downs—past the financial false leads, wrong turns, and dead ends in the footnotes and line items of a company's reports—to get to the essence of its operations and prospects for growth.

This book will show you the way.

Where the Truth Can Be Found

1

THE ROLE OF THE SECURITIES AND EXCHANGE COMMISSION

AMONG ITS VAST RANGE OF DUTIES, the U.S. Securities and Exchange Commission (SEC) is concerned foremost with enforcing the concept that all investors, whether large institutions or private individuals, should have equal access to certain basic facts about an investment prior to buying it. The SEC's stated mission is to protect investors and maintain the integrity of the securities market.

That's a tall order. In fact, the SEC has come under a growing chorus of criticism for failing to monitor corporations and protect investors. Making the case are the hundreds of thousands of investors who lost large chunks of their life savings thanks to scandals at Enron, WorldCom, Global Crossing, Tyco, Arthur Anderson, ImClone, Adelphia, Halliburton, Dynergy, Xerox, and others. Shareholders and employees of those companies, as well as members of Congress who have reviewed the scandals, contend that the SEC has not been vigilant enough in policing America's publicly traded corporations. They feel that the SEC should have done more to fulfill its obligation to protect investors from the hidden debts, falsely-inflated earnings figures, and unethical accounting gimmicks that the scandal-ridden companies used to pump up their stock prices and line their own pockets. Clearly, if the SEC had done a better job, some of those scandals could have been avoided, and investors would have avoided billions of dollars in losses.

That's not to say, however, that the SEC has an easy row to hoe. Its mission to protect investors and the integrity of the market requires a complex set of regulations and a vast bureaucracy of about 3000 employees to administer and enforce the regulations. The SEC is comprised of five commissioners appointed by the President of the United States and approved by the Senate, four divisions and 18 offices. Based in Washington, D.C., it has 11 regional and district offices throughout the country.

Promoting full disclosure of information is one of the SEC's most important roles. To achieve this, the SEC requires public companies to disclose detailed financial and other information to the public, which provides a common pool of knowledge for all investors to use to judge whether a company's securities are a good investment.

The SEC also oversees other key participants in the securities world, including stock exchanges, broker-dealers, investment advisors, mutual funds, and public utility holding companies. Once again, the key role for the SEC is promoting disclosure of important information, enforcing the securities laws, and protecting investors involved with these organizations and individuals.

As we learned in the recent corporate scandals, sometimes that includes conducting civil and criminal investigations and filing charges. Each year, the SEC brings 400 to 500 civil enforcement actions against individuals and companies that break the securities laws. Typical infractions include insider trading, accounting fraud, and providing false or misleading information about securities and the companies that issue them.

The SEC also provides the tools for investors to make informed decisions. Through its EDGAR online database, it provides access to all disclosure documents that public companies are required to file.

CREATION OF THE SEC

The first chairman of the SEC was Joseph Kennedy, father of President John F. Kennedy. Kennedy was appointed to the position by President Franklin D. Roosevelt shortly after the creation of the SEC in 1934. The agency and its powers have grown steadily ever since.

It's no coincidence that the SEC was created shortly after the Great Crash of 1929. Before the crash, there was little support for federal regulation of the securities markets because of the market's strong performance. But the investing public learned a valuable lesson when the market crashed. During the 1920s, approximately 20 million large and small shareholders invested in the stock market in hopes of making their fortune. But more fortunes were lost than made. Of the estimated $50 billion in new securities issued during this period, half became worthless.

When the stock market crashed in October of 1929, countless investors lost their fortunes, and many banks, which were also heavily invested in the markets, were driven to the brink of bankruptcy. An ensuing "run" on the banking system by panicked customers pushed many banks over the brink and out of business. The Crash and the Great Depression helped erode the public's confidence. Suddenly, there was a strong consensus that for the economy to recover, the public's faith in the capital markets needed to be restored. Congress held hearings to identify the problems and search for solutions.

Congress used the hearings to establish the Securities Act of 1933 and the Securities Exchange Act of 1934. These laws were designed to restore investor confidence in the capital markets by providing more structure and government oversight. The laws focused on the following two key objectives:

- Companies offering securities for investment dollars must tell the public the truth about their businesses, the securities they are selling, and the risks involved in investing.

- People who sell and trade securities—brokers, dealers, and exchanges—must treat investors fairly and honestly, putting investors' interests first.

The SEC was set up to enforce the newly passed securities laws, to promote stability in the markets, and to protect investors.

SECURITIES INDUSTRY LAWS

The SEC is charged with promoting and enforcing the laws set up by Congress to regulate the securities industry. The Securities Act of 1933—often referred to as the "truth in securities" law—has the following two basic objectives:

- to require that investors receive financial and other significant information concerning securities being offered for public sale

- to prohibit deceit, misrepresentations, and other fraud in the sale of securities. (The full text of this act is available at: *http://www.law.uc.edu/ CCL/sldtoc.html.*)

Because companies are required to disclose important financial information through the registration of securities, investors are able to make informed judgments about whether to purchase a company's securities. While the SEC requires that the information provided be accurate, it does not guarantee it. Investors who purchase securities and suffer losses have important recovery rights if they can prove that there was incomplete or inaccurate disclosure of important information—unless, of course, the company goes out of business.

THE REGISTRATION PROCESS

Publicly traded companies must file a series of forms that provide essential facts while minimizing the burden and expense of complying with the law. In general, registration forms call for the following:

- a description of the company's properties and business
- a description of the security to be offered for sale
- information about the management of the company
- financial statements certified by independent accountants

Registration statements and prospectuses become public shortly after filing with the SEC. If filed by U.S. domestic companies, the statements are available on the EDGAR database accessible at *www.sec.gov*. Registration statements are subject to examination for compliance with disclosure requirements.

There are a few exceptions to the registration requirement:

- private offerings to a limited number of persons or institutions
- offerings of limited size
- intrastate offerings
- securities of municipal, state, and federal governments

The SEC allows exceptions for small offerings in order to promote capital formation by lowering the cost of offering securities to the public.

SECURITIES EXCHANGE ACT OF 1934

The SEC was created by Congress in 1934 through the Securities Exchange Act. The act gives the SEC broad authority over all aspects of the securities industry, including the power to register, regulate, and oversee brokerage firms, transfer agents, clearing agencies, and securities self regulatory organizations (SROs). The various stock exchanges, such as the New York Stock Exchange and the American Stock Exchange are SROs, as is the National Association of Securities Dealers, which operates the NASDAQ system.

The Securities Exchange Act also identifies and prohibits certain types of conduct in the markets and provides the SEC with disciplinary powers over regulated entities and persons associated with them.

The act also gives the SEC the power to require periodic reporting of information by companies with publicly traded securities. Here are some of the leading areas of authority for the SEC:

- **Corporate Reporting.** Companies with more than $10 million in assets whose securities are held by more than 500 owners must file annual and other periodic reports. These reports are available to the public through the SEC's EDGAR database.

- **Proxy Solicitations.** The Securities Exchange Act also governs the disclosure in materials used to solicit shareholders' votes in annual or special meetings held for the election of directors and the approval of other corporate action. This information, contained in proxy materials, must be filed with the SEC in advance of any solicitation to ensure compliance with the disclosure rules. Solicitations must disclose all important facts concerning the issues on which shareholders are asked to vote.

- **Tender Offers.** The Securities Exchange Act requires disclosure of important information by anyone seeking to acquire more than five percent of a company's securities by direct purchase or tender offer. Such offers are often extended in an effort to gain control of the company. This full-disclosure requirement allows shareholders to make informed decisions on these important corporate events.

- **Insider Trading.** The securities laws broadly prohibit fraudulent activities of any kind in connection with the offer, purchase, or sale of securities. These provisions are the basis for many types of disciplinary actions, including actions against fraudulent insider trading. Insider trading is illegal when a person trades a security while in possession of material, nonpublic information in violation of a duty to withhold the information or refrain from trading.

- **Registration of Exchanges, Associations, and Others.** The act requires a variety of market participants to register with the SEC, including exchanges, brokers and dealers, transfer agents, and clearing agencies. Registration for these organizations involves filing disclosure documents that are updated on a regular basis. (The full text of this act can be read online at: *http://www.law.uc. edu/CCL/sldtoc.html.)*

REGULATING THE INVESTMENT INDUSTRY

In addition to the Securities Acts of 1933 and 1934, Congress passed four other related acts to govern the investment industry, including the following:

- **Trust Indenture Act of 1939.** This act applies to debt securities such as bonds, debentures, and notes that are offered for public sale. Even though such securities may be registered under the Securities Act, they may not be offered for sale to the public unless a formal agreement between the issuer of bonds and the bondholder, known as the trust indenture, conforms to the standards of this act. The full text of this act can be read online at: *http://www4.law.cornell.edu/uscode/15/ch2A.html.* (The SEC does not control or maintain this site.)

- **Investment Company Act of 1940.** This act regulates the organization of companies, including mutual funds, that engage primarily in investing, reinvesting, and trading in securities, and whose own securities are offered to the investing public. The regulation is designed to minimize conflicts of interest that arise in these complex operations. The act requires these companies to disclose their financial conditions and investment policies to investors when stock is initially sold, and subsequently, on a regular basis. The focus of this act is on disclosure to the investing public of information about the fund and its investment objectives, as well as on investment company structure and operations. It is important to remember that the act does not permit the SEC to supervise the investment decisions or activities of these companies directly or judge the merits of their investments. The text of the Investment Company Act of 1940 is part of the Internet Web page located at: *http://www.law.uc.edu/CCL/sldtoc.html.* (The SEC does not control or maintain this site.)

- **Investment Advisers Act of 1940.** This law regulates investment advisers. With certain exceptions, this act requires that firms or sole practitioners compensated for advising others about securities investments must register with the SEC and conform to regulations designed to protect investors. Since the act was amended in 1996, generally only advisers who have at least $25 million of assets under management or advise a registered investment company must register with the SEC. (The text of this act can be read at: *www.law.cornell.edu/uscode/15/ch2D.html.)*

- **Public Utility Holding Company Act of 1935.** Interstate holding companies engaged, through subsidiaries, in the electric utility business or in the retail distribution of natural or manufactured gas are subject to regulation under this act. These companies, unless specifically exempted, are required to submit reports providing detailed information concerning the organization, financial structure, and operations of the holding company and its subsidiaries. Holding companies are subject to SEC regulations on matters such as the structures of their utility systems, transactions among companies that are part of the holding company utility system, acquisitions, business combinations, the issue and sale of securities, and financing transactions. (The full text of this act is available online at: *http://www.law.cornell.edu/uscode/15/ch2C.html.*)

THE SEC RULE-MAKING PROCESS

The series of acts passed by Congress to regulate the investment industry marked just the beginning of the regulation process. The acts served as a framework of principles and objectives to follow in overseeing the investment industry, but the SEC continues to fine-tune and augment the original acts with new rules to keep up with changes and advances in the investment industry. Its rule-making process typically involves three key steps:

- **Concept Release:** The rule-making process usually begins with a rule proposal, but sometimes an issue is so unique or complex that the SEC asks for public feedback. A concept release is issued describing the area of interest and the SEC's concerns, identifying different approaches to address the problem. That is followed by a series of questions that seek the views of the public on the issue. The public's feedback is supposed to be considered by the SEC in deciding which approach, if any, is appropriate.

- **Rule Proposal:** The staff of the SEC drafts a detailed formal rule proposal and presents it to the full SEC. Unlike a concept release, a rule proposal is specific in its objectives and methods for achieving its goals. Following approval by the SEC, the rule proposal is presented to the public for a specified period of time, typically between 30 and 60 days, for review and comment. Again, the SEC considers the public's input in drafting the final rule.

- **Rule Adoption:** Finally, the staff of the SEC presents a final rule to the full SEC for its consideration. If adopted, the measure becomes part of the official rules that govern the securities industry. If the rule is a major rule, it may be subject to congressional review and veto prior to becoming effective.

COMMON VIOLATIONS

One of the SEC's most important responsibilities is to enforce the laws and investigate individuals and companies suspected of violating securities regulations. The most common violations include the following:

- insider trading—buying or selling a security in breach of a relationship of trust and confidence while in possession of material, nonpublic information about the security

- misrepresentation or omission of important information about securities

- manipulating the market prices of securities

- stealing customers' funds or securities

- violating broker-dealers' responsibility to treat customers fairly

- selling securities without proper registration

Under the securities laws, the SEC can bring enforcement actions either in the federal courts or internally before an administrative law judge. The factors considered by the SEC in deciding how to proceed include: the seriousness of the wrongdoing, the technical nature of the matter, tactical considerations, and the type of sanction or relief to obtain. For example, the SEC may bar someone from the brokerage industry in an administrative proceeding, but an order barring someone from acting as a corporate officer or director must be obtained in federal court. Often, when the misconduct warrants it, the SEC will bring both proceedings.

The SEC can proceed on an enforcement matter in one of two ways:

- **Civil Action.** In civil matters, the SEC files a complaint with a U.S. district court that describes the misconduct, identifies the laws and rules violated, and identifies the sanction or remedial action that is sought. Typically, the SEC asks the court to issue an order, called an injunction, that prohibits the actions or practices that violate the law or SEC rules. A court's order can also require various actions, such as audits, accounting for frauds, or special supervisory arrangements. In addition, the SEC often seeks civil monetary penalties and the return of illegal profits, known as disgorgement. The courts may also bar or suspend an individual from serving as a corporate officer or director. A person who violates the court's order may be found in contempt and be subject to additional fines or imprisonment.

- **Administrative Action.** In an administrative action, the SEC can seek a variety of sanctions. Administrative proceedings differ from civil court actions in that they are heard by an administrative law judge, who is independent of the SEC. The judge presides over a hearing and considers the evidence presented by the SEC staff, as well as any evidence submitted by the subject of the proceeding. Following the hearing, the judge issues an initial decision in which he or she makes findings of fact and reaches legal conclusions. The initial decision also contains a recommended sanction. Both the SEC staff and the defendant may appeal all or any portion of the initial decision to the SEC. The SEC may affirm the decision of the judge, reverse the decision, or remand it for additional hearings. Administrative sanctions include cease and desist orders, suspension or revocation of broker-dealer and investment advisor registrations, censures, bars from association with the securities industry, payment of civil monetary penalties, and return of illegal profits.

SEC STRUCTURE

The SEC is a large organization with many divisions. It is directed by five commissioners. Their terms last five years and are staggered so that one commissioner's term ends on June 5 of each year. To ensure that the SEC remains nonpartisan, no more than three commissioners may belong to the same political party. The President also designates one of the commissioners as chairman, the SEC's top executive.

The commissioners meet to discuss and resolve a variety of issues the staff brings to their attention. At these meetings, the commissioners do the following:

- interpret federal securities laws
- amend existing rules; propose new rules to address changing market conditions
- enforce rules and laws

These meetings are open to the public and the news media unless the discussion pertains to confidential subjects, such as whether to begin an enforcement investigation.

The SEC divides its operations into four divisions and 18 offices, discussed in the following section.

DIVISION OF CORPORATION FINANCE

The Division of Corporation Finance oversees corporate disclosure of important information to the investing public. Corporations are required to comply with regulations pertaining to disclosure that must be made when stock is initially sold, and then on a continuing and periodic basis. The division's staff routinely reviews the disclosure documents filed by companies. The staff also provides companies with assistance interpreting the commission's rules and recommends to the SEC new rules for adoption.

The division of Corporation Finance reviews documents that publicly held companies are required to file with the SEC, including:

- registration statements for newly offered securities
- annual and quarterly filings (Forms 10-K and 10-Q)
- proxy materials sent to shareholders before an annual meeting
- annual reports to shareholders
- documents concerning tender offers. (A tender offer is an offer to buy a large number of shares of a corporation, usually at a premium above the current market price.)
- filings related to mergers and acquisitions

These documents disclose information about the companies' financial conditions and business practices to help investors make informed investment decisions. Through the division's review process, the staff checks to see if publicly held companies are meeting their disclosure requirements and seeks to improve the quality of the disclosure. To meet the SEC's requirements for disclosure, a company issuing securities or whose securities are publicly traded must make available all information, whether it is positive or negative, that might be relevant to an investor's decision to buy, sell, or hold the security.

The division also provides administrative interpretations of the Securities Act of 1933, the Securities Exchange Act of 1934, and the Trust Indenture Act of 1939, and recommends regulations to implement these statutes. Working closely with the Office of the Chief Accountant, the division monitors the activities of the accounting profession, particularly the Financial Accounting Standards Board (FASB), that result in the formulation of generally accepted accounting principles (GAAPs).

The division's staff also provides guidance and counseling to registrants, prospective registrants, and the public to help them comply with the law. The division uses no-action letters to issue guidance in a more formal manner. A company seeks a no-action letter from the staff of the SEC when it plans to enter uncharted legal territory in the securities industry. For example, if a company wants to try a new marketing or financial technique, it can ask the staff to write a letter indicating whether it would or would not recommend that the SEC take action against the company for engaging in its new practice.

DIVISION OF MARKET REGULATION

The chief objective of the Division of Market Regulation is to establish and maintain standards for fair, orderly, and efficient markets. It does this primarily by regulating the major securities' market participants: broker-dealer firms; self-regulatory organizations (SROs), which include the stock exchanges and the National Association of Securities Dealers (NASD), Municipal Securities Rulemaking Board (MSRB), and clearing agencies that help facilitate trade settlement; transfer agents (parties that maintain records of stock and bond owners); and securities information processors.

The division also oversees the Securities Investor Protection Corporation (SIPC), which is a private, nonprofit corporation that insures the securities and cash in the customer accounts of member brokerage firms against the failure of those firms. (SIPC insurance does not cover investor losses arising from market declines or fraud.) The division's responsibilities include the following:

- executing the SEC's financial integrity program for broker-dealers
- reviewing and approving proposed new rules and proposed changes to existing rules filed by the self-regulatory organizations such as the stock exchanges
- establishing rules and issuing interpretations on matters affecting the operation of the securities markets
- surveillance of the markets

DIVISION OF INVESTMENT MANAGEMENT

The Division of Investment Management oversees and regulates the $15 trillion investment management industry and administers the securities laws affecting investment companies (including mutual funds) and investment advisers. In applying the federal securities laws to this industry, the division works to improve disclosure and minimize risk for investors without imposing undue costs on regulated entities. The division:

- interprets laws and regulations for the public and SEC inspection and enforcement staff
- responds to no-action requests and requests for exemptive relief
- reviews investment company and investment adviser filings
- reviews enforcement matters involving investment companies and advisers
- develops new rules and amendments to adapt regulatory structures to new circumstances

The division also exercises oversight of registered and exempt utility holding companies under the Public Utility Holding Company Act of 1935. In this area, the division:

- reviews proposals and applications and proposes new rules and amendments under the act
- examines annual and periodic reports of holding companies and their subsidiaries
- participates in audits of these companies

DIVISION OF ENFORCEMENT

The Division of Enforcement investigates possible violations of securities laws, recommends SEC action when appropriate, either in a federal court or before an administrative law judge, and negotiates settlements on behalf of the SEC. While the SEC has civil enforcement authority only, it works closely with various criminal law enforcement agencies throughout the country to bring criminal cases when the misconduct warrants more severe action.

The division obtains evidence of possible violations of the securities laws from many sources, including its own surveillance activities, other divisions of the SEC, the self-regulatory organizations and other securities industry sources, press reports, and investor complaints.

All SEC investigations are conducted privately. Facts are developed to the fullest extent possible through informal inquiry, interviewing witnesses, examining brokerage records, reviewing trading data, and other methods. Once the SEC issues a formal order of investigation, the division's staff may compel witnesses by subpoena to testify and produce books, records, and other relevant documents. Following an investigation, SEC staff present their findings to the SEC for its review. The SEC can authorize the staff to file a case in federal court or bring an administrative action. Individuals and companies charged sometimes choose to settle the case, while others contest the charges.

SEC OFFICES

The SEC is divided into several special offices. Here are some of the key offices:

- **Office of Administrative Law Judges.** Administrative law judges conduct hearings and rule on allegations of securities law violations brought by the SEC staff. After cases are referred to them by the SEC, the judges conduct hearings in a manner similar to nonjury trials in the federal district courts. Among other actions, administrative law judges issue subpoenas, rule on motions, and rule on the admissibility of evidence. At the conclusion of hearings, the parties involved submit proposed findings of fact and conclusions of law. The administrative law judges prepare and file initial decisions including factual findings and legal conclusions. Parties may appeal decisions to the commission, which can affirm or deny the administrative law judges' rulings or remand the case back for additional hearings.

- **Office of Administrative and Personnel Management.** The office develops, implements, and evaluates the SEC's programs for human resource and personnel management. Its responsibilities include position management and pay administration; recruitment, placement, and staffing; payroll; performance management and awards; employee training and career development; employee relations; personnel management evaluation; employee benefits and counseling; the processing and maintenance of employee records; and ethics and financial disclosure. The office develops and executes programs for office services, such as telecommunications; procurement and contracting; property management; contract and lease administration; space acquisition and management; management of official vehicles; safety programs; emergency preparedness programs; physical security; mail receipt and distribution; and publications, printing, and desktop publishing.

- **Office of the Chief Accountant.** The chief accountant is the principal adviser to the SEC on accounting and auditing matters. An audit is an examination of a company's financial books and records done to ensure that it keeps fair, consistent documents in accordance with SEC regulations. The office works closely with domestic and international private-sector accounting and auditing-standards-setting bodies, such as the Financial Accounting Standards Board and the International Accounting Standards Committee. It also consults with registrants, auditors, and other SEC staff regarding the application of accounting standards and financial disclosure requirements, and assists in addressing problems that may warrant enforcement actions.

- **Office of Compliance Inspections and Examinations.** This office administers the SEC's nationwide examination and inspection program for registered self-regulatory organizations, broker-dealers, transfer agents, clearing agencies, investment companies, and investment advisers. The office conducts inspections to foster compliance with the securities laws, to detect violations of the law, and to keep the SEC informed of developments in the regulated community. Among the more important goals of the examination program is the quick and informal correction of compliance problems. When the office finds deficiencies, it issues a "deficiency letter" identifying the problems that need to be rectified and monitors the situation until it is resolved. Violations that appear too serious for informal correction are referred to the Division of Enforcement.

- **Office of Filings and Information Services.** This office receives and initially handles all public documents filed with the SEC. The office is also responsible for custody and control of the SEC's official records, development and implementation of the records management program, and authentication of all documents produced for administrative or judicial proceedings. Through the office's Public Reference Branch, the public may obtain a wide range of information from quarterly and annual reports, registration statements, proxy materials, and other reports submitted by SEC filers. All public documents are available for inspection in the Public Reference Room in Washington, D.C. Copies of documents may be obtained for a fee. Most corporate disclosure documents filed since May of 1996 are available on the SEC Internet Web site at *www.sec.gov* and on the terminals located in the public reference rooms in the SEC's offices in New York and Chicago.

- **Office of the General Counsel.** The general counsel is the chief legal officer of the SEC. Primary duties of the office include representing the SEC in certain civil, private, or appellate proceedings; preparing legislative material; and providing independent advice and assistance to the SEC, the divisions, and the offices. Through its amicus curiae program, the office often intervenes in private appellate litigation involving novel or important interpretations of the securities laws.

- **Office of Information Technology.** This office operates the Electronic Data Gathering Analysis and Retrieval (EDGAR) system, which electronically receives, processes, and disseminates more than 500,000 financial statements every year. The office also maintains a very active Web site that contains a wealth of information about the SEC, the securities industry, and also hosts the entire EDGAR financial database for free public access. It is responsible for organizing and implementing an integrated program designed to support the SEC staff in all aspects of information technology. The office has overall management responsibility for the SEC's information technology program, including headquarters, regional and district operations support, applications development, information technology program management, network engineering, security, and enterprise architecture.

- **Office of the Inspector General.** The inspector general conducts internal audits and investigations of SEC programs and operations. Through these audits and investigations, the inspector general seeks to identify and mitigate operational risks, enhance government integrity, and improve the efficiency and effectiveness of SEC programs.

- **Office of International Affairs.** The SEC works extensively in the international arena to promote cooperation and assistance and to encourage the adoption of high regulatory standards worldwide. The Office of Internal Affairs aids in the development and implementation of the SEC's international enforcement and regulatory initiatives. The office negotiates and oversees the implementation of information-sharing arrangements for enforcement and regulatory matters, conducts a technical-assistance program for countries with emerging securities markets, and ensures that the SEC's interests are furthered through participation in international meetings and organizations.

- **Office of Investor Education and Assistance.** This office serves individual investors, ensuring that their problems and concerns are known throughout the SEC and considered when the agency takes action. Investor assistance specialists answer questions, analyze complaints, and seek informal resolutions. In addition to handling questions and complaints, the office organizes investors' town meetings in cities throughout the country to help Americans learn how to save and invest wisely, prepare for retirement, and achieve financial security. The office also publishes free brochures and other educational materials on numerous investing topics. The office, and the SEC in general, cannot act as a personal lawyer to members of the public engaged in private disputes with the securities industry. It also cannot force a broker to settle or resolve a private dispute. The office can assist an investor by explaining how these disputes can be resolved through binding arbitration, mediation, or private litigation.

- **Office of Municipal Securities**. This office coordinates the SEC's municipal securities activities and advises the SEC on policy matters relating to the municipal securities market. States, cities, and other political subdivisions, such as school districts, issue municipal securities to raise money. The office assists the Division of Enforcement and other divisions on municipal securities matters. The office also provides technical assistance in the development and implementation of major SEC initiatives in the municipal securities area, including the coordination of municipal enforcement actions. The office works closely with the municipal securities industry to educate state and local officials about risk-management issues and to foster a thorough understanding of the SEC's policies.

- **Office of the Secretary.** The Office of the Secretary schedules SEC meetings, administers the SEC's seriatim—the process by which the SEC takes collective action without convening a meeting of the commissioners—and duty-officer process, and prepares and maintains records of SEC actions. The office reviews all SEC documents submitted to and approved by the SEC. These include rule-making releases, SEC enforcement orders and litigation releases, self-regulating organizations' rule-making notices and orders, as well as other actions taken by SEC staff pursuant to delegated authority. The office also provides advice to the SEC and the staff on questions of practice and procedure. In addition, it receives and tracks documents filed in administrative proceedings, requests for confidential treatment, and comment letters on rule proposals. The office is responsible for publishing official documents and releases of SEC actions in the Federal Register and the SEC Docket, and it posts them on the SEC Internet Web site, *www.sec.gov.* The office also monitors compliance with the government in the Sunshine Act, and maintains records of financial judgments imposed in enforcement proceedings.

HOW YOU CAN FILE A COMPLAINT WITH THE SEC

If you should ever have problems with your broker, or with a company in which you won stock, you can file a complaint with the SEC either directly over the Internet, or through the regular mail. The EDGAR site provides an online complaint form you can file on the spot, or print out and send in.

At the SEC.com home page, click on "Complaint Center," under the category, "Investor Information."

If you wish to mail a complaint rather than file it electronically, you can send it to:

SEC Complaint Center
450 Fifth Street, NW
Washington, D.C. 20549-0213
Fax: 202-942-9634

If you receive spam (junk email) from investment companies, you can forward or send copies of message board postings to the email address, enforcement@sec.gov. (Please do not use this email box for general complaints or questions.)

Complaints should include the following:

- your name, mail and email addresses, and telephone numbers

- the name, mail and email addresses, telephone numbers, and Web site address of any individual or company you mention in the complaint

- Specific details of how, why, and when you were defrauded or encountered problems with investments or your broker or adviser

Once you file the complaint, the SEC reviews and evaluates it to see if they can refer you to the appropriate SEC office. According to the EDGAR site: The Office of Investor Education and Assistance will handle certain general questions about the securities laws and complaints relating to financial professionals or a complainant's personal financial matters. The professionals in this office can counsel you regarding possible remedies and may, under appropriate circumstances, approach brokerage firms, advisers, or other financial professional concerning matters you have raised.

"Attorneys in the Division of Enforcement evaluate complaints implicating violations of the federal securities laws. It is the general policy of the SEC to conduct its investigations on a confidential basis to preserve the integrity of its investigative process as well as to protect persons against whom unfounded charges may be made or where the SEC determines that enforcement action is not necessary or appropriate.

While the SEC will not represent you in a civil legal case, they can help investigate your complaint, and offer some guidance on appropriate action. It's yet another function of the SEC.

This complex matrix of divisions and offices that makes up the SEC is in business for one primary purpose: to protect you and other investors from unscrupulous dealings by public corporations, brokers, and investment companies. While the system has proven to be *far* from foolproof, it does help keep order and credibility in the markets, and that helps keep America's free enterprise system running as smoothly as possible.

WHAT IS EDGAR? A DAY SPENT WATCHING THE FILINGS ACCUMULATE

EVERY BUSINESS DAY, THE **SEC** and its EDGAR online information site bustle with activity. Corporate filings, legal proceedings,
and other noteworthy actions are promptly recorded in the SEC's
online news directory at *www.sec.gov.* EDGAR electronically
receives, processes, and disseminates more than 500,000 financial statements every year. That's about 2000 filings each business day. And
that is just part of the action at the SEC site.

Let's look at a day in the life of EDGAR and the SEC. I've randomly
picked Thursday, July 18, 2002. On that day, the SEC got its usual truckload
of corporate filings and announced some other legal matters.

Here is a diary of the action for that July day:

Broker fraud.   The SEC filed civil charges against a Merrill Lynch broker,
and reached a settlement in which the broker agreed to pay nearly $675,000 in
disgorgement and penalties. According to the release, the broker sold several of
his clients' money market securities and then forged their signatures on autho-
rizations to transfer the proceeds into his own bank and securities accounts.

Pinching PNC.   The SEC announced a simultaneous proceeding and settlement with PNC Financial Services Group for reporting irregularities. The SEC

release summarized the charges this way: "PNC endeavored to remove certain volatile, troubled or underperforming loans and venture capital investments from its financial statements by transferring them to certain special purpose entities that were specially created to receive these assets and in which PNC held a substantial interest...The Commission found that PNC's accounting with respect to these entities was improper under GAAP, in that it should have consolidated them."

Fallen Knight.   The SEC fined Knight Securities $75,000 for violating the limit order display rule between 1997 and 1999. The SEC said Knight, which is the largest market maker in the over-the-counter market, failed to display customer limit orders properly that were priced better than the market maker's quote.

Piranha attack.   The SEC announced that it received approval from a U.S. district court for an investigative subpoena against the former chief financial officer of Piranha, Inc.

In other business, the SEC also did the following that day:

- approved a rule change that allowed the American Stock Exchange to permit limited side-by-side trading and integrated market making
- announced a rule change for equity options charges at the Philadelphia Stock Exchange
- approved a request by the Philadelphia Stock Exchange to strike from listing and registration certain call and put options contracts issued by The Options Clearing Corp.
- granted Xcel Energy, Inc. authority to expand appliance warranty and repair programs offered to residential customers and engage in energy marketing and brokering activities in Canada.
- approved a request by Progress Energy, Inc. to increase its aggregate investment in exempt wholesale generators and foreign utility companies to $4 billion
- announced hearing request deadlines for applications filed by Met Investors Series Trust, Met Investors Advisory LLC, MassMutual Institutional Funds, and Armstrong World Industries, Inc.
- approved a request by Magnum Hunter Resources, Inc. to withdraw its common stock, $.002 par value, from listing and registration on the American Stock Exchange

CORPORATE FILINGS

On that day—as on every business day—the SEC received hundreds of financial disclosure forms, registration statements, and current reports from companies such as General Electric, Anheuser-Busch, Bank of America, Bank One, Bear Stearns, Continental Airlines, Ford Motor, Dole Food, IBM, Intel, Office Depot, and UPS. The forms pour in, also, from foreign companies who do business here, and small companies interested in going public.

Following is a summary of the types of forms received each day by the SEC:

- **Annual Report to Shareholders.** The annual report is the primary document used by most public companies to disclose corporate information to shareholders. It is usually a state-of-the-company report including an opening letter from the chairman, president, or CEO; financial data; results of continuing operations; market segment information; new product plans; subsidiary activities; and research and development activities on future programs. Most companies use their annual reports to put the most positive spin possible on the company's operations and future prospects.

- **Form 10-K.** Perhaps the most the most important and relevant form for analysts and investors who want details of a company's operation, the 10-K is the annual report that most reporting companies file with the SEC. It provides a comprehensive overview of the registrant's business. Unlike the annual report, which is often packed with fluff about the company's products or services, the prospectus is strictly business. It is expected to stick to the facts and to disclose all relevant information about the company—even information that is troubling or unflattering. The report must be filed within 90 days after the end of the company's fiscal year.

- **Registration Statements.** Companies are required to file registration statements to disclose important business and financial information. The registration statement is divided into two parts. Part one is the prospectus (see following bullet), and part two contains information not required to be in the prospectus, including information on expenses of issuance and distribution, indemnification of directors and officers, and recent sales of unregistered securities, as well as undertakings and copies of material contracts.

- **Prospectus.** The prospectus, which constitutes part one of the registration statement, contains the basic business and financial information on an issuer with respect to a particular securities offering. Investors may use the prospectus to help appraise the merits of the offering and make educated investment decisions. A prospectus in its preliminary form is frequently called a "red herring" prospectus and is subject to completion or amendment before the registration statement becomes effective, after which a final prospectus is issued and sales can be consummated. One of the most common filings is the 425, which is typically filed in connection with business combination transactions.

- **Form 10-Q.** The Form 10-Q is a report filed quarterly by most reporting companies. It includes unaudited financial statements and provides a continuing view of the company's financial position during the year. The report must be filed for each of the first three fiscal quarters of the company's fiscal year and is due within 45 days of the close of the quarter.

- **Proxy Solicitation Materials (Regulation 14A/Schedule 14A).** State law governs the circumstances under which shareholders are entitled to vote. When a shareholder vote is required and any person solicits proxies with respect to securities registered under Section 12 of the 1934 Act, that person generally is required to furnish a proxy statement containing the information specified by Schedule 14A. The proxy statement is intended to provide security holders with the information necessary to enable them to vote in an informed manner on matters intended to be acted upon at security holders' meetings, whether the traditional annual meeting or a special meeting. Typically, a security holder is also provided with a "proxy card" to authorize designated persons to vote his or her securities on the security holder's behalf in the event that the holder does not vote in person at the meeting.

FORM 8-K

The 8-K is the most common SEC filing. Hundreds of 8-Ks pour into the SEC every business day. The 8-K is considered the "current report," and is used to report the occurrence of any material events or corporate changes that are of importance to investors or security holders and previously have not been reported. It is used specifically for several key purposes:

- changes in control of registrant

- acquisition or disposition of assets

- bankruptcy or receivership

- changes in registrant's certifying accountant

- other materially important events

- resignations of registrant's directors
- financial statements and exhibits
- change in fiscal year
- regulation FD disclosure

OTHER REGISTRATION FORMS

In addition to the prospectus, there are many other types of registration forms. Here are the most common:

- **S-1.** This is the basic registration form. It can be used to register securities for which no other form is authorized or prescribed, except securities of foreign governments or political subdivisions thereof.

- **S-2.** This is a simplified optional registration form that may be used by companies that have been required to report under the 1934 act for a minimum of three years and have timely filed all required reports during the 12 calendar months and any portion of the month immediately preceding the filing of the registration statement. Unlike Form S-1, it permits incorporation by reference from the company's annual report to stockholders (or annual report on Form 10-K) and periodic reports. Delivery of these incorporated documents as well as the prospectus to investors may be required.

- **S-3.** This is the most simplified registration form, and it may only be used by companies that have been required to report under the 1934 act for a minimum of 12 months and have met the timely filing requirements set forth under Form S-2. Also, the offering and issuer must meet the eligibility tests prescribed by the form. The form maximizes incorporating by reference information from 1934 act filings.

- **S-4.** This form is used to register securities in connection with business combinations and exchange offers.

- **S-8.** This form is used for the registration of securities to be offered to an issuer's employees pursuant to certain plans.

- **S-11.** This form is used to register securities of certain real estate companies, including real estate investment trusts.

- **SB-1.** This form may be used by certain "small business issuers" to register offerings of up to $10 million of securities, provided that the company has not registered more than $10 million in securities offerings during the preceding 12 months. This form requires less detailed information about the issuer's business than Form S-1. Generally, a "small business issuer" is a U.S. or Canadian company with revenues and public market float of less than $25 million.

- **SB-2.** This form may be used by "small business issuers" to register securities to be sold for cash. This form requires less detailed information about the issuer's business than Form S-1.

- **S-20.** This form may be used to register standardized options where the issuer undertakes not to issue, clear, guarantee, or accept an option registered on Form S-20, unless there is a definitive options disclosure document meeting the requirements of Rule 9b-1 of the 1934 act.

- **Sch B.** Schedule B is the registration statement used by foreign governments (or political subdivisions of foreign governments) to register securities. Generally, it contains a description of the country and its government, the terms of the offering, and the uses of proceeds.

- **F-1.** This is the basic registration form authorized for certain foreign private issuers. It is used to register the securities of those eligible foreign issuers for which no other, more specialized form is authorized or prescribed.

- **F-2.** This is an optional registration form that may be used by certain foreign private issuers that have an equity float of at least $75 million worldwide, or are registering nonconvertible investment-grade securities, or have reported under the 1934 act for a minimum of three years. The form is somewhat shorter than Form F-1 because it uses delivery of filings made by the issuer under the 1934 act, particularly Form 20-F.

- **F-3.** This form may only be used by certain foreign private issuers that have reported under the 1934 act for a minimum of 12 months and that have a worldwide public market float of more than $75 million. The form also may be used by eligible foreign private issuers to register offerings of nonconvertible investment-grade securities, securities to be sold by selling security holders, or securities to be issued to certain existing security holders. The form allows 1934 act filings to be incorporated by reference.

- **F-4.** This form is used to register securities in connection with business combinations and exchange offers involving foreign private issuers.

- **F-6.** This form is used to register depository shares represented by American Depositary Receipts ("ADRs") issued by a depositary against the deposit of the securities of a foreign issuer.

- **F-7.** This form is used by certain eligible publicly traded Canadian foreign private issuers to register rights offers extended to their U.S. shareholders. Form F-7 acts as a wraparound for the relevant Canadian offering documents. To be registered on Form F-7, the rights must be granted to U.S. shareholders on terms no less favorable than those extended to other shareholders.

- **F-8.** This form may be used by eligible large publicly traded Canadian foreign private issuers to register securities offered in business combinations and exchange offers. Form F-8 acts as a wraparound for the relevant Canadian offering or disclosure documents. The securities must be offered to U.S. holders on terms no less favorable than those extended to other holders.

- **F-9.** This form may be used by eligible large publicly traded Canadian foreign private issuers to register nonconvertible investment-grade securities. Form F-9 acts as a wraparound for the relevant Canadian offering documents.

- **F-10.** This form may be used by eligible large publicly traded Canadian foreign private issuers to register any securities (except certain derivative securities). Form F-10 acts as a wraparound for the relevant Canadian offering documents. Unlike Forms F-7, F-8, F-9, and F-80, however, Form F-10 requires the Canadian issuer to reconcile its financial statements to U.S. Generally Accepted Accounting Principles ("GAAP").

- **F-80.** This form may be used by eligible large publicly traded Canadian foreign private issuers to register securities offered in business combinations and exchange offers. Form F-80 acts as a wraparound for the relevant Canadian offering or disclosure documents. The securities must be offered to U.S. holders on terms no less favorable than those extended to other holders.

- **SR.** This form is used as a report by first-time registrants under the act of sales of registered securities and use of proceeds therefrom. The form is required at specified periods of time throughout the offering period, and a final report is required after the termination of the offering.

OTHER LEADING REGISTRATION FORMS

- **Form TA-1.** This form is used to apply for registration as a transfer agent or to amend such registration. It provides information on the company's activities and operation.

- **Form X-17A-5.** Every broker or dealer registered pursuant to Section 15 of the exchange act must file annually, on a calendar or fiscal year basis, a report audited by an independent public accountant.

- **Forms 3, 4, and 5.** Every director, officer, or owner of more than 10 percent of a class of equity securities registered under Section 12 of the 1934 act must file with the commission a statement of ownership regarding such security. The initial filing is on Form 3 and changes are reported on Form 4. The annual statement of beneficial ownership of securities is on Form 5. The forms contain information on the reporting person's relationship to the company and on purchases and sales of such equity securities.

- **Form 6-K.** This report is used by certain foreign private issuers to furnish information: (i) required to be made public in the country of its domicile; (ii) filed with and made public by a foreign stock exchange on which its securities are traded; or (iii) distributed to security holders. The report must be furnished promptly after such material is made public. The form is not considered "filed" for Section 18 liability purposes. This is the only information furnished by foreign private issuers between annual reports, since such issuers are not required to file on Forms 10-Q or 8-K.

- **Form 8-K.** This is the "current report" that is used to report the occurrence of any material events or corporate changes that are of importance to investors or security holders and previously have not been reported by the registrant. It provides more current information on certain specified events than would Forms 10-Q or 10-K.

- **Form 10-C.** This form must be filed by an issuer whose securities are quoted on the Nasdaq interdealer quotation system. Reported on the form is any change that exceeds five percent of the number of shares of the class outstanding and any change in the name of the issuer. The report must be filed within 10 days of such change.

- **Form 10-KSB.** This is the annual report filed by reporting "small business issuers." It provides a comprehensive overview of the company's business, although its requirements call for slightly less detailed information than required by Form 10-K. The report must be filed within 90 days after the end of the company's fiscal year.

- **Form 10-QSB.** The Form 10-QSB is filed quarterly by reporting small business issuers. It includes unaudited financial statements and provides a continuing view of the company's financial position and results of operations throughout the year. The report must be filed for each of the first three fiscal quarters and is due within 45 days of the close of the quarter.

- **Form 11-K.** This form is a special annual report for employee stock purchase, savings, and similar plans, interests in which constitute securities registered under the 1933 act. The Form 11-K annual report is required in addition to any other annual report of the issuer of the securities (e.g., a company's annual report to all shareholders or Form 10-K).

- **Form 12b-25.** This form is used as a notification of late filing by a reporting company that determines that it is unable to file a required periodic report when first due without unreasonable effort or expense. If a company files a Form 12b-25, it is entitled to relief, but must file the required report within 5 calendar days (for a Form 10-Q or 10-QSB) or within 15 calendar days (for a Form 10-K, 10-KSB, 20-F, 11-K, or N-SAR).

- **Form 13F.** This is a quarterly report of equity holdings by institutional investment managers having equity assets under management of $100 million or more. Included in this category are certain banks, insurance companies, investment advisers, investment companies, foundations, and pension funds.

- **Form 15.** This form is filed by a company as notice of termination of registration under Section 12(g) of the 1934 act, or suspension of the duty to file periodic reports under Sections 13 and 15(d) of the 1934 act.

- **Form 18.** This form is used for the registration on a national securities exchange of securities of foreign governments and political subdivisions thereof.

- **Form 18-K.** This form is used for the annual reports of foreign governments or political subdivisions thereof.

- **Schedule 13D.** This schedule discloses beneficial ownership of certain registered equity securities. Any person or group of persons who acquire a beneficial ownership of more than five percent of a class of registered equity securities of certain issuers must file a Schedule 13D reporting such acquisition together with certain other information within 10 days after such acquisition. Moreover, any material changes in the facts set forth in the schedule generally precipitate a duty to file promptly an amendment on Schedule 13D. The commission's rules define the term "beneficial owner" to be any person who directly or indirectly shares voting power or investment power (the power to sell the security).

- **Schedule 13G.** Schedule 13G is a much abbreviated version of Schedule 13D that is only available for use by a limited category of "persons" (such as banks, broker/dealers, and insurance companies) and even then only when the securities were acquired in the ordinary course of business and not with the purpose or effect of changing or influencing the control of the issuer.

- **Schedule 13E-3.** This schedule must be filed by certain persons engaging in "going private" transactions. The schedule must be filed by any company or an affiliate of a company who engages in a business combination, tender offer, or stock purchase that has the effect of causing a class of the company's equity securities registered under the 1934 act (i) to be held by fewer than 300 persons, or (ii) to be delisted from a securities exchange or interdealer quotation system. The filer must disclose detailed information about the transaction, including whether the filer believes the transaction to be fair.

- **Schedule 13E-4.** This schedule (called an "Issuer Tender Offer Statement") must be filed by certain reporting companies that make tender offers for their own securities. In addition, Rule 13e-4 under the 1934 act imposes additional requirements than an issuer must comply with when making an issuer tender offer.

- **Information Statement (Regulation 14C/Schedule 14C).** Schedule 14C sets forth the disclosure requirements for information statements. Generally, a company with securities registered under Section 12 of the 1934 act must send an information statement to every holder of the registered security who is entitled to vote on any matter for which the company is not soliciting proxies. (If the company solicits proxies, Regulation 14C/Schedule 14A may be required.)

- **Schedule 14D-1.** Any person, other than the issuer itself (see Schedule 13E-4), making a tender offer for certain equity securities registered pursuant to Section 12 of the 1934 act, which offer, if accepted, would cause that person to own over five percent of that class of the securities, must at the time of the offer file a Schedule 14D-1. This schedule must be filed with the Commission and sent to certain other parties, such as the issuer and any competing bidders. In addition, Regulation 14D sets forth certain requirements that must be complied with in connection with a tender offer.

- **Schedule 14D-9.** This schedule must be filed with the commission when an interested party, such as an issuer, a beneficial owner of securities, or a representative of either, makes a solicitation or recommendation to the shareholders with respect to a tender offer that is subject to Regulation 14D.

In all, between the litigation announcements, the rule changes, the delistings, and the numerous corporate forms, the SEC receives a mountain of paperwork so large each day that even Evelyn Woods couldn't speed-read through it all. But at the SEC and its EDGAR online databank, it's all in a day's work.

ANNUAL REPORTS:
GETTING PAST THE FLUFF

IRONICALLY, ONE OF THE MOST IMPORTANT DOCUMENTS companies file with the SEC is not always available for viewing at EDGAR—but you can readily find it elsewhere online. The annual report to shareholders, which is one of the essential documents you need to review in analyzing a stock, is more difficult for companies to submit electronically than other filings because the reports typically contain fancy graphics, color photographs, and unconventional layouts. Instead, the SEC gives companies the option of filing either a standard paper report or an electronic version, and the vast majority of companies opt for the paper version. That rule may change soon, however, as advances in computer technology make it easier to submit and display high-level graphics content.

In the meantime, you can still readily find annual reports of nearly all of America's leading companies—in their complete graphics-enhanced formats—online. All the leading companies now have Web sites that contain their annual reports, typically available for viewing on your computer as a PDF file (Adobe Portable Document Format), which is the standard document-reading format on the Web. If you're not sure whether you can read a PDF file on your computer, just go to the Web site of one of your favorite stocks, click on "annual report" and see what happens. It's very likely that your computer will have no problem displaying the report. Otherwise, just call or write the company shareholder relations person, and he or she will happily send you an annual report at no charge. If you do use the online version, you may find it easier to page through and study if you print it out.

WHERE'S THE BEEF?

The first thing you need to remember about an annual report is that the dazzling graphs, stunning artwork, and flowery praise typical of today's corporate annual reports has very little to do with the company's true level of success. In fact, fancy graphics and hyperbole are sometimes used to camouflage ho-hum financial returns. In reading through the annual report, you need to focus on substance, not sizzle.

We hope to answer several key questions in reviewing the annual report, such as:

* What is the company's principal business?

* How does management assess its performance?

* Is the company profitable and growing?

One of the first things you'll see in an annual report is the letter to shareholders from the CEO, chairman, or president (or a combination of the three). That letter will put the most positive spin possible on the company's past performance and future prospects. Read it with a fair dose of skepticism. It can give you some insights into the company's operations and future plans, but there's no guarantee that the optimism the letter expresses will be realized in the real world. For example, take a look at the following excerpts from annual report letters to shareholders from two prominent companies:

> ...Our results put us in the top tier of the world's corporations. We have a proven business concept that is eminently scalable in our existing businesses and adaptable enough to extend to new markets....Taken together, these markets present a $3.9 trillion opportunity for (the company), and we have just scratched the surface. Add to that the other big markets we are pursuing—forest products, metals, steel, coal and air-emissions credits— and the opportunity rises by $830 billion to reach nearly $4.7 trillion...Our talented people, global presence, financial strength and massive market knowledge have created our sustainable and unique businesses...We plan to leverage all of these competitive advantages to create significant value for our shareholders.

> Kenneth L. Lay
> *Chairman*
>
> Jeffrey K. Skilling
> *President and Chief Executive Officer*

That letter from Enron's Kenneth Lay and Jeffrey Skilling, brimming with confidence and optimism, was published in early 2001, just months before the company collapsed into bankruptcy as part of one of the biggest bookkeeping scandals in stock market history.

Here's another sample letter from a different company:

We are pleased to report to you the progress that (our company) has made during the year 2000. Our efforts over the past year have culminated in some of the Company's greatest achievements to date. We are poised to leverage our assets and experience in areas such as research and clinical development, regulatory affairs, and manufacturing to transition from the development stage toward the final regulatory review phase and product commercialization. . . (Our company's) success and its vision for the future of oncology treatment have continued into 2001... As we attain new product development and regulatory milestones and realize our goal of becoming a fully integrated commercial biotechnology company, we would like to thank the (company's) family for helping us achieve our success...

Sincerely,
Samuel D. Waksal, Ph.D.
President and Chief Executive Officer

That letter to shareholders from Imclone CEO and president, Sam Waksal came just months before the company's stock went into a dizzying freefall when Imclone lost its bid for FDA approval for its major product. The collapse also landed Waksal in jail on insider trading charges, and put his close friend, Martha Stewart, into hot water for dumping about 4000 shares of Imclone stock the day before the big plunge.

In analyzing a company and its prospects, it's important to look past the fluff and hyperbole of an annual report and focus on more quantitative elements.

In addition to the letter from the key officers, what else should you look for in an annual report? Here are some sections worth examining in researching and analyzing a stock:

Company description. Near the front of the annual report—often inside the front cover—there is usually a brief one- to three-paragraph description of the company that's worth reading. It provides a quick overview of the company's operations and its leading products or services.

Some companies also put their "mission statements" up front. Don't waste your time. The mission statement is typically mumbo jumbo about the company's commitment to "shareholder value"—whatever that means. For example, here was Qwest's 2001 "vision" statement: "To build shareholder value by becoming the customer-focused market leader for worldwide broad-band Internet communications and applications services." Qwest Chairman and Chief Executive Joseph Nacchio was so concerned about "building share-holder value" that he collected more than $100 million in salary, stock options, and other compensation in 2001, while orchestrating a plunge in the company's stock price from nearly $50 a share to under $2.

Performance graphs. You can often get a very good indication of a company's success within the first two or three pages of the report, based on what the company chooses to feature up front—or, just as importantly, what it chooses not to feature. The deeper you have to page into a report to find anything about the company's financial results, the worse those results are likely to be. But if the returns have been stellar, you can rest assured the company will put it right up front.

If a company is doing well, it will nearly always publish at least three performance graphs near the front of the book—one showing *revenue* (or sales) growth over the past few years, one showing *net income* growth, and one showing *earnings per share* growth. When you see those three graphs, they will very likely show steady growth during the years featured. But if those graphs aren't present, you should be immediately suspicious. It probably means the recent results have been disappointing. Often, companies will put in other graphs in the report instead, such as growth of number of employees, assets, inventory, or cash and cash investments—anything the corporate PR people can come up with to show some type of positive growth. But if the graphs don't cover revenue, net income, and earnings per share, that's probably a bad sign for the company.

Three-year financial table. Also near the front of the report (along with the graphs), companies often include a condensed financial table covering the past 2 or 3 years in such financial categories as sales (or revenue), net income, earnings per share, stockholders' equity, return on equity, and dividends paid. A quick review of that table will give you a good indication of the company's recent success and growth rate. But for a better look at the company's financial history, most reports include a more detailed table of "selected financial data" in the back half of the report. In most reports, that table covers results for the past 5 to 10 years. (More on that table is discussed later.) Figure 3-1 shows the 3-year financial table from page two of the 2001 annual report of Johnson & Johnson:

As you can see, the company has increased its sales, net earnings, cash dividends, and shareholder equity each year, as well as its earnings per share. That indicates a very healthy company.

FIGURE 3-1

Three Years in Brief—Worldwide

(Dollars in Millions Except Per Share Figures)	2001	2000	1999	% Change 2001	% Change 2000
Sales to customers	$33.004	29,846	28,007	10.6	6.6
Net earnings*	5,668	4,953	4,273	14.4	15.9
Cash dividends paid	2,047	1,724	1,479	18.7	16.6
Shareowners' equity	24,233	20,395	16,995	18.8	20.0
Percent return on average shareholders' equity*	25.4	26.5	27.0	—	—
Per share					
Net earning-basic*	$ 1.87	1.65	1.43	13.3	15.4
-diluted*	1.84	1.61	1.39	14.3	15.8
Cash dividends paid	0.70	0.62	0.55	12.9	12.7
Shareholders' equity	7.95	6.77	5.70	17.4	18.8
Market price (year end close)	59.86	52.53	46.63	14.0	12.7
Average shares outstanding (millions)					
-basic	3,033.8	2,993.5	2,978.2	1.3	0.5
-dilluted	3,099.3	3,099.2	3,100.4	0.0	(0.0)
Number of employees (thousands)	101.8	100.9	99.8	0.9	1.1

Net earnings and earnings per share for 2001, 2000 and 1999 include special charges of $231 million or $.07 diluted earnings per share for 2001, $45 million or $.01 diluted earnings per share for 2000 and $75 million or $.02 diluted earnings per share in1999. These special charges relate to the ALZA merger and In-Process Reseach and Development (IPR&D) in 2001, IPR&D and restructuring gain in 2000, and the Centocor and SEQUUS mergers in 1999. Excluding the impact of these charges, 2001 net earnings increased 18.0% over 2000. For detailed discussion of thses charges, refer to Nate 17 of the Notes to Consolidated Finacial Staements.

Glossy content.   Most annual reports include a fairly extensive section after the letter from the chairman that includes glossy photos, creative layout, and several pages of copy about the company or some aspect of its operations. Sometimes companies use this space constructively to give shareholders an idea of its newest products or its leading products, its ongoing research, international operations, or other important aspects of the operations. But far too often, this glossy content section is filled with useless babble that teaches you nothing about the company. You may see page after page highlighting the noble efforts of their employees or praising their leading customers, or discussing their commitment to excellence. All trite babble. Don't waste your time. If you want a good, detailed description of the company's operations, you can find it in the 10-K report (next chapter), so you don't need to spend a lot of time wading throught the annual report to learn about the company. If it's of interest, read it, otherwise skip it and move on to the back half of the report.

FINANCIALS

After the glossy section comes the "management's discussion and analysis of results of operations and financial condition." Dull and dry as it may seem, this is where the real meat of the annual report can be found.

In analyzing any type of financial data, the key is not the numbers themselves, but how this year's numbers compare with last year's numbers, the previous year's numbers, and so forth. What you are looking for is consistent growth from one year to the next. Consistent companies tend to make better stocks, so the ideal company would be one that shows annual growth of 5 to 25 percent in all the major categories (such as revenue, net income, and earnings per share) year in and year out. For a turnaround stock, you would hope to see growing returns in the most recent year or two.

What types of financial information should you look for in the annual report? Here are some of the most important elements of the financial section:

Five- to ten-year financial tables.   This is a good place to get a long-term view of the company. Typically, companies include a table of leading financial data covering the past 5 to 10 years. Look through the data to see if the company has had consistent growth in all the important categories, and to make sure that the growth momentum is continuing in the most recent years. The tables usually cover leading financial categories, such as sales (or revenue), cost of sales, gross profit, operating expenses (such as research and development, marketing, and administrative), income (or loss) from operations, income taxes, net income, earnings per share, dividends, total assets, working capital, stockholders' equity, and return on average equity.

Figure 3-2 shows a 10-year financial table from the annual report of Johnson & Johnson:

If you look under "Total Sales" (third line from the top), you'll see that the company's sales have increased every year since 1991. That is a very good sign that indicates a solid, consistent growing company. Near the bottom of the table, you'll see that dividends paid per share has also increased every year since 1991. That is also the sign of a solid, growing company. Net income and earnings per share have increased 7 of the past 8 years, and 8 of the past 10. That is also a good indication of the company's consistent growth. Ideally, you would like to see a company with 10 straight years of record earnings, but 8 out of the past 10 is not bad. Notice also, the company has made money every year—no losses. That, too, is a good sign of a solid company.

You'll see one other good sign of a strong company when looking under "selling, marketing, administrative expenses," and "research expense." The company has increased its marketing and research budgets every single year. That means the company is focused on the future, and focused on building an operation that will continue to do well for the long term.

Balance sheet.   The balance sheet is a snapshot of the company's present financial condition. The balance sheet typically includes financial data for the

FIGURE 3-2

Summary of Operations and Statistical DatA 1991-2001[3]   Johnson & Johnson and Subsidiaries

(Dollars in Millions Except Per Share Figures)	2001	2000	1999	1998	1997	1996	1995	1994	1993	1992	1991
Sales to customers-Domestic	$ 20,204	17,707	15,921	13,251	12,183	11,215	9,372	7,986	7,358	7,111	6,364
Sales to customers-International	12,800	12,139	12,086	11,147	10,935	10,769	9,696	7,930	6,944	6,868	6,207
Total sales	33.004	29,846	28,007	24,398	23,118	21,984	19,068	15,916	14,302	13,985	12,571
Cost of products sold	9,536	8,908	8,498	7,646[2]	7,291	7,130	6,303	5,350	4,869	4,748	4,248
Selling marketing and administrative expenses	11,992	11,218	10,756	9,166	8,840	8,500	7,530	6,406	5,828	5,776	5,202
Research expense	3,591	3,105	2,768	2,506	2,373	2,109	1,788	1,416	1,296	1,282	1,092
Purchased in-process research and development	105	66	—	298	108	—	—	37	—	—	171
Interest income	(456)	(429)	(266)	(302)	(263)	(196)	(151)	(85)	(104)	(122)	(123)
Interest expense, net of portion capitalized	153	204	255	186	179	176	184	182	165	162	156
Other expense, net	38	(61)	37	12	(10)	122	70	(5)	(71)	20	24
Special charges	147	(33)	82	553	258	—	—	—	—	—	—
	25,106	22,978	22,130	20,065	18,776	17,841	15,724	13,301	11,983	11,866	10,770
Earnings before provision for taxes on income	7,898	6,868	5,877	4,333	4,342	4,143	3,344	2,615	2,319	2,119	1,801
Provision for taxes on income	2,230	1,915	1,604	1,232	1,237	1,185	926	654	533	547	531
Earnings before cumulative effect of accounting charges	5,668	4,953	4,273	3,101	3,105	2,958	2,418	1,961	1,786	1,572	1,270
Cumulative effect of accounting charges (net of tax)	—	—	—	—	—	—	—	—	—	(595)	—
Net earnings	$ 5,668	4,953	4,273	3,101	3,105	2,958	2,418	1,961	1,786	977	1,270
Percent of sales to customers	17.2	16.6	15.3	12.7[2]	13.4	13.5	12.7	12.3	12.5	7.0[1]	10.1
Diluted net earnings per share of common stock*	$ 1.84[1]	1.61[1]	1.39[1]	1.02[1]	1.02[1]	.98	.84	.69	.63	.34[1]	.44
Percent return on average shareholders' equity	25.4	26.5	27.0	22.2[2]	24.6	27.2	27.6	28.4	30.1	16.4[1]	22.1
Percent increase (decrease) over previous year:											
Sales to customers	10.6	6.6	14.8	5.5	5.2	15.3	19.8	11.3	2.3	11.2	10.6
Diluted net earnings per share	14.3[1]	15.8[1]	36.3[1]	—[2]	4.1[1]	16.7	21.7	9.5	85.3[1]	(22.7)[1]	12.8
Supplementary expense data:											
Cost of materials and services[4]	$ 15,333	14,113	13,922	11,779	11,702	11,341	9,984	8,104	7,168	7,736	6,573
Total employment costs	7,749	7,085	6,537	5,908	5,586	5,447	4,849	4,401	4,181	4,166	3,605
Depreciation and amortization	1,605	1,592	1,510	1,335	1,117	1,047	886	754	649	576	505
Maintenance and repairs[5]	372	327	322	286	270	285	257	222	205	215	206
Total tax expense[6]	2,995	2,619	2,271	1,881	1,824	1,753	1,458	1,132	957	975	929
Total tax expense per share[7]	.99	.87	.76	.63	.62	.60	.52	.40	.34	.34	.33
Supplementary balance sheet data:											
Property, plant and equipment, net	$ 7,719	7,409	7,155	6,767	6,204	6,025	5,544	5,230	4,717	4,443	3,962
Additions to property, plant and equipment	1,731	1,689	1,822	1,610	1,454	1,427	1,307	979	1,001	1,162	1,052
Total assets	38,488	34,245	31,064	28,966	23,615	22,248	19,355	17,027	13,372	13,087	11,653
Long-term debt	2,217	3,163	3,429	2,652	2,084	2,347	2,702	2,776	1,761	1,832	1,773
Operating cash flow	8,864	6,903	5,920	5,106	4,210	4,001	3,436	2,984	2,202	2,136	1,558
Common stock information*											
Dividends paid per share	$ .70	.62	.55	.49	.425	.368	.32	.283	.253	.223	.193
Shareowners' equity per share	$ 7.95	6.77	5.70	4.93	4.51	4.07	3.46	2.76	2.16	2.03	2.17
Market price per share (year-end close)	$ 59.86	52.53	46.63	41.94	32.44	25.25	21.38	13.69	11.19	12.63	14.31
Average shares outstanding (millions)-basic	3,033.8	2,993.5	2,978.2	2,973.6	2,951.9	2,938.0	2,820.1	2,796.9	2,816.6	2,845.8	2,847.2
-diluted	3,099.3	3,099.2	3,100.4	3,082.7	3,073.0	3,046.2	2,890.0	2,843.2	2,840.8	2,876.4	2,901.2
Employees (thousands)	101.8	100.9	99.8	96.1	92.6	91.5	84.2	83.4	83.2	86.9	84.9

*Adjusted to reflect the 2001 two-for-one stock split.
[1] Excluding the cumulative effect of accounting changes of $595 million. –1992 earnings percent of sales to customers before accounting changes is 11.2%. –1992 earnings per share before accounting change is $.55. –1992 earnings percent return on average shareowners' equity before accounting changes is 25.1%. –1993 diluted net earnings per share percent increase over prior year before accounting changes is 14.5%; 1992 diluted net earnings per share increase over prior year is 25.0%.
[2] Excluding Special and In-Process Research and Development charges –1997 diluted net earnings per share before special charges is $1.11. –1997 diluted net earnings per share increase over prior year before special charges is 13.3%. –1998 earnings percent of sales to customers before special charges is 15.6%. –1998 diluted net earnings per share before special charges is $1.24. –1998 percent return on average shareowners' equity before special charges is 26.5%. –1998 diluted net earnings per share increase over prior year before special charges is 11.7%; –1998 cost of products sold includes $60 million of inventory write-offs for restructuring; – 1999 diluted net earnings per share before special charges is $1.42. 1999 excluding special charges diluted net earnings per share percent increase over prior year is 14.5%; – 2000 diluted net earnings per share before special charges is $1.63. 2000 excluding special charges diluted net earnings per share increase over prior year is 14.8%; –2001 diluted net earnings per share before special charges is $1.91. –2001 excluding special charges diluted net earnings per share increase over prior year is 17.2%.
[3] All periods have been adjusted to include the effects of the ALZA merger.
[4] Net of interest and other income.
[5] Also included in cost of materials and services category.
[6] Includes taxes on income, payroll, property and other business taxes; per share data calculated using average basic shares.

most recent two years. You'll find information on assets, liabilities, inventory, and stockholders' equity. In a quick glance comparing the past two years, you can see whether the company is growing, earning a good return on capital, paring down its inventories, or piling up more debt. Figure 3-3 shows the balance sheet from Johnson & Johnson's annual report:

FIGURE 3-3

Consolidated Balance Sheets   Johnson & Johnson and Subsidiaries

At December 30, 2001 and December 31, 2000 (Dollars in Millions) (Note 1)	2001	2000
Assets		
Current assets		
Cash and cash equivalents (Notes 1, 14 and 15)	$3,758	4,278
Marketable securities (Notes 1, 14 and 15)	4,214	2,479
Accounts receivable trade, less allowances for doubtful accounts $197 (2000, $182)	4,630	4,601
Inventories (Notes 1 and 2)	2,992	2,905
Deferred taxes on income (Note 8)	1,192	1,174
Prepaid expenses and other receivables	1,687	1,254
Total current assets	18,473	16,691
Marketable securities, non-current (Notes 1, 14 and 15)	969	657
Property, plant and equipment, net (Notes 1 and 3)	7,719	7,409
Intangible assets, net (Notes 1 and 7)	9,077	7,535
Deferred taxes on income (Note 8)	288	240
Other assets	1,962	1,713
Total assets	$38,488	34,245
Liabilities and Shareowners' Equity		
Current liabilities		
Loans and notes payable (Note 6)	$565	1,489
Accounts payable	2,838	2,122
Accrued liabilities	3,135	2,793
Accrued salaries, wages and commissions	969	529
Taxes on income	537	322
Total current liabilities	8,044	7,255
Long-term debt (Note 6)	2,217	3,163
Deferred tax liability (Note 8)	493	255
Employee related obligations (Note 5)	1,870	1,804
Other liabilities	1,631	1,373
Shareowners' equity		
Preferred stock—without par value (authorized and unissued 2,000,000 shares)	—	—
Common stock—par value $1.00 per share (Note 20)		
(authorized 4,320,000,000 shares; issued 3,119,842,000 shares)	3,120	3,120
Note receivable from employee stock ownership plan (Note 16)	(30)	(35)
Accumulated other comprehensive income (Note 11)	(530)	(461)
Retained earnings	23,066	18,113
	25,626	20,737
Less: common stock held in treasury, at cost (Note 20) (72,627,000 and 105,218,000)	1,393	342
Total shareowners' equity	24,233	20,395
Total liabilities and shareowners' equity	$38,488	34,245

See Notes to Consolidated Financial Statements

As you can see, total current assets as well as total assets (what the company owns) have gone up. Liabilities (what the company owes) have also edged up a little, but not as much as the assets. You will also see that total liabilities and shareholder equity (the part of the company owned through stock ownership) is exactly the same as the total assets ($38,488 million). That should always be the case with a normally functioning company.

Income statement. (also referred to as "earnings statement," "revenue statement," "profit or loss statement," "consolidated statement of earnings," or "statements of operations.") The income statement gives a three-year breakdown of sales, cost of sales, interest income and expense, taxes, and other sources of income or expense. Are total earnings rising? How about per share earnings? Are expenses being held in check? Did the company have a major jump in interest income, or are there any extraordinary items—sales of fixed assets, one-time tax carry-forwards—that might make for a distorted view of the company's true profitability?

Also look closely at two other important factors. Is the company continuing to add to its research and development expenditures and its marketing and selling costs? If you see a sudden drop in either of those categories, that may mean that the company is being forced to cut back there to cover shortfalls elsewhere in the budget. That's a bad sign. Cutting back on research or marketing does not bode well for the long term. The ideal company is one that continues to pump up its marketing and research to develop more products and sell more products because that means they're focused on long-term growth.

Figure 3-4 shows a copy of Johnson & Johnson's earnings statement. Notice that the company's sales and profits have increased the past two years, as have the costs of "selling, marketing and administrative expenses," and "research expenses." You'll also see that net earnings have also gone up both

FIGURE 3-4

Consolidated Statements of Earnings

Johnson & Johnson and Subsidiaries

(Dollars in Millions Except Per Share Figures) (Note 1)	2001	2000	1999
Sales to customers	$33,004	29,846	28,007
Cost of products sold	9,536	8,908	8,498
Gross profit	23,468	20,938	19,509
Selling, marketing and administrative expenses	11,992	11,218	10,756
Research expense	3,591	3,105	2,768
Purchased in-process research and development (Note 17)	105	66	—
Interest income	(456)	(429)	(266)
Interest expense, net of portion capitalized (Note 3)	153	204	255
Other (income) expense, net	185	(94)	119
	15,570	14,070	13,632
Earnings before provision for taxes on income	7,898	6,868	5,877
Provision for taxes on income (Note 8)	2,230	1,915	1,604
Net earnings	$ 5,668	4,953	4,273
Basic net earnings per share (Notes 1 and 19)	$ 1.87	1.65	1.43
Diluted net earnings per share (Notes 1 and 19)	$ 1.84	1.61	1.39

See Notes to Consolidated Financial Statements

years, as have basic net earnings per share and diluted net earnings per share. That's the sign of a healthy company.

Business segments.   If the company does business in several different business segments, it may break down its financial numbers into segment results. Those are often published in the annual report or the 10-K—or both. Figures 3-5 and 3-6 show segment results from Johnson & Johnson's annual report:

In the previous examples, the company does a nice job of showing the segment financial information both in table and graph format. While it's difficult to get a true grasp of growth and momentum from just two years worth of results, you can glean some important facts from the information. For instance,

FIGURE 3-5

Segments of Business

Financial information for the Company's three worldwide business segments is summarized below. See Note 12 for additional information on segments of business.

Sales by Seqment of Business
(Millions of Dollars)

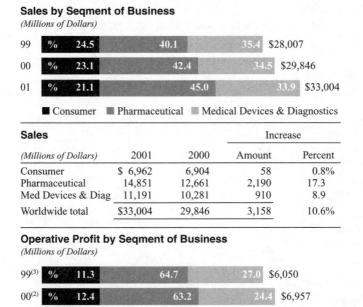

Sales			Increase	
(Millions of Dollars)	2001	2000	Amount	Percent
Consumer	$ 6,962	6,904	58	0.8%
Pharmaceutical	14,851	12,661	2,190	17.3
Med Devices & Diag	11,191	10,281	910	8.9
Worldwide total	$33,004	29,846	3,158	10.6%

Operative Profit by Seqment of Business
(Millions of Dollars)

FIGURE 3-6

Operating Profit

(Millions of Dollars)	2001[1]	2000[2]	Percent of Sales 2001	Percent of Sales 2000
Consumer	$1,004	867	14.4%	12.6%
Pharmaceutical	4,928	4,394	33.2	34.7
Med Devices & Diag	2,001	1,696	17.9	16.5
Segments total	7,933	6,957	24.0	23.3
Expenses not allocated to segments	(35)	(89)		
Earnings before taxes on income	$7,898	6,868	23.9%	23.0%

if you look at the two graphs, "sales by segment of business" and "operating profit by segment of business," you'll see that the most important segment is the pharmaceutical division. It accounts for 45 percent of sales and 63.2 percent operating profit. Next is medical devices and diagnostics, with 33.9 percent of sales and 25 percent of operating profit, followed by the consumer division, at 21 percent of sales and just 12.7 percent of the operating profit. The numbers indicate that not only is the pharmaceutical division the largest segment, but also the most profitable, since it accounts for almost two-thirds of the company's operating profit while collecting less than half the revenue.

You'll also notice that sales revenue in the pharmaceutical segment is growing faster than the other two segments. That's a good sign, since the pharmaceutical segment is the most profitable of the three segments. On the other hand, the segment growing the most slowly is the consumer segment, which also happens to be the least profitable segment. In looking over the operating profit table, you'll see that all three segments experienced solid profit growth in 2001. That's an excellent sign of a healthy company.

AUDITOR'S LETTER *(YOU LIE, I'LL SWEAR TO IT.)*

> CEO: "What's 1 plus 1?"
> Auditor: "Whatever you want it to be."

The recent rash of corporate scandals has given a well-deserved black eye to the accounting industry. You may recall that the Enron scandal thrust its auditor, Arthur Anderson, into public humiliation, and ultimately, bankruptcy because the company failed to report any inconsistencies in Enron's financials.

An auditor's job is to check a company's financial statements, and report its findings—pro or con. But as we learned in the Enron case, auditors may have conflicts of interest that taint their judgment. Arthur Anderson received millions of dollars in consulting fees from Enron, and apparently that helped persuade them to overlook Enron's vast matrix of bookkeeping irregularities. Instead of raising a red flag, Arthur Anderson continued to give Enron full approval. But once Enron fell into financial trouble, Arthur Anderson also became embroiled in the investigation, and had its reputation—and its business—permanently damaged because of its inability to provide an accurate, honest audit of Enron's financials. In the wake of the Arthur Anderson scandal, other accounting firms face a powerful incentive to do an honest job of assessing a company's financials. That incentive is desperately needed, however, to outweigh the inherent conflict of interest that an accounting firm faces when its livelihood depends on the very companies it is auditing.

A more logical system would be to have the SEC hire independent auditors to audit the financials of each publicly traded company, and then bill the company for the service, rather than to let the company hire and pay its own auditing firm.

A letter from the auditor is included in every annual report (near the footnotes and financial tables). The letter either approves the financials or comments on possible discrepancies. In the vast majority of cases, the auditor gives the company full approval.

When reviewing the auditor's letter, here's a rule of thumb: if the letter runs no more than two paragraphs, you can assume that the auditor reviewed the corporation's financials and found them to be "in conformity with generally accepted accounting practices." But if the letter is longer than two paragraphs, take a closer look. It probably means the auditor uncovered some discrepancies in the financials worth noting. Figure 3-7 shows an auditor's letter in the Johnson & Johnson annual report that gives the company a clean bill of health.

Footnotes. (or "notes to consolidated financial statements.") You'll see several pages of footnotes in the back that will offer some information on the company's operations regarding such areas as long-term debt, accounts receivable, taxes, benefit plans, stock options, acquisitions, mergers, business segments, and discontinued operations.

Other sections. In most annual reports, you can also find some other interesting lists, such as board of directors, divisional office locations, the stock symbol, recent stock price and dividend data, information on the company's

FIGURE 3-7

Independent Auditor's Report

To the Shareowners and Board of Directors of
Johnson & Johnson:

In our opinion, the accompanying consolidated balance sheets and the related consolidated statements of earnings, consolidated statements of equity and consolidated statements of cash flows present fairly, in all material respects, the financial position of Johnson & Johnson and subsidiaries at December 30, 2001 and December 31, 2000, and the results of their operations and their cash flows for each of the three years in the period ended December 30, 2001, in conformity with accounting principles generally accepted in the United States of America. These financial statements are the responsibility of the Company's management; our responsibility is to express an opinion on these financial statements based on our audits. We conducted our audits of these statements in accordance with auditing standards generally accepted in the United States of America which require that we plan and perform the audit to obtain reasonable assurance about whether the financial statements are free of material misstatement. An audit includes examining, on a test basis, evidence supporting the amounts and disclosures in the financial statements, assessing the accounting principles used and significant estimates made by management, and evaluating the overall financial statement presentation. We believe that our audits provide a reasonable basis for our opinion.

PricewaterhouseCoopers LLP

New York, New York
January 21, 2002

dividend reinvestment and stock purchase plan (if one exists), and other facts about the company. In all, the annual report can give you a pretty good look at a company's operations, although the 10-K and other reports filed with the SEC would provide you with an even broader view of the company and its management.

There are a number of other financial ratios and formulas you can use to get a truer picture of the company's financials. We take an in-depth look at those measures in the next chapter.

KEY MEASURES OF FINANCIAL STRENGTH

THERE ARE SEVERAL SIMPLE FORMULAS you can use to analyze a company's financial strength. In this chapter, we'll provide you with a close look at many of the ratios and measures that Wall Street analysts use to evaluate a company. You can use the same measures in your own research while reviewing a company's income statement, balance sheet, and other financial tables available in their 10-K and annual reports. We'll refer back to many of these ratios in later chapters as we discuss the 10-K and other financial reports. Here are some of the leading ratios and measures:

RETURN ON EQUITY

Return on equity is considered to be one of the most important measures of a company's financial strength. It helps you determine how much shareholders are making for their investment dollars, and whether they are making more for their investment dollars this year than they did in previous years. Here is the formula for determining return on equity (ROE):

Net income for the year (after taxes) ÷ Shareholders' equity
(from the start of the year) = Return on equity

Not everyone calculates ROE using shareholders' equity from the start of the year. Some analysts (including the well-known ValueLine Investment Survey) calculate the ROE using shareholders' equity at the end of the year. But that does not represent a true return on equity. As a business, you start with a certain amount of money and capital investment in the company (the equity), and you spend the next 12 months generating revenue and income using that equity. The ROE is supposed to demonstrate the return that shareholders earned on their investment that year. That's why it's important to use the equity the company starts the year with rather than what it ends the year with.

Example: If ABC Corporation has a net income of $10 million for the year 2002, and shareholders' equity of $70 million at the start of 2002, to calculate ROE, you would divide the $10 net income by the $70 million shareholder equity. The return on equity is 14 percent—a pretty healthy return.

While ROEs tend to vary dramatically by industry, here is a very rough guideline: over 40 percent would be considered an excellent ROE, 15 to 30 percent would be about average, and under 10 percent would be considered mediocre to poor.

To get a better perspective on the ROE, see how it compares with the previous year's return, how it compares with the return of other companies in the same industry, and how it compares with current interest rates on corporate bonds. In its 2001 annual report, Johnson & Johnson included its return on shareholder equity in its three-year financial table. (See Figure 3-1.) Its ROE was 27.0 in 1999, 26.5 in 2000, and 25.4 in 2001. A dropping ROE is not a particularly good sign, but even at 25.4 percent, that's a very good ROE.

Let's see how that compares to the ROE for General Motors. In GM's annual report, the company does not list its ROE, so we have to calculate it ourselves. The following figures were extracted from a financial table in GM's 10-K report:

GENERAL MOTORS CORPORATION AND SUBSIDIARIES

Years Ended December 31				
2001	**2000**	**1999**	**1998**	**1997**
(dollars in millions except per-share amounts)				
Net income	$601	$ ÷ 4,452	$6,002	$2,956	$6,698
Stockholders' equity	$19,707	$30,175	$20,644	$15,052	$17,584

In 2000, GM earned net income of $4452 million. It began the year with stockholder's equity of $20,644 million (the equity listed under 1999). Let's use the formula to calculate GM's ROE:

$4452 million (Net income) ÷ $20,644 million (Stockholders' equity
                   at the start of the year) = 0.21 (21%) (Return on equity)

A return on equity of 21 percent is considered very healthy.

But the following year, 2001, GM's net income plummeted, and so did its ROE. The company posted net income of $601 million (compared with $4452 million the previous year), on shareholder equity of $30,175 million. Follow the formula again, and you come up with an ROE of just 2 percent—a very low return for the shareholders' investment.

GROSS PROFIT MARGIN ON SALES

Has the company been able to widen its margin between costs and revenues, or is competition in its industry forcing it to keep prices down and costs up? To calculate the gross profit margin on goods sold, follow this formula:

$$\frac{\text{Sales} - \text{Cost of goods sold}}{\text{Gross profit margin}}$$

(Be aware that "cost of goods sold" does not include marketing, selling, administrative, or research and development costs. It merely refers to the actual costs of producing the products.)

Here's an example: If ABC had sales of $50 million, and its cost of goods sold was $30 million, its gross profit margin on sales would be $20 million.

Johnson & Johnson spells out its gross profit margin in its Consolidated Statements of Earnings. (See Figure 3-4.) It had sales of $33,004 and cost of goods sold of $9536. Subtract the $9536 from the $33,004 to get a gross profit margin of $23,468. You'll also notice in the table that the company's gross profit margin increased from 1999 to 2000 and from 2000 to 2001. That's a positive sign for the company.

GROSS PROFIT MARGIN RATIO

In and of itself, the gross profit margin provides only a one-dimensional view of the company's profits. It's difficult to make a valid comparison from one company to another based on the profit margin because the size of the company makes such a dramatic difference in the profit margin.

To get a better perspective of the company's profitability (as compared with others in its industry), you can quickly calculate the company's *gross profit margin ratio*. To calculate gross profit margin ratio, divide profit margin by gross sales. Here's the formula:

Sales
− Cost of goods sold

Gross profit margin ÷ Sales = Gross profit margin ratio

With our ABC Company example, divide the $20 million profit margin by the $50 million in gross sales. That would give you a very respectable gross profit margin ratio of 40 percent. Again, to get a true reading, compare this ratio to the previous year's gross margin ratio, and if possible, to the gross margin ratios of other companies in the industry.

Let's calculate Johnson & Johnson's gross profit margin ratio:

$33,004 (Sales)
−   9,536 (Cost of goods sold)

23,468 ÷ 33,004 (Sales) = 0.71 (71%)

A 71-percent gross profit margin ratio is outstanding, although gross profit margins in the medical products field tend to be higher than average because the cost of their goods is relatively cheap. But they do spend sizable sums on research and development that is not included in "costs of goods sold."

Let's look at the gross profit margin of companies in two other industries. Here's Wal-Mart's numbers for its fiscal year 2002:

$217,799 million (Net sales)
− 171,562 million (Cost of sales)

46,237 ÷ 217,799 = 21.2%

As the figures indicate, Wal-Mart had a 21.2-percent gross operating margin ratio. As expected, that is far below Johnson & Johnson's because Wal-Mart faces the high cost of purchasing and transporting the goods for its stores with a relatively low margin for its retail sales. But the company does make up for its lower margins with very high sales volume.

Let's look at a heavy manufacturing company. Boeing Corp., the leading aircraft manufacturer, posts its operating margin ratio in its financial highlights table in its annual report. According to its table, the ratio varied from about 5.5 to 6.7 percent over the most recent three years. What the low numbers indicate is that Boeing has a high cost of goods and production to produce its aircraft and related products, and a relatively low margin of profit on each product sold.

That is why it is important to compare a company's profit margin ratio to other companies in the same type of industry, rather than with companies in unrelated industries where the economic dynamics may be entirely different.

But what do you do for a service company that doesn't sell any products, and therefore, does not have a "cost of goods sold?" Figure 4-1 shows a copy of the Statements of Consolidated Earnings for Automatic Data Processing, a corporate services company that processes payroll checks for thousands of companies. It sells no products.

Although you will see no category for cost of goods sold, underneath total revenue you will see a line for "operating expenses." You can use that

FIGURE 4-1

Statements of Consolidated Earnings   Automatic Data Processing, Inc. and Subsidiaries

(In thousands, except per share amounts) Years ended June 30,	2001	2000	1999
Revenues other than interest on funds held for clients and PEO revenues	$6,264,030	$5,729,042	$5,110,262
Interest on funds held for clients	518, 956	348,596	269,496
PEO revenues (A)	234,584	209,874	160,383
Total Revenues	7,017,570	6,287,512	5,540,141
Operating expenses	2,900,124	2,564,496	2,376,172
General, administrative and selling expenses	1,665,447	1,643,360	1,379,026
Systems development and programming costs	514,279	460,275	412,380
Depreciation and amortization	320,856	284,282	272,807
Interest expense	14,260	13,140	19,090
Realized (gains)/losses on investments	77,594	32,359	(3,834)
	5,492,560	4,997,912	4,455,641
Earnings before income taxes	1,525,010	1,289,600	1,084,500
Provision for income taxes	600,290	448,800	387,660
Net earnings	$ 924,720	$ 840,800	$ 696,840
Basic earnings per share	$ 1.47	$ 1.34	$ 1.13
Diluted earnings per share	$ 1.44	$ 1.31	$ 1.10
Basic shares outstanding	629,035	626,766	615,630
Diluted shares outstanding	645,989	646,098	636,892

(A) Net of pass-though costs of $2,446,768, $2,197,323, and $1,748,841 respectively.

See notes to consolidated financial statements.

to calculate gross profit margin. The company had $6,264,030 (thousand) in normal revenue and $2,900,124 (thousand) in operating expenses. So, to use the formula again:

$$\begin{array}{r} \$6,264,030 \text{ (Revenue)} \\ -\quad 2,900,124 \text{ (Operating expenses)} \\ \hline 3,363,906 \div 6,264,030 \text{ (Revenue)} = 0.537 \ (53.7\%) \end{array}$$

That gives ADP a gross profit margin ratio of 53.7 percent—a very healthy ratio. As you can see in examining some of the other results from ADP's financial statement, the company also had increasing revenue, net earnings, and earnings per share each of the years shown. For an investor interested in a solid stock, ADP's results are right on target.

BOOK VALUE (PER COMMON SHARE)

Theoretically, book value tells you what one share of common stock would be worth if all of the company's assets were liquidated and the proceeds returned to the stockholders. The assets would include the company's real estate, patents, brand names, and all other assets, minus debts and other liabilities. Most of the time, however, a company is worth far more than its book value because it has more than just valued assets. It also has a corporate infrastructure in place to produce and sell goods or services, and presumably, has some name recognition or marketing ties that should help guarantee the future success of the company. That all goes into a company's total value—which is what you're paying for when you buy the stock—but goodwill and future prospects are not included in calculating a company's book value. Book value only takes into account the company's actual assets.

But the book value (or book value per share) does give you another factor to consider in evaluating a stock. You can compare the book value with the actual stock price (the book value will be lower in the vast majority of cases), and you can compare it to the book values of other companies in the same industry. Generally, the closer a book value is to the actual stock price, the better the value to the shareholders. It may also be helpful to compare it to the book values of preceding years to see if—and how fast—the book value is increasing. That gives you another good indicator of the company's overall growth.

Here is the formula to use in calculating book value per share:

$$\begin{array}{l} \text{Total common shareholders' equity} \\ -\text{Intangible assets (goodwill, copyrights, patents, etc.)} \\ \hline \text{Balance} \div \text{number of shares of stock outstanding} = \text{Book value per share} \end{array}$$

Figure 4-2

Click here for info.

Free From Multex

Click here to download
MarketBrowser

Forbes

Download our
Media Kit

Price & Volume		Valuation Ratios	
Recent Price $	41.15	Price/Earnings (TTM)	51.18
52 Week High $	51.68	Price/Sales (TTM)	7.86
52 Week Low $	32.50	Price/Book (MRQ)	7.78
Avg Daily Vol (Mil)	4.56	Price/Cash Flow (TTM)	38.35
Beta	0.68	**Per Share Data**	
Share Related Items		Earnings (TTM) $	0.80
Mkt. Cap. (Mil) $	49,929.85	Sales (TTM) $	5.24
Shares Out (Mil)	1,213.36	Book Value (MRQ) $	5.29
Float (Mil)	1,208.50	Cash Flow (TTM) $	1.07
Dividend Information		Cash (MRQ) $	0.44
Yield %	0.61	**Mgmt Effectiveness**	
Annual Dividend	0.25	Return on Equity (TTM)	16.56
Payout Ratio (TTM) %	28.33	Return on Assets (TTM)	10.91
Financial Strength		Return on Investment (TTM)	15.76
Quick Ratio (MRQ)	0.52	**Profitability**	
Current Ratio (MRQ)	0.88	Gross Margin (TTM) %	74.22
LT Debt/Equity (MRQ)	0.00	Operating Margin (TTM) %	23.78
Total Debt/Equity (MRQ)	0.39	Profit Margin (TTM) %	15.35

Mil = Millions   MRQ = Most Recent Quarter   TTM = Trailing Twelve Months
Asterisks (*) Indicates numbers are derived from Earnings Announcements
Pricing and volume data as of 08/16/2002

Fundamental Data provided by:

market guide

You may find that it is easier to come up with book value per share—and a number of other ratios—by going to one of the many online financial sites that offer basic stock information absolutely free. Among the top sites are multexinvestor.com and hoovers.com. Figure 4-2 (above) is a "Snapshot report" on Medtronic from multexinvestor.com:

As you can see in the right column near the top, the company has a book value per share of $5.29. That's a far cry from the stock's actual trading price (top left), which is $41.15 a share.

The table also gives a variety of other data and ratios that can be helpful to investors in analyzing a stock.

Let's go over some of the other key measures and ratios:

PRICE-TO-BOOK VALUE RATIO

Instead of comparing a stock's current price to the company's earnings, you can compare the price to the worth of the company's assets—its book value. To compute the ratio, divide the stock's price by the book value per share. Here's an example:

ABC Company has a $20 stock price and a $5 book value per share. Here's how you calculate its price-to-book ratio:

$20 Current stock price ÷ $5 Book value per share = 4.0 Price-book ratio

A stock that is selling over its book value indicates that investors think highly of the company and therefore have put a high value on its assets. A stock selling at or below its book value indicates that investors have low expectations for the company and do not prize its assets. Investors who specialize in buying undervalued stocks peruse stocks selling at or below book value because they think they are getting a bargain if they can buy the stock for less than the company's assets are worth. Such stocks might also be takeover bait because another company or a raider may smell the same bargain, acquire the company, and sell off its pieces for more than their current price. Most of the time, however, these stocks do not recover. For comparative reference, a price-to-book ratio of under 2 is very good, 3 to 5 is about average, 6 to 8 is a bit below average, and over 8 is cause for some concern.

OTHER VITAL RATIOS

Here are some other important financial measures you may want to use to analyze a company's investment value:

Cash flow.   The cash flow helps measure the company's ability to generate cash. A positive cash flow means the company has more cash coming in than going out, while a negative cash flow means the company has more money going out than coming in. Some analysts consider this to be a company's most important measure of financial health. The more cash flow a company can generate, the easier it can pay its bills, dole out dividends to shareholders, and invest in new assets. To calculate cash flow, start with net income after taxes and add all other noncash charges, such as depreciation, depletion, and amortization.

> Net income after taxes
> +Depreciation and other noncash charges
> _____
> Cash Flow

Cash flow per share.   Divide the cash flow by the number of shares outstanding. Compare within industries. Generally speaking, the higher the better, and a growing cash flow per share is also a positive sign. But to get a better reading, you need to take one more step and calculate the "price-to-cash-flow-per-share ratio." To calculate that, divide the current stock price by cash flow per share. The lower the price-to-cash-flow-per-share, the cheaper the stock (relative to its cash flow). Compare with companies in the same industry.

Current ratio. A measure of the company's financial strength, the current ratio is calculated by dividing the total current assets by total current liabilities. This ratio is more applicable to product-oriented rather than to service-oriented companies. A healthy ratio for a company that keeps inventories is two to one or higher. A ratio of one is also okay, but if it's under one, it indicates that current liabilities have become greater than current assets, which is a riskier short-term financial position.

> Total current assets ÷ Total current liabilities = Current ratio

Debt-to-assets ratio. Used to help measure a company's reliance on leveraging, it is also known as the "debt ratio." The debt ratio is calculated by dividing total long-term and short-term liabilities by total assets. The lower the better (the more conservative the company). Higher leveraging can increase company's returns, but it also puts the company at higher risk in bad times. While the ratio level tends to vary by the industry, the debt should make up no more than about two-thirds to three-quarters of the company's assets—a debt-to-assets ratio of 66 to 75 percent.

> Total long-term liabilities + Total short-term liabilities
> ÷ Total assets = Debt-to-assets ratio

Debt-to-equity ratio. Also known as the *leverage ratio*, it helps measure the company's financial strength by comparing its debt financing to equity ownership. To calculate, divide long-term debt for the most recent fiscal quarter by total shareholder equity for the same period. Lower is better. For a loose reference, less than 0.1 would be considered excellent, 0.1 to 0.9 would be considered good, 1.0 to 2.0 would be considered fair, 2.1 to 4.0 would be considered below average, and more than 4 would be considered to be poor.

Diluted shares. The number of shares of common stock that would be outstanding if all convertible securities were converted to common stock. (**Diluted earnings per share** is the company's net income divided by its total number of diluted shares.)

Dividend Yield (%).   As a shareholder, dividend yield measures the percentage of the dividend payment, based on the price of the stock. It's similar to an interest rate. For instance, if you pay $100 for a share of stock that pays a $1 dividend, your dividend yield is 1 percent ($1 divided by $100). Calculate by dividing the annual dividend payment by the current price of the stock. If ABC Corp. pays a $1 dividend, and its stock is trading at $50, here is the calculation: $1 ÷ $50 = 0.02 (2 percent). So the company has a dividend yield of 2 percent.

Annual dividend payment ÷ stock price = Dividend yield

Earnings per share.   The net income divided by the number of common stock shares outstanding gives you earnings per share. A company with one million shares outstanding, and net income of $2 million, would have earnings per share of $2.

Inventory turnover ratio.   How quickly does the company sell off its products? The inventory turnover ratio, which measures the number of times inventory is turned over (or is sold) each year, helps you compare the sales success of companies in the same industry. Calculate by dividing cost of goods sold by inventory. A high ratio is preferable, and indicates that the company is selling out its goods quickly, while a low ratio means that products are not moving. But there are vast differences in inventory turnover ratios from one industry to another.

Cost of goods sold ÷ Inventory = Inventory turnover ratio

Net-sales-to-working capital ratio.   How efficiently is the company using its working capital? This ratio gives you a broad idea. To calculate, divide net sales by net working capital. (See "working capital," later in this section.) A very low ratio means you may not be getting enough out of your working capital, while a very high ratio could put you at risk of a cash shortfall if sales suddenly sink.

Operating Margin.   One measure of a company's profitability, the operating margin measures the percent of revenues remaining after paying all operating expenses. It is calculated by dividing operating income by total revenue. It is expressed as a percentage. This tends to vary by industry, but for a very rough guideline, over 50 percent would be considered excellent, 20 to 40 percent would be good, and under 10 percent would be poor.

> Operating income ÷ Total revenue = Operating margin

Price-to-cash-flow-per-share ratio. To calculate this, divide the current stock price by cash flow per share. Compare within industries—generally the lower the better. (See "cash flow" and "cash flow per share.")

Price-to-sales ratio. Refers to the stock price divided by the sales per share. This measure has gained growing importance, particularly with stocks that have little or no earnings. With no earnings—and no price-earnings ratio—the price-to-sales ratio can give you a comparative reference point in valuing a stock. As a very loose point of reference, you might consider a price-to-sales ratio of under 4 to be excellent, 5 to 8 above average, 8 to 12 about average, 13 to 18 a little higher than normal, and over 18 dangerously high. Here's the formula:

> Total revenue ÷ Shares outstanding = Revenue per share
> Stock price ÷ Revenue per share = Price-to-sales ratio

Quick ratio. Also known as the "acid test ratio," the quick ratio is a good measure of the company's current liquidity and ability to meet short-term obligations. To calculate, divide the company's current assets—its cash, short-term investments, and accounts receivable (but not its inventory)—by its current liabilities. Inventory is not included because it's not liquid—it takes time to convert inventory to cash. The higher the better, but a quick ratio of 0.5 to 1.0 is considered satisfactory.

> Current assets (not including inventory)
> ÷ Current liabilities = Quick ratio

Return on Assets. Another measure of a company's profitability, return on assets, is calculated by dividing the company's income after taxes by its total assets. It is expressed as a percentage. For rough reference, over 30 percent is considered excellent, 15 to 20 percent is very good, 10 to 15 percent is about average, 5 to 10 percent is a little below average, and under 5 percent is generally considered very poor.

> Net income (after taxes) ÷ Total assets = Return on assets

Return on Investment. (ROI). Determined by dividing the net income by assets, the ROI helps measure how effectively management is using its assets to make money. A more telling calculation sometimes used by analysts to determine ROI is to divide operational earnings by assets. "Operational earnings" refers to earnings from the company's main operations, and would not include earnings received from unrelated investments. That gives you a truer picture of how effectively the management is running the company's core operations. An ROI of more than 20 percent is excellent, 10 to 20 percent is good, and under 10 is mediocre to poor.

> Net income ÷ Total assets = Return on investment

Sales-to-receivables ratio. Is the company collecting on its sales? This ratio, which measures the number of times a company turns over its accounts receivables each period, helps illustrate how effective a company is at collecting its debts. Calculate by dividing net sales (from the income statement) by net receivables (from the balance sheet). A higher ratio is better, indicating efficient collection of debts. However, this ratio can vary dramatically by industry, so it is best used to compare companies in the same industry.

Working capital. A measure of the company's cash flow, working capital, is calculated by subtracting current liabilities from current assets (such as cash, accounts receivable, short-term investments, and inventory). The higher the working capital, the more financially secure the company.

$$\begin{array}{r} \text{Current liabilities} \\ -\text{Current assets} \\ \hline \text{Working capital} \end{array}$$

THE PE—WALL STREET'S FAVORITE RATIO

Without a doubt, the price-earnings ratio is Wall Street's most commonly used measure of a stock's value. All other ratios and formulas pale in comparison to the price-to-earnings ratio—generally referred to, simply, as the "PE."

Literally translated, the price-earnings ratio means *the stock price divided by the earnings per share.* For example, a $10 stock with annual earnings of $1 per share would have a PE of 10 ($10 divided by $1). Normally, the PE is based on the most recent (trailing) four quarters of earnings. A stock with no earnings or losses would not have a PE.

> Price of the stock
> ÷ Earnings per share
> Price-to-earnings ratio

PEs are a lot like golf scores—the lower the better. That's why on Wall Street, a low stock price doesn't necessarily mean the stock is cheap. In fact, in value terms, a $100 stock could be cheaper than a $3 stock. It all depends on the *price-earnings ratio*.

Many professionals and individual investors decide which stocks to buy and sell based largely on the PE. (The PEs are listed every day in the stock tables of most major newspapers, as well as at nearly any Internet financial site.) Investors often watch the PEs as closely as the stock price itself. In the late 1990s, when investors ignored the PE and bought tech stocks with astronomical PEs, they ultimately paid the price when tech stocks crashed. But investors who owned stocks with reasonable PE ratios (primarily outside the tech sector) escaped the market crash relatively unscathed. That's why the PE is a measure every serious investor should understand.

Which of the following stocks would be cheaper in Wall Street terms?

• A $30 stock with earnings of $1 per share (a PE of 30)?

• A $100 stock with earnings of $10 a share (a PE of 10)?

In value terms, the $100 stock would be cheaper than the $30 stock, because the PE of the $100 stock is one-third that of the $30 stock.

Most established blue chip stocks have PEs in the range of 10 to 30. The average PE for a stock on the Dow Jones Industrial Average over the past 50 years has been about 13, although over the past 10 years that figure has climbed to about 18. In fact, the average PE jumped to over 20 during the bull market run of the late 1990s, and hit a peak just before the market started its downward slide.

In comparing PEs, think of buying a stock in much the same way as you would think of buying a business. If you can buy a business for $10 that earns $1 a year (10 PE), that would seem to be a much better value than to buy a business for $30 with that same $1 of earnings (30 PE).

So why doesn't everyone buy stocks with the lowest possible PE? Because some companies really are worth more than others. Great companies with fast earnings growth command a premium over slow-growing companies, as well they should.

For a stock to be fairly priced, its PE should roughly reflect its earnings growth rate. If earnings are growing at 30 to 40 percent, then the PE should be in the 30 to 50 range. If earning are growing at 15 percent per year, the PE should be closer to 15 to 20.

Picking stocks based on PEs can be tricky. Some industries command higher PEs than others. Tobacco and military stocks, for instance, often have very low PEs, while technology and medical stocks tend to support fairly high ratios.

The best point of comparison may be the stock's own historical PEs. If a stock has had a 20 PE through most of its history, and its earnings are continuing to grow at the same pace, then you would probably be safe to buy the stock when its PE is around 20 or less. If the PE has climbed closer to 30—and the earnings growth has remained the same—you might be better served to look for other opportunities and wait for the PE of that stock to drop back down before buying.

The PE, however, is just one factor to use in judging a stock. Never buy a stock based on its PE alone. But for stocks that meet your other standards, the PE can help you sift out the bargains, and decide when to buy and when to sell.

LOW-PE STOCKS

Some investors focus exclusively on low-PE stocks, often with good success. In fact, studies have shown that low-PE stocks, as a group, tend to outperform the overall market. But that's not to say that there is no risk to low-PE stocks. Keep in mind, those stocks have a low PE for a reason. It might be because their earnings growth has been slow, or the company is facing legal problems, or its prospects for future growth are considered poor. But for whatever reason, Wall Street has put a low value on that stock. Fortunately for low-PE investors, Wall Street makes plenty of mistakes. That's why low-PE investors continue their search for the diamonds in the rough—low-PE companies with solid growth and strong future prospects that Wall Street has overlooked.

There is one big problem with investing exclusively in low-PE stocks, according to money manager Lee Kopp. People who only buy low-PE stocks will never own the great companies. "They're missing out on some great opportunities," says Kopp. "They have their heads in the sand." The great stocks always command a premium. You'll never find the fastest growing, most dynamic companies in the bargain bin. For short-term investments, low-PE stocks can provide some surprising returns. Just don't build your entire portfolio around them. If you keep an eye out for low-PE stocks, you may be able to catch some big gains on the turnaround. Or as Minneapolis business-man Dennis Kleve puts it: "I'm not cheap. I just want a good deal."

Where can you find low-PE stocks? Price-earnings ratios are listed in the stock tables of the *Wall Street Journal, Investor's Business Daily,* and most major newspapers, as well as on most online investment sites. (See my list of favorites, Chapter 12.) An easier way to find cheap stocks is through the *Value*

Line Investment Survey (which should be available at your public library). Value Line publishes a list of the lowest-PE stocks in each of its weekly updates. A number of online investment sites also allow you to do special screens to identify low-PE and high-PE stocks.

HIGH-PE SECTORS
It is not unusual for the price-earnings ratios of an entire sector to become irrationally high from time to time. If you own stocks in an overpriced sector, you can save yourself some heavy losses by unloading those stocks before they begin to plummet.

There have been several times in recent history when PEs of certain sectors became dangerously high. Those times are usually easy to recognize, because the rationale for the high prices from the experts on Wall Street is almost always the same: "This time it's different. These stocks can support exorbitantly high PEs because (fill in the blank)." Sometimes the claim is that the dynamics of valuing stocks has changed; sometimes it's because a particular sector has "unlimited" potential. There have been many rationales for exorbitant PEs, but none have held up over time. Stocks with high PEs have always come back to earth.

Here is a brief history lesson. The most recent example was the Internet stock phenomenon. Stocks of little-known companies were carrying PEs of 100 to 200 (and beyond). In fact, many Internet stocks had no earnings at all and no prospect for achieving earnings any time in the foreseeable future. Yet the hype surrounding the Internet sector was so pervasive that investors poured billions of dollars into those stocks. And the higher those stocks climbed, the faster the money poured into the market. But when the bubble burst, it took down hundreds of Internet companies along with the millions of investors who had staked much of their retirement dollars on those stocks.

But the Internet meltdown was just one example in a long history of market madness. In the early 1980s, high-tech start-up stocks and biotech stocks were the rage with investors who believed that there could be no end to their spectacular growth. It mattered little that many of those companies still had no earnings, or very small earnings, and no track records. Investors still were bidding up the prices. PEs climbed into the 50-to-100 range. And the rationalizations from Wall Street's experts began: "These stocks are different from the blue chips. They can support higher PEs because of their potential for rapid growth." When the rapid growth never materialized, investors lost interest in the sector and prices fell through the floor. Stocks trading as high as $30 or $40 per share were suddenly going begging at $6 or $8.

In the late 1980s, Japanese stocks roared to record levels. Many stocks carried PEs as high as 100 to 200—levels that were virtually unheard of in the history of the stock market. Unfazed investors continued to buy, while Japanese brokers continued to tout the stocks. "This time it's different," they said. "This is the great Japanese financial empire, an empire that is taking over the world's financial markets, the world's manufacturing markets, and the world's high technology markets. These stocks can support the higher PEs because they are part of this great Japanese economic machine." But suddenly the machine ground to a halt, the bottom fell out of the Japanese economy, and hundreds of stocks dropped to a fraction of their former highs. Some 15 years later, Japan's Nikkei Stock Exchange was trading at less than one-third of its peak level of the late 1980s.

In 1991, medical stocks suddenly caught fire. Merck climbed 80 percent. Pfizer went from $40 to $84 a share. Stryker went from $16 to $50. Across the board, medical stocks were climbing far faster than the market averages. PEs were moving into the 40-to-70 range. And once again, the rationalizations from Wall Street analysts began: "This time it's different. The world's population is aging, and the need for medical products will continue to expand. That's why these stocks can support high PEs." But once the frenzy wore off in 1992, those stocks began to slide, continuing to decline for about two years to the point where great stocks with great earnings such as Merck and Bristol-Myers Squibb were actually carrying PEs in the low teens. They went from overpriced to underpriced—until Wall Street finally rediscovered them in 1995 and pushed their prices back up to fair market value.

If you own stocks of a sector with PEs that seem way out of whack, be prepared to lighten your position. Your sell signal will be those wise words from Wall Street: "But this time it's different." Get out, take your profit, and move on. Invoke the Greater Fool's Theory to your own benefit and let the next guy take the fall. Or as General George Patton once put it: "The object of war is not to die for your country but to make the other bastard die for his."

THE REPORT TYPES AND WHAT THEY MEAN

FORM 10-K: GETTING TO THE MEAT OF THE MATTER

"Facts. Facts alone are wanted in life. Plant nothing else, and root out everything else."

— *Charles Dickens*, *Hard Times*

THERE ARE TWO SIDES TO EVERY STORY (and sometimes more). In the corporate world, if you want the *varnished* version of a company's story, the annual report is your best source. But for the unvarnished version, the 10-K is the answer. No graphics, no photos, no puff pieces about the corporate mission, the 10-K contains page after page of in-depth information and cold, hard facts about the company's operation and its financial performance over the past fiscal year. Dull, dry, and matter-of-fact, 10-Ks are single-spaced documents printed on plain white paper—and now, of course, on file electronically at EDGAR in the simplest html or text formats. The 10-K offers details of the company's history, its industry, its corporate marketing strategy, its product mix, its distribution system, its customers, competitors, employees, key officers, and its international operations, as well as reams of financial information. Any significant lawsuits or other significant legal matters in which the company is involved would also be discussed in the 10-K.

The 10-K is no puff piece. It is a long, factual, detailed report that reveals an immense amount of information about all aspects of the corporation. It's the key document that analysts on Wall Street use to size up a company and its investment potential, and it's the essential document you need to make a comprehensive analysis of a company's operations and prospects.

In this chapter and the next one, we go over all the key elements of a 10-K report in detail, offering some real-life examples of reports filed with the SEC.

We hope to answer several important questions in the report:

- What is the company's principal line of business?

- What are its leading business segments?

- How does the company market its products?

- Does it have any international operations?

- What type of competition does it face?

- Is it involved in any significant legal battles?

- Who are the top officers of the company?

- Is the company profitable and growing? (more on that in Chapter 6)

FINDING THE 10-K

Before you can read it, the first thing you need to do is find the 10-K report at the EDGAR site. Let's say you are doing research on Johnson & Johnson, and you want to find its 10-K report or any other report filed with the SEC. It's very quick and very simple. Here is a short step-by-step guide:

1. Go to the EDGAR Web site at *www.sec.gov*. (See Figure 5-1.)

2. Look under the second column on the left: "Filings and Forms (EDGAR)." You'll see the subhead, "Search for Company Filings." Click on that. (Web site home pages are constantly being updated, so the page you see may be somewhat different than the example we use in Figure 5-1. Regardless of any change in the home page, you should still be able to find the "Search for Company Filings" link with little problem.)

3. That will lead you to the company search page. (See Figure 5-2.) Simply enter the name "Johnson & Johnson" in the box, and click.

4. That will bring you to a directory of filings from Johnson & Johnson. (See Figure 5-3.) Look down the list until you find "10-K" and click on that. That will bring you to the 10-K report, so you can begin to research the company.

FIGURE 5-1 SEC home page.

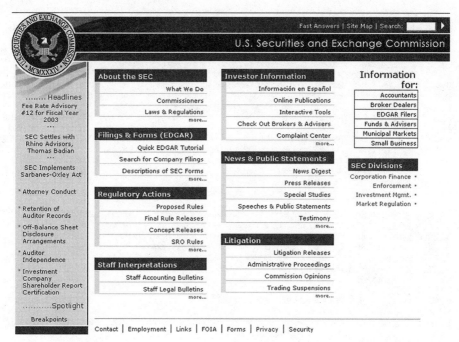

FIGURE 5-2 Company search.

EDGAR Company Search

From this page, you can search the EDGAR database for company information, including real-time filings. If more than one company name matches your search keyword(s), you will be presented with a list of possible matches from which to pick. Company filings are available for **1993** through **2003**.

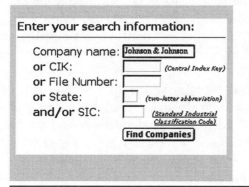

FIGURE 5-3 Filings directory.

Items 81–160

Form	Formats	Description	Filing Date	File Number
8-K	[html][text] 9 KB	Current report	2002-08-13	001-03215
10-Q	[html][text] 58 KB	Quarterly report [Sections 13 or 15(d)]	2002-08-12	001-03215
S-8	[html][text] 25 KB	Securities to be offered to employees in employee benefit plans	2002-07-16	333-96541
10-K/A	[html][text] 295 KB	[Amend]Annual report [Section 13 and 15(d), not S-K Item 405]	2002-06-27	001-03215
10-Q	[html][text] 42 KB	Quarterly report [Sections 13 or 15(d)]	2002-05-14	001-03215
424B3	[html][text] 4 KB	Prospectus [Rule 424(b)(3)]	2002-05-10	333-67020
S-8	[html][text] 28 KB	Securities to be offered to employees in employee benefit plans	2002-05-07	333-87736
8-K/A	[html][text] 11 KB	[Amend]Current report	2002-04-30	001-03215
8-K	[html][text] 8 KB	Current report	2002-04-16	001-03215
424B3	[html][text] 5 KB	Prospectus [Rule 424(b)(3)]	2002-04-12	333-67020
SC 13G/A	[html][text] 13 KB	[Amend]Statement of acquisition of beneficial ownership by individuals	2002-04-05	
5	[html][text] 19 KB	Annual statement of changes in beneficial ownership of securities	2002-03-27	
10-K	[html][text] 285 KB	Annual report [Section 13 and 15(d), not S-K Item 405]	2002-03-20	001-03215
DEF 14A	[html][text] 101 KB	Other definitive proxy statements	2002-03-13	001-03215
ARS	[html][text] 1 KB	[Paper]Annual Report to Security Holders Film# = 02024008	2002-03-13	001-03215
SC 13G/A	[html][text] 11 KB	[Amend]Statement of acquisition of beneficial ownership by individuals	2002-02-14	
SC 13G/A	[html][text] 11 KB	[Amend]Statement of acquisition of beneficial ownership by individuals	2002-02-14	
SC 13G/A	[html][text] 12 KB	[Amend]Statement of acquisition of beneficial ownership by individuals	2002-02-14	
SC 13G	[html][text] 15 KB	Statement of acquisition of beneficial ownership by individuals	2002-02-14	
NO ACT	[html][text] 1 KB	[Paper]Film# = 02020226	2002-02-13	001-03215
NO ACT	[html][text] 1 KB	[Paper]Film# = 02024541	2002-02-12	001-03215
NO ACT	[html][text] 1 KB	[Paper]Film# = 02016351	2002-01-30	001-03215
NO ACT	[html][text] 1 KB	[Paper]Film# = 02016311	2002-01-25	001-03215
NO ACT	[html][text] 1 KB	[Paper]Film# = 02016313	2002-01-25	001-03215
8-K/A	[html][text] 7 KB	[Amend]Current report	2001-11-30	001-03215
S-8 POS	[html][text] 37 KB	Securities to be offered to employees in employee benefit plans, post-effective amendments	2001-11-29	333-67370

BREAKING DOWN THE 10-K

We go through the 10-K section by section, to identify areas of interest, and to point out the significance of each section:

Opening page. The opening page usually gives the name, address, and phone number of the company. Figure 5-4 shows the opening page from the William Wrigley report:

Table of Contents. After the opening page comes a rather lengthy table of contents. 10-K reports tend to be long documents that can exceed 100 pages of single-spaced copy. If you're looking for specific tables or categories of information, the table of contents can often help you locate it much more quickly.

All 10-Ks contain four parts. The first covers information on the operation of the company; the second provides information on the financial condition of the company; the third discusses the directors and executives; and the fourth covers exhibits, schedules, and other reports. Typically, section three simply refers readers to the proxy statement for more information about the company's directors and executives.

FIGURE 5-4 Opening page of 10-K report.

10-K 1 form10k01.htm SEC FORM 10-K FOR THE PERIOD ENDING 12/31/01

SECURITIES AND EXCHANGE COMMISSION
WASHINGTON, D.C. 20549

FORM 10-K

[X]   **ANNUAL REPORT PURSUANT TO SECTION 13 OR 15(d)**
OF THE SECURITIES EXCHANGE ACT OF 1934

[ ]   **TRANSITION REPORT PURSUANT TO SECTION 13 OR 15(d)**
OF THE SECURITIES EXCHANGE ACT OF 1934

For the fiscal year ended December 31, 2001   Commission file number 1-800

WM. WRIGLEY JR. COMPANY
(Exact name of registrant as specified in its charter)

Delaware	36-1988190
(State or other jurisdiction of incorporation or organization)	(I.R.S. Employer Identification No.)
410 North Michigan Avenue Chicago, Illinois	60611
(Address of principal executive offices)	(Zip Code)

Registrant's telephone number, including Area Code: (312) 644-2121

Securities registered pursuant to Section 12(b) of the Act:

Title of each class	Name of each exchange on which registered
Common Stock, no par value	New York Stock Exchange Chicago Stock Exchange

Securities registered pursuant to Section 12(g) of the Act:
Title of each class
Class B Common Stock, no par value

Indicate by check mark whether the Registrant (1) has filed all reports required to be filed by Section 13 or 15(d) of the Securities Exchange Act of 1934 during the preceding 12 months (or for such shorter period that the Registrant was required to file such reports), and (2) has been subject to such filing requirements for the past 90 days.   Yes X   No __

This sample table of contents from the 2001 Johnson & Johnson 10-K report lists all the key elements of a 10-K report:

PART I

PART II

PART III

PART IV

BUSINESS SUMMARY

This section of the 10-K report (under the heading "Item 1. Business") is usually brief, fact-filled, and well worth reading. You can usually learn a lot about the company in a quick glance. The opening paragraph or two (and in some cases several paragraphs) usually provides a brief summary of the company's business and perhaps some historical information, as well. Here are some examples of opening sections:

ITEM 1. BUSINESS

GENERAL

Johnson & Johnson, employing approximately 101,800 people worldwide, is engaged in the manufacture and sale of a broad range of products in the health care field. With over 190 operating companies, it conducts business in virtually all countries of the world. Johnson & Johnson's primary interest, both historically and currently, has been in products related to human health and well-being. Johnson & Johnson was organized in the State of New Jersey in 1887.

Johnson & Johnson is organized on the principle of decentralized management. The Executive Committee of Johnson & Johnson is the principal management group responsible for the allocation of the resources of the Company. This Committee oversees and coordinates the activities of U.S. and international companies related to each of the Consumer, Pharmaceutical and Medical Devices & Diagnostics businesses. Each international subsidiary is, with some exceptions, managed by citizens of the country where it is located.

You learn a lot in those paragraphs. You learn that the company is a significant employer with more than 100,000 employees around the world. You learn that it is involved in manufacturing health care products, that it has 190 different operating companies in the organization, and that it has operations in virtually every country in the world. You also learn that the company was founded in New Jersey in 1887. As an investor, you've learned in a single paragraph that this company is a worldwide force in the healthcare industry that has been around for more than 100 years. While that is just part of the picture, those are strong points that should give you confidence in the company's business model and long-term prospects. Clearly, this is not a fly-by-night operation.

In the second paragraph, you get some insight into the company's management strategy—190 separate operating companies in a decentralized structure. You also learn that the company breaks its operations into three key business segments, Consumer, Pharmaceutical, and Medical Devices & Diagnostics.

Let's look at another example, the opening paragraph of the Automatic Data Processing 10-K report:

Automatic Data Processing, Inc., incorporated in Delaware in 1961 (together with its subsidiaries "ADP" or the "Registrant"), is one of the largest providers of computerized transaction processing, data communication, and information services in the world.

Obviously, ADP's opening business summary is not as complete as Johnson & Johnson's—every report is a little different—but you do learn that ADP is one of the largest companies in the world in the transaction processing business.

You also learn something that is a little bit deceiving. The opening line states that ADP was incorporated in Delaware in 1961, which might lead you to believe that ADP began business in 1961, or at least, first incorporated as a business in 1961. Both assumptions are wrong. ADP began business in the late 1940s—and was probably incorporated originally in its home state of New Jersey. But because of favorable tax laws, many U.S. corporations formally incorporate their businesses in Delaware to get the tax breaks—even though their operations are conducted from home offices in other states. You will see the same thing in many 10-K reports. Sometimes, the report will mention when the company was originally founded, and the year it was incorporated in Delaware. But companies do not always include their founding year in the report, nor are they required to.

Here's another opening section from Medtronic's 10-K report. Rather than a brief one- or two-paragraph opening, Medtronic opens with several paragraphs on its operations and history:

Medtronic is a world-leading medical technology company, providing lifelong solutions for people with chronic disease. We are committed to offering market-leading therapies worldwide to restore patients to fuller, healthier lives. With roots in the treatment of heart disease, we have expanded well beyond our historical core business and today provide a wide range of products and therapies that help solve many challenging, life-limiting medical conditions. We hold market-leading positions in almost all of the major markets in which we compete.

We currently operate in five operating segments that manufacture and sell device-based medical therapies. Our business units are:
• Cardiac Rhythm Management ("CRM")
• Vascular
• Cardiac Surgery
• Neurological and Diabetes
• Spinal and ENT

With innovation and market leadership, we have pioneered advances in medical technology in all of our business units and enjoyed steady growth. Over the last five years, our net sales have more than doubled, from $3,010.3 million in fiscal 1997 to $6,410.8 million in fiscal 2002. We attribute this growth to our continuing commitment to develop or acquire new products to treat an expanding array of medical conditions. Medtronic was founded in 1949, incorporated as a Minnesota corporation in 1957 and today serves physicians, clinicians and patients in more than 120 countries worldwide. Beginning with the development of the heart pacemaker in the 1950s, we have assembled a broad and diverse portfolio of progressive technology expertise both through internal development of core technologies as well as acquisitions. We remain committed to a mission written by our founder more than 40 years ago that directs the Company "to contribute to human welfare by application of biomedical engineering in the research, design, manufacture and sale of products that alleviate pain, restore health and extend life.

The opening section gives you some history and perspective on Medtronic—founded in 1949; does business in 120 countries; developed a heart pacemaker in the 1950s; holds "market-leading positions" in several medical product segments; has net sales of $6.4 billion. That's all helpful material in assessing the company. But some of the copy is more promotional in tone than you'll find in other 10-Ks. Phrases like "innovation and market leadership," "broad and diverse portfolio of progressive technology expertise," "challenging, life-limiting medical conditions," and "restore patients to fuller, healthier lives," are usually reserved for the annual report. Serious investors prefer not to wade through fluff to get the facts in the 10-K. And generally, that's the case—all the details laid out in a straight, business-like format.

BUSINESS SEGMENTS

After the brief opening section, the 10-K generally moves onto a fuller description of the company's operations. Many 10-Ks offer details of each of the company's business segments, as we see in the Enron 10-K report:

BUSINESS SEGMENTS

Enron's operations are classified into the following four business segments:
1) Transportation and Operation: Interstate transmission of natural gas; construction, management and operation of natural gas pipelines and clean fuels plants; and investment in crude oil transportation activities.
2) Domestic Gas and Power Services: Purchasing, marketing and financing of natural gas, natural gas liquids, crude oil and electricity; price risk management in connection with natural gas, natural gas liquids, crude oil and electricity transactions; intrastate natural gas pipelines; development, acquisition and promotion of natural gas-fired power plants in North America; and extraction of natural gas liquids.
3) International Operations and Development: Independent (non-utility) development, acquisition and promotion of power plants, natural gas liquids facilities and pipelines outside of North America.
4) Exploration and Production: Natural gas and crude oil exploration and production primarily in the United States, Canada, Trinidad and India.

As you can see, the business segments section gives you some pretty informative details on each of the key areas of the company's operations.

Here's a similar section from the Johnson & Johnson 10-K:

SEGMENTS OF BUSINESS; GEOGRAPHIC AREAS

Johnson & Johnson's worldwide business is divided into three segments: Consumer, Pharmaceutical and Medical Devices & Diagnostics. Additionalinformation required by this item is incorporated herein by reference to the narrative and tabular (but not the graphic) descriptions of segments and geographic areas captioned "Management's Discussion and Analysis of Results ofOperations and Financial Condition—Segments of Business, Consumer, Pharmaceutical, Medical Devices & Diagnostics and Geographic Areas" on pages 27 through 29 and 49 of Johnson & Johnson's Annual Report to Shareowners for fiscal year 2001.

CONSUMER

The Consumer segment's principal products are personal care and hygienic products, including nonprescription drugs, adult skin and hair care products, baby care products, oral care products, first aid products and sanitary protection products. Major brands include AVEENO skin care products; BAND-AID Brand Adhesive Bandages; BENECOL food products; CARE-FREE Panty Shields; CLEAN & CLEAR teen skin care products; IMODIUM A-D, an antidiarrheal; JOHNSON'S Baby line of products; JOHNSON'S pH 5.5 skin and hair care products; LACTAID lactose-intolerance products; MONISTAT, a remedy for vaginal yeast infections; adult and children's MOTRIN IB ibuprofen products; MYLANTA gastrointestinal products and PEPCID AC Acid Controller from the Johnson & Johnson - Merck Consumer Pharmaceuticals Co.; NEUTROGENA skin and hair care products; o.b. Tampons; PENATEN and NATUSAN baby care products; PIZ BUIN and SUNDOWN sun care products; REACH toothbrushes; RoC skin care products; SHOWER TO SHOWER personal care products; SPLENDA, a non-caloric sugar substitute; STAYFREE sanitary protection products; the broad family of TYLENOL acetaminophen products; and VIACTIV calcium supplements. These products are marketed principally to the general public and distributed both to wholesalers and directly to independent and chain retail outlets.

PHARMACEUTICAL

The Pharmaceutical segment's principal worldwide franchises are in the antifungal, anti-infective, cardiovascular, dermatology, gastrointestinal, hematology, immunology, neurology, oncology, pain management, psychotropic, urology and women's health fields. These products are distributed both directly and through wholesalers for use by health care professionals and the general public. Prescription drugs in the antifungal field include NIZORAL (ketoconazole), SPORANOX (itraconazole), TERAZOL (terconazole) and DAKTARIN (miconazole nitrate) antifungal products. Prescription drugs in the anti-infective field include FLOXIN (ofloxacin) and LEVAQUIN (levofloxacin). Prescription drugs in the cardiovascular field include RETAVASE (reteplase), a recombinant biologic cardiology care product for the treatment of acute myocardial infarction to improve blood flow to the heart, and REOPRO (abciximab) for the treatment of acute cardiac disease. Prescription drugs in the dermatology field include RETIN-A MICRO (tretinoin), a dermatological cream for acne. Prescription drugs in the gastrointestinal field include ACIPHEX (rabeprazole sodium, sold outside the U.S. as PARIET), a proton pump inhibitor for treating erosive gastroesophageal reflux disease (GERD), symptomatic GERD and duodenal ulcers; IMODIUM (loperamide HCl), an antidiarrheal; MOTILIUM (domperidone), a gastrointestinal mobilizer; and REMICADE (infliximab), a novel monoclonal antibody for treatment of certain Crohn's disease patients. REMICADE is also indicated for the treatment of rheumatoid arthritis.

Prescription drugs in the hematology field include PROCRIT (epoetin alfa, sold outside the U.S. as EPREX), a biotechnology derived version of the human hormone erythropoietin that stimulates red blood cell production, which accounted for 10.4% of the Company's total revenues in 2001. Prescription drugs in the immunology field include ORTHO-CLONE OKT-3 (muromonab-CD3), for reversing the rejection of kidney, heart and liver transplants. Prescription drugs in the neurology field include REMINYL (galantamine), TOPAMAX (topiramate) and STUGERON (cinnarizine). Prescription drugs in the oncology field include DOXIL (doxorubicin), an anti-cancer treatment, ERGAMISOL (levamisole hydrochloride), a colon cancer drug, and LEUSTATIN (cladribine), for hairy cell leukemia. Prescription drugs in the pain management field include DURAGESIC (fentanyl transdermal system, sold abroad as DUROGESIC), a transdermal patch for chronic pain; ULTRACET (tramadol hydrochloride/acetaminophen) for the short-term management of acute pain; and ULTRAM (tramadol hydrochloride), an analgesic for moderate to moderately severe pain. Prescription drugs in the psychotropics (central nervous system) field include RISPERDAL (risperidone) and HALDOL (haloperidol), antipsychotic drugs, and CONCERTA (methylphenidate) for Attention Deficit/Hyperactivity Disorder. Prescription drugs in the urology field include DITROPAN XL (oxybutynin) for treatment of overactive bladder. Prescription drugs in the women's health field include ORTHO-NOVUM (norethindrone/ethinyl estradiol) and TRICILEST (norgestimate/ethinyl estradiol, sold in the U.S. as ORTHO TRI-CYCLEN) group of oral contraceptives and ORTHO-PREFEST (17 (beta)- estradiol/norgestimate) for hormone replacement therapy. In 2001, sales to three distributors, McKesson HBOC, Cardinal Distribution and AmerisourceBergen Corp. accounted for 10.4%, 10.3% and 10.2%, respectively, of total revenues. These sales were concentrated in the Pharmaceutical segment.

MEDICAL DEVICES & DIAGNOSTICS

The Medical Devices & Diagnostics segment includes a broad range of products used by or under the direction of health care professionals,

including, suture and mechanical wound closure products, surgical equipment and devices, wound management and infection prevention products,
interventional and diagnostic cardiology products, diagnostic equipment
and supplies, joint replacements and disposable contact lenses. These
products are used principally in the professional fields by physicians,
nurses, therapists, hospitals, diagnostic laboratories and clinics. Distribution to these markets is done both directly and through surgical supply
and other dealers.

Not exactly compelling, edge-of-your-seat drama, but the section does
offer a detailed review of each of Johnson & Johnson's business segments,
including a listing of nearly every product the company manufactures. It's the
kind of detailed information you need to know before deciding if it's the type
of company that is worthy of your investment dollars.

INTERNATIONAL OPERATIONS

Next in the 10-K comes information about international operations—if the
company actually does business outside the United States. Generally, international operations are summarized in a quick paragraph or two. The paragraph
often states the number of countries in which the company does business and
the percentage of revenue generated outside the United States. Here is the section on international operations from the Johnson & Johnson 10-K:

INTERNATIONAL

The international business of Johnson & Johnson is conducted by subsidiaries located in 54 countries outside the United States, which are selling
products in more than 175 countries throughout the world. The products
made and sold in the international business include many of those
described above under "Business—Consumer, Pharmaceutical and Medical Devices & Diagnostics." However, the principal markets, products and
methods of distribution in the international business vary with the country
and the culture. The products sold in the international business include not
only those which were developed in the United States but also those which
were developed by subsidiaries abroad. Investments and activities in some
countries outside the United States are subject to higher risks than comparable domestic activities because the investment and commercial climate is
influenced by restrictive economic policies and political uncertainties.

You'll notice that the above paragraph does not give a percentage breakdown of international revenue versus U.S. revenue. That information would be
available elsewhere in the report or in the financial section of the annual
report.

In Pitney Bowe's 10-K report, the company offers even less information
in the international section:

Operations Outside the United States

Our manufacturing operations outside the U.S. are in the United Kingdom, France and Germany.

That's the extent of Pitney's international details, although more information is probably available elsewhere in the 10-K or annual report.

Here's one more example from the international section of the Merck 10-K report:

Geographic Area and Segment Information

The Company's operations outside the United States are conducted primarily through subsidiaries. Sales of the Company's human health products by subsidiaries outside the United States were 37% of the Company's human health sales in 2001, and 36% and 40% in 2000 and 1999, respectively.

The Company's worldwide business is subject to risks of currency fluctuations, governmental actions and other governmental proceedings abroad. The Company does not regard these risks as a deterrent to further expansion of its operations abroad. However, the Company closely reviews its methods of operations and adopts strategies responsive to changing economic and political conditions.

In recent years, the Company has been expanding its operations in countries located in Latin America, the Middle East, Africa, Eastern Europe and Asia Pacific where changes in government policies and economic conditions are making it possible for the Company to earn fair returns. Business in these developing areas, while sometimes less stable, offers important opportunities for growth over time.

Financial information about geographic areas and operating segments of the Company's business is incorporated by reference to page 37 of the Company's 2001 Annual Report to stockholders.

As you can see, Merck provides some details of its international operations, and then refers readers to page 37 of the annual report where they can find more information on the subject.

MARKETING

Some 10-Ks also include a section on marketing, although it is generally fairly brief, like the following one from the Pitney Bowes report:

Marketing

Our products and services are marketed through an extensive network of offices in the U.S. and through a number of our subsidiaries and independent distributors and dealers in many countries throughout the world. We also use direct marketing, outbound telemarketing, and the Internet. We sell to a variety of business, governmental, institutional and other organizations. We believe we have a broad base of customers, and we are not dependent upon any one customer or type of customer for a significant part of our business. The company does not have significant backlog or seasonality relating to its businesses.

In its 10-K report, Harley-Davidson discusses the marketing of its motorbikes as well as the type of customer most likely to buy a Harley:

> Studies by the Company indicate that the average U.S. Harley-Davidson motorcycle purchaser is a married male in his mid-forties, with a household income of approximately $78,300, who purchases a motorcycle for recreational purposes rather than to provide transportation and is an experienced motorcycle rider. Over two-thirds of the Company's U.S. sales of Harley-Davidson motorcycles are to buyers with at least one year of education beyond high school, and 31% of the buyers have college degrees. Approximately 9% of the Company's Harley-Davidson U.S. retail motorcycle sales are to female buyers.

RESEARCH AND DEVELOPMENT

Most 10-Ks include a short section on research and development—generally no longer than one or two paragraphs. Here is an example from the Merck 10-K:

> Research and Development/Patents
>
> We have research and development programs that are directed toward developing new products and service methods. Our expenditures on research and development totaled $133.1 million, $120.5 million, and $108.9 million in 2001, 2000, and 1999, respectively.
>
> As a result of our research and development efforts, we have been awarded a number of patents with respect to several of our existing and planned products. However, we believe our businesses are not materially dependent on any one patent or any group of related patents. We also believe our businesses are not materially dependent on any one license or any group of related licenses.

You may have noticed that the company includes R&D expenditures for the most recent three years. When looking at R&D numbers, consider it a healthy sign if research spending goes up every year (as was the case with Merck). You want to invest in companies that value a growing commitment to R&D. Here is another example from the Johnson & Johnson 10-K:

RESEARCH

Research activities are important to all segments of Johnson & Johnson's business. Major research facilities are located not only in the United States but also in Australia, Belgium, Brazil, Canada, Germany, Switzerland and the United Kingdom. The costs of Johnson & Johnson's worldwide research activities relating to the development of new products, the improvement of existing products, technical support of products and compliance with governmental regulations for the protection of the consumer amounted to $3,591, $3,105, and $2,768 million for fiscal years 2001, 2000 and 1999, respectively. These costs are charged directly to income in the year in which incurred. All research was sponsored by Johnson & Johnson.

As you see, Johnson & Johnson also reported research expenditures for the most recent three-year period—and those expenditures increased each year.

Not all research sections are the same, however. In the Merck 10-K, the company provides a great depth of information about many aspects of its research efforts:

Research and Development

The Company's business is characterized by the introduction of new products or new uses for existing products through a strong research and development program. Approximately 11,900 people are employed in the Company's research activities. Expenditures for the Company's research and development programs were $2.5 billion in 2001, $2.3 billion in 2000 and $2.1 billion in 1999 and will be approximately $2.9 billion in 2002. The Company maintains its ongoing commitment to research over a broad range of therapeutic areas and clinical development in support of new products. Total expenditures for the period 1992 through 2001 exceeded $16.7 billion with a compound annual growth rate of 10%.

The Company maintains a number of long-term exploratory and fundamental research programs in biology and chemistry as well as research programs directed toward product development. Projects related to human health are being carried on in various fields such as bacterial and viral infections, cardiovascular functions, cancer, diabetes, pain and inflammation, kidney function, obesity, mental health, the nervous system, ophthalmic research, prostate therapy, the respiratory system, fungal diseases, bone diseases, endoparasitic and ectoparasitic diseases, companion animal diseases and production improvement.

In the development of human health products, industry practice and government regulations in the United States and most foreign countries provide for the determination of effectiveness and safety of new chemical compounds through preclinical tests and controlled clinical evaluation. Before a new drug may be marketed in the United States, recorded data on preclinical and clinical experience are included in the NDA or the biological Product License Application to the FDA for the required approval. The development of certain other products is also subject to government regulations covering safety and efficacy in the United States and many foreign countries. There can be no assurance that a compound that is the result of any particular program will obtain the regulatory approvals necessary for it to be marketed.

New product candidates resulting from this research and development program include Arcoxia (etoricoxib), a second COX-2 specific inhibitor potentially useful for the treatment of osteoarthritis, rheumatoid arthritis, acute pain, chronic pain and dysmenorrhea, for which the Company filed an NDA with the FDA on August 8, 2001. The Company plans to submit an expanded NDA for Arcoxia to the FDA in order to include new efficacy data that will better position the product to compete successfully in the coxib class, where there already are three entrants. Accordingly, on March 13, 2002, the Company withdrew the original U.S. NDA for the investigational medicine. The Company is submitting the additional efficacy data to support a new indication for ankylosing spondylitis, which is a chronic, inflammatory disorder primarily involving the spine. In addition to the indications listed above, the Company is seeking an indication for acute gouty arthritis. Timing of the expanded submission has not been determined. The regulatory process for Arcoxia outside the United States continues uninterrupted.

Other products in development include an oral compound potentially useful for treatment of chemotherapy-induced emesis; an oral compound potentially useful for the treatment of depression and other neuropsychiatric diseases; a compound potentially useful for the treatment of diabetes and diabetic dyslipidemia; a compound potentially useful for the treatment of anxiety; a compound potentially useful for the treatment of Chronic Obstructive Pulmonary Disease and asthma; a compound potentially useful to treat AIDS; and certain new vaccines including a Human Papillomavirus vaccine ("HPV"), potentially useful to prevent HPV infection; a rotavirus vaccine potentially useful for the prevention of infant diarrhea and dehydration caused by rotavirus; and a vaccine potentially useful for the prevention and treatment of human immunodeficiency virus.

All product or service marks appearing in type form different from that of the surrounding text are trademarks or service marks owned by or licensed to Merck & Co., Inc., its subsidiaries or affiliates (including Zetia, a trademark owned by an entity of the Merck/Schering-Plough Pharmaceuticals partnership). Cozaar and Hyzaar are registered trademarks of E.I. du Pont de Nemours and Company, Wilmington, DE. Claritin is a trademark of Schering Corporation and Prilosec and Nexium are trademarks of the AstraZeneca group.

Research and development is a vital part of Merck's corporate success, and as you can see from the previous example, the company offers investors a great deal of insight into the company's R&D program in its 10-K.

COMPETITION

Nearly every 10-K report includes some mention of competition—specifically the competition the company faces in its key categories. Typically, the section (usually one or two paragraphs) discusses the challenges the company faces in squaring off against its competitors. Here is an example from the McDonald's 10-K:

> Competition
>
> McDonald's restaurants compete with international, national, regional and local retailers of food products. The Company competes on the basis of price, convenience and service and by offering quality food products. The Company's competition in the broadest perspective includes restaurants, quick-service eating establishments, pizza parlors, coffee shops, street vendors, convenience food stores, delicatessens and supermarkets.
>
> In the U.S., there are about 515,000 restaurants that generate $303 billion in annual sales. McDonald's restaurant business accounts for 2.5% of those restaurants and 6.6% of the sales. No reasonable estimate can be made of the number of competitors outside the U.S.; however, the Company's business in foreign markets continues to grow.

In just two short paragraphs, you learn a great deal about the restaurant business, and McDonald's stake in that business. You learn that there are more than half a million restaurants in the United States generating more than $300 billion in sales, and you learn that McDonald's accounts for 2.5 percent of all U.S. restaurants—even though it may seem like much more. (In fact, if you travel the highways, it seems like McDonald's makes up about 20 percent of all restaurants.) You also learn that McDonald's restaurants tend to do much greater volume than the average U.S. restaurant. While it accounts for just 2.5 percent of all restaurants, McDonald's generates 6.6 percent of all sales.

The following example from Pitney Bowes offers a detailed discussion of competitive life in the postage meter and mailing machine business:

> Competition
>
> Historically we have been a leading supplier of products and services in our business segments, particularly postage meters and mailing machines. Our meter base and our continued ability to place meters in key

markets is a significant contributor to our current and future revenue and profitability. However, all of our segments face strong competition from a number of companies. In particular, we face competition in many countries for new placements from several postage meter and mailing machine suppliers, and our mailing systems products face competition from products and services offered as alternative means of message communications. PBMS, a major provider of business support services to the corporate, financial services, and professional services markets, competes against national, regional and local firms specializing in facilities management. We believe that our long experience and reputation for product quality, and our sales and support service organizations are important factors in influencing customer choices with respect to our products and services.

The financing business is highly competitive with aggressive rate competition. Leasing companies, commercial finance companies, commercial banks and other financial institutions compete, in varying degrees, in the several markets in which our finance operations do business. Our competitors range from very large, diversified financial institutions to many small, specialized firms. In view of the market fragmentation and absence of any dominant competitors, we believe that it is not possible to provide a meaningful description of our finance operations' competitive position in these markets.

What are the competitive pressures of the medical industry? The Johnson & Johnson report gives you some insight:

COMPETITION

In all its product lines, Johnson & Johnson companies compete with companies both large and small, located in the United States and abroad. Competition is strong in all lines without regard to the number and size of the competing companies involved. Competition in research, involving the development of new products and processes and the improvement of existing products and processes, is particularly significant and results from time to time in product and process obsolescence. The development of new and improved products is important to Johnson & Johnson's success in all areas of its business. This competitive environment requires substantial investments in continuing research and in multiple sales forces. In addition, the winning and retention of customer acceptance of Johnson & Johnson's consumer products involve heavy expenditures for advertising, promotion and selling.

Companies in different industries face different types of competition. While Johnson & Johnson talks about the need to continue to invest in research and development to stay ahead of the competition in the medical products industry, the following paragraph from the Best Buy annual report highlights the type of competition the company faces in the retail business:

Competition

Best Buy stores' industry is highly competitive. Best Buy stores compete nationally against other consumer electronics retailers, specialty home office retailers, mass merchants, home improvement superstores, entertainment software superstores, electronics boutiques and a growing number of direct-to-consumer alternatives. Best Buy stores also compete against independent dealers, regional chain discount stores, wholesale clubs, mail-order and Internet retailers, video rental stores and other specialty retail stores. Mass merchandisers continue to increase their assortment of consumer electronics products—primarily those that are less complex to sell, install and operate. Similarly, large home improvement retailers are expanding their assortment of appliances. In addition, consumers are increasingly downloading entertainment and computer software directly via the Internet.

We believe Best Buy stores' formats and brand marketing strategies distinguish them from most competitors by positioning Best Buy retail stores as the destination for new technology and entertainment products in a fun, informative and no-pressure shopping environment. Best Buy stores compete by aggressively advertising and emphasizing a broad product assortment, value pricing and financing alternatives. In addition, we believe our e-commerce operations, coupled with the knowledgeable sales associates and service capabilities of Best Buy retail stores, have effectively positioned us to compete successfully despite an increasingly competitive environment.

EMPLOYEES

The 10-K report typically includes a paragraph or two on the employees. It is usually a very matter-of-fact paragraph that gives very basic information, such as the number of workers—full and part time—that the company employs, and a little bit about its employee relations and labor union status. Here is an example from the Pitney Bowes 10-K:

Employee Relations

At December 31, 2001, we employed 26,698 persons in the U.S. and 6,026 persons outside the U.S. We believe that employee relations are satisfactory. The majority of our employees are not represented by any labor union. Our management follows the policy of keeping employees informed of decisions, and encourages and implements employee suggestions whenever practicable.

In this short paragraph, you learn that the company employees 26,698 persons in the United States and about 6000 abroad, and that most of its employees are not represented by a labor union. Here is another example from the Best Buy 10-K:

Our Employees

At the end of fiscal 2002, we employed approximately 94,000 full-time, part-time and seasonal employees across all of our operating segments. There are currently no collective bargaining agreements covering any of our employees with the exception of unions that represent hourly employees at 13 Musicland stores. We have not experienced a strike or work stoppage and we believe that we have favorable employee relations.

Again, you learn how many employees the company has, although it is not broken down by full and part time, and you learn about its labor situation.

PROPERTIES

Does the company own any significant real estate? Does it own its own office buildings or does it lease? The "properties" section gives details of the company's holdings, as the following example from the Pitney Bowes 10-K illustrates:

ITEM 2—PROPERTIES

Our World Headquarters and certain other office and manufacturing facilities are located in Stamford, Connecticut. We have additional office facilities located in Shelton, Connecticut. We maintain research and development operations at a corporate engineering and technology center in Shelton, Connecticut. A sales and service training center is located near Atlanta, Georgia. We believe that our current manufacturing, administrative and sales office properties are adequate for the needs of all of our operations.

Global Mailing

Global Mailing products are manufactured in a number of plants principally in Connecticut, as well as in Harlow, England; Friedberg, Germany; Lyon, France and St. Denis, France. Most of these facilities are owned by the company. At December 31, 2001, there were 134 sales, support services, and finance offices, substantially all of which are leased, located throughout the U.S. and in a number of other countries.

Enterprise Solutions

Our Document Messaging Technologies business is headquartered in Danbury, Connecticut. We lease five facilities located throughout the U.S. Our management services business is headquartered in Stamford, Connecticut and leases 37 facilities located throughout the U.S. and facilities in Canada, England, Belgium, Denmark, France, Germany, Norway, Netherlands and Sweden. Our headquarters of the financing operations within the U.S. are located in Shelton, Connecticut. Offices of the financing operations outside the U.S. are maintained in Mississauga, Ontario, Canada; London, England; Heppenheim, Germany; Paris, France; Oslo, Norway; Dublin, Ireland; French's Forest, Australia; Vienna, Austria; Effretikon, Switzerland; Milan, Italy; Barcelona, Spain; and Stockholm, Sweden.

Capital Services

Our wholly-owned subsidiary, Pitney Bowes Credit Corporation (PBCC), leases an executive and administrative office in Shelton, Connecticut, which is owned by Pitney Bowes Inc. There are nine leased regional and district sales offices located throughout the U.S.

RAW MATERIALS

Raw materials are not a key factor in many industries, but are vital in others. Here is a section on raw materials from the Anheuser-Busch 10-K report:

SOURCES AND AVAILABILITY OF RAW MATERIALS

The products manufactured by the Company require a large volume of various agricultural products, including barley for malt; hops, malt, rice, and corn grits for beer; and rice for the rice milling and processing operations of BARI. The Company fulfills its commodities requirements through purchases from various sources, including purchases from its subsidiaries, through contractual arrangements, and through purchases on the open market.

The Company believes that adequate supplies of the aforementioned agricultural products are available at the present time, but cannot predict future availability or prices of such products and materials. The above referenced commodity markets have experienced and will continue to experience price fluctuations. The price and supply of raw materials will be determined by, among other factors, the level of crop production both in the U.S. and around the world, weather conditions, export demand, and government regulations and legislation affecting agriculture.

Anheuser-Busch offers details of the type of products used in its brewing process, and assures readers that the materials should always be in adequate supply.

Now let's look at the raw materials section from the William Wrigley 10-K report:

(ii) *Sources and availability of raw materials.* Raw materials blended to make chewing gum base are available from suppliers and in the open market.

Sugar, corn syrup, flavoring oils, polyols and aspartame are obtained in the open market, or under contracts, from suppliers in various countries. All other ingredients and necessary packaging materials are also purchased and available on the open market.

As the report mentions, Wrigley expects to have no problem finding the ingredients for its famous chewing gums.

MISCELLANEOUS CATEGORIES

Different companies include different subsections in their 10-Ks. Some discuss raw materials; others talk about patents and trademarks, environmental matters, distribution, or other matters that affect their business. For instance, as a retailer, Best Buy faces some challenges that are not necessarily a factor in other industries, such as seasonal demand and distribution to its stores. As a result, retailers like Best Buy include some sections in their 10-Ks that you won't always find in 10-Ks from companies in other industries. This excerpt from the Best Buy 10-K report discusses operations, distribution, and seasonality:

Operations

Best Buy stores follow standardized and detailed operating procedures called Standard Operating Platform (SOP). The SOP includes procedures for inventory management, transaction processing, customer relations, store administration, product sales and merchandise display.

Best Buy store operations are organized into three divisions. Each division is divided into regions and is under the supervision of a senior vice president who oversees store performance through regional vice presidents. Regional vice presidents have responsibility for a number of districts within their respective region. District managers monitor store operations closely and meet regularly with store managers to discuss merchandising, new product introductions, sales promotions, customer loyalty programs, employee satisfaction surveys and store operating performance. Similar meetings are conducted at the corporate level with divisional and regional management. A senior vice president of retail operations has overall responsibility for retail store processing and operations including labor management. Each district also has a loss prevention manager, with product security personnel employed at each store to control inventory shrinkage. Advertising, merchandise buying and pricing, and inventory policies for Best Buy stores are centrally controlled.

Best Buy stores are open seven days a week for approximately 73 hours a week. A store is typically staffed by one manager and four to five assistant managers. The average staff ranges from 65 to 150 people, depending on store size and sales volume.

Distribution

Generally, merchandise is shipped to Best Buy stores from six distribution centers located in California, Georgia, Minnesota, Ohio, Oklahoma and Virginia. Best Buy stores also currently operate a dedicated distribution center for entertainment software in Minnesota. In fiscal 2004, we expect to open an additional general distribution center in upstate New York. The majority of Best Buy stores' merchandise, except for major appliances and large-screen televisions, is shipped directly from manufacturers to a distribution center. Major appliances and large-screen televisions are shipped to satellite warehouses in each major market. Best Buy stores are dependent upon the distribution centers for inventory storage and shipment of most merchandise. However, in order to meet release dates for selected products and to improve inventory management, certain merchandise is shipped directly to the stores from manufacturers and distributors. We believe distribution centers can most effectively service Best Buy stores within a 600 to 700-mile radius and that our current distribution centers, and the planned addition of the New York distribution center in fiscal 2004, will accommodate expansion plans for the next several years. On average, Best Buy stores receive product shipments two or three times a week depending on sales volume. Generally, e-commerce merchandise sales are either picked up at Best Buy retail stores, or fulfilled through the distribution centers.

Seasonality

Similar to many retailers, Best Buy stores' business is seasonal. Revenues and earnings are typically greater during the second half of the fiscal year, which includes the holiday selling season.

In addition to its own chain of Best Buy stores, the company also owns several other retail chains, including Musicland, Sam Goody's, and Magnolia Hi-Fi. As a result, the company includes details of the operations of all of its store divisions in the 10-K, including operations, distribution, seasonality, and competition.

In the following Wells Fargo 10-K, the company includes a section entitled "History and Growth:"

HISTORY AND GROWTH

The Company is the product of the merger of equals involving Norwest Corporation and the former Wells Fargo & Company, completed on November 2, 1998 (the WFC Merger). On completion of the WFC Merger, Norwest Corporation changed its name to Wells Fargo & Company.

Norwest Corporation, prior to the WFC Merger, provided banking services to customers in 16 states and additional financial services through subsidiaries engaged in a variety of businesses including mortgage banking and consumer finance.

The former Wells Fargo & Company's principal subsidiary, Wells Fargo Bank, N.A., was the successor to the banking portion of the business founded by Henry Wells and William G. Fargo in 1852. That business later operated the westernmost leg of the Pony Express and ran stagecoach lines in the western part of the United States. The California banking business was separated from the express business in 1905, was merged in 1960 with American Trust Company, another of the oldest banks in the Western United States, and became Wells Fargo Bank, N.A., a national banking association, in 1968.

The former Wells Fargo & Company acquired First Interstate Bancorp in April 1996. First Interstate's assets had an approximate book value of $55 billion. The transaction was valued at approximately $11.3 billion and was accounted for as a purchase. The Company expands its business, in part, by acquiring banking institutions and other companies engaged in activities that are financial in nature.

The Company continues to explore opportunities to acquire banking institutions and other financial services companies. Discussions are continually being carried on related to such possible acquisitions. The Company cannot predict whether, or on what terms, such discussions will result in further acquisitions. As a matter of policy, the Company generally does not comment on such discussions or possible acquisitions until a definitive acquisition agreement has been signed.

This section gives readers a good perspective on Wells Fargo and its storied history. The more you know about a company's history and operations, the easier it is to make an informed decision on the investment potential of that company.

Environmental matters are also discussed in some 10-K reports. In the following paragraph, Merck discusses the details of its environmental situation:

Environmental Matters

The Company believes that it is in compliance in all material respects with applicable environmental laws and regulations. In 2001, the Company incurred capital expenditures of approximately $197.5 million for environmental protection facilities. Capital expenditures for this purpose are forecasted to exceed $500.0 million for the years 2002 through 2006. In addition, the Company's operating and maintenance expenditures for environmental protection facilities were approximately $88.7 million in 2001. Expenditures for this purpose for the years 2002 through 2006 are forecasted to approximate $520.0 million. The Company is also remediating environmental contamination resulting from past industrial activity at certain of its sites. Expenditures for remediation and environmental liabilities were $34.2 million in 2001, and are estimated at $137.0 million for the years 2002 through 2006. These amounts do not consider potential recoveries from insurers or other parties. The Company has taken an active role in identifying and providing for these costs, and in management's opinion, the liabilities for all environmental matters which are probable and reasonably estimable have been accrued. Although it is not possible to predict with certainty the outcome of these environmental matters, or the ultimate costs of remediation, management does not believe that any reasonably possible expenditures that may be incurred in excess of those provided should result in a materially adverse effect on the Company's financial position, results of operations, liquidity or capital resources.

Companies in specialized industries will cover topics in their 10-Ks that are of no relevance to other industries. In the following example, Delta Airlines details its "Fares and Rates" and "Route Authority:"

Fares and Rates

Airlines are permitted to set ticket prices in most domestic and international city pairs without governmental regulation, and the industry is characterized by significant price competition. Certain international fares and rates are subject to the jurisdiction of the DOT and the governments of the foreign countries involved. Most of Delta's tickets are sold by travel agents, and fares are subject to commissions, overrides and discounts paid to travel agents, brokers and wholesalers.

Route Authority

Delta's flight operations are authorized by certificates of public convenience and necessity and, to a limited extent, by exemptions issued by the DOT. The requisite approvals of other governments for international operations are provided by bilateral agreements with, or permits or approvals issued by, foreign countries. Because international air transportation is governed by bilateral or other agreements between the United States and the foreign country or countries involved, changes in United States or foreign government aviation policies could result in the alteration or termination of such agreements, diminish the value of Delta's international route authorities or otherwise affect Delta's international operations. Bilateral agreements between the United States and various foreign countries served by Delta are subject to renegotiation from time to time.

Delta gives you some insight into how fares are set and routes assigned. You can learn a lot about a company and its industry by carefully reading through some of the key subsections of the 10-K report.

COMPANY OFFICERS

One of the most valuable parts of the 10-K is the section on "Executive Officers" which lists the leading officers of the company, and usually gives some background information on each officer. Most investors look for companies with an outstanding, experienced management team. The 10-K is the place to find out just how experienced the company's management team is. Here is the executive section from the Anheuser-Busch 10-K report:

EXECUTIVE OFFICERS OF THE REGISTRANT

AUGUST A. BUSCH III (age 64) is presently Chairman of the Board and President, and a Director of the Company and has served in such capacities since 1977, 1974, and 1963, respectively. Since 1979 he has also served as Chairman of the Board of the Company's subsidiary, Anheuser-Busch, Incorporated and also previously served as its Chief Executive Officer (1979–2000).

PATRICK T. STOKES (age 59) is presently Senior Executive Vice President and a Director of the Company and has served in such capacities since 2000. He previously served as Vice President and Group Executive of the Company since 1981. He is also presently Chief Executive Officer and President of the Company's subsidiary, Anheuser-Busch, Incorporated, and has served in such capacities since 2000 and 1990 respectively, and Chairman of the Board of the Company's subsidiary, Anheuser-Busch International, Inc., and has served in such capacity since 1999.

W. RANDOLPH BAKER (age 55) is presently Vice President and Chief Financial Officer of the Company and has served in such capacity since 1996. He previously served as Vice President and Group Executive of the Company (1982–1996).

STEPHEN K. LAMBRIGHT (age 59) is presently Group Vice President and General Counsel of the Company and has served in such capacity since 1997. He previously served as Vice President and Group Executive of the Company (1984–1997).

DONALD W. KLOTH (age 60) is presently Vice President and Group Executive of the Company and has served in such capacity since

1994. He is also Chairman of the Board and Chief Executive Officer of the Company's subsidiary, Busch Agricultural Resources, Inc., and has served in such capacity since 1994.

JOHN E. JACOB (age 67) is presently Executive Vice President and Chief Communications Officer, and a Director of the Company and has served in such capacities since 1994 and 1990, respectively.

THOMAS W. SANTEL (age 43) is presently Vice President—Corporate Development of the Company and has served in such capacity since 1996.

STEPHEN J. BURROWS (age 50) is presently Vice President—International Operations of the Company and has served in such capacity since 1999. He previously served as Vice President—International Marketing of the Company (1992–1998). He is also presently Chief Executive Officer and President of the Company's subsidiary, Anheuser-Busch International, Inc., and has served as Chief Executive Officer since 1999 and as President since 1994. During the past five years, he also served as Chief Operating Officer of Anheuser-Busch International, Inc. (1994–1998).

VICTOR G. ABBEY (age 46) is presently Chairman of the Board and President of the Company's subsidiary, Busch Entertainment Corporation, and has served in such capacities since 2000. During the past five years, he also served as Executive Vice President and General Manager of the SeaWorld theme park in Orlando, Florida (1997–2000), and Executive Vice President and General Manager of the former SeaWorld theme park in Cleveland, Ohio (1995–1997).

AUGUST A. BUSCH IV (age 37) is presently Vice President and Group Executive of the Company and has served in such capacity since 2000. He is also presently Group Vice President—Marketing and Wholesale Operations of the Company's subsidiary, Anheuser-Busch, Incorporated, and has served in such capacity since 2000 and had previously served as its Vice President—Marketing (1996–2000).

MARK T. BOBAK (age 42) is presently Vice President—Corporate Human Resources of the Company and has served in such capacity since 2000. He had previously served as Vice President and Deputy General Counsel of the Company (1998–2000) and Vice President-Litigation (1996–1998) of the Company.

JOSEPH P. SELLINGER (age 56) is presently Vice President and Group Executive of the Company and has served in such capacity since 2000. He is also presently Chairman, Chief Executive Officer and President of the Company's direct subsidiaries, Anheuser-Busch Packaging Group, Inc., Anheuser-Busch Recycling Corporation, Metal Container Corporation, Eagle Packaging, Inc., and Precision Printing and Packaging, Inc., and has served in all such capacities since 2000. He had previously served as Vice President—Operations of the Company's subsidiary, Anheuser-Busch, Incorporated (1992–2000).

DOUGLAS J. MUHLEMAN (age 48) is presently Group Vice President—Brewing Operations and Technology of the Company's subsidiary, Anheuser-Busch, Incorporated, and has served in such capacity since October, 2001 and had previously served as its Vice President—Brewing (1996–September, 2001).

As you can see, the executive officers section affords you a good opportunity to check out the background and experience of each of the key officers. Evaluating the management team gives you yet another measure to use in assessing the prospects of the stock. Unfortunately, not every 10-K gives the amount of detail on key officers that the Anheuser-Busch report provides, but most do give a helpful bio on each of the officers.

LEGAL TROUBLE? FIND IT IN THE 10-K

Some 10-K reports include several pages of information on legal proceedings and potential liability. Other companies that face very little in legal challenges may spend no more than a sentence or two summarizing their legal status. The following paragraph from the Best Buy 10-K is typical of most 10-K reports:

Item 3. Legal proceedings

We are involved in various legal proceedings arising during the normal course of conducting business. The resolution of those proceedings is not expected to have a material impact on our results of operations and financial condition.

Here is another example from the McDonald's 10-K. With its thousands of customers, suppliers, employees, and franchise owners, it will always be subject to a steady stream of legal challenges—most of which are ultimately dismissed. Here is how McDonald's summarizes its legal proceedings:

Item 3. Legal proceedings

The Company has pending a number of lawsuits which have been filed from time to time in various jurisdictions. These lawsuits cover a broad variety of allegations spanning the Company's entire business. The following is a brief description of the more significant of these categories of lawsuits. In addition, the Company is subject to various federal, state and local regulations that impact various aspects of its business, as discussed below. The Company does not believe that any such claims, lawsuits or regulations will have a material adverse effect on its financial condition or results of operations.

Franchising

A substantial number of McDonald's restaurants are franchised to independent entrepreneurs operating under arrangements with the Company. In the course of the franchise relationship, occasional disputes arise between the Company and its franchisees relating to a broad range of subjects including, without limitation, quality, service and cleanliness issues, contentions regarding grants or terminations of franchises, franchisee claims for additional franchises or rewrites of franchises, and delinquent payments. Additionally, on occasion, disputes arise between the Company and individuals who claim they should have been granted a McDonald's franchise.

Suppliers

The Company and its affiliates and subsidiaries do not supply, with minor exceptions outside the U.S., food, paper, or related items to any McDonald's restaurants. The Company relies upon numerous independent suppliers that are required to meet and maintain the Company's high standards and specifications. On occasion, disputes arise between the Company and its suppliers on a number of issues including, by way of example, compliance with product specifications and the Company's business relationship with suppliers. In addition, on occasion, disputes arise on a number of issues between the Company and individuals or entities who claim that they should be (or should have been) granted the opportunity to supply products or services to the Company's restaurants.

Employees

Thousands of people are employed by the Company and in restaurants owned and operated by subsidiaries of the Company. In addition, thousands of people, from time to time, seek employment in such restaurants. In the ordinary course of business, disputes arise regarding hiring, firing and promotion practices.

Customers

The Company's restaurants serve a large cross-section of the public and in the course of serving so many people, disputes arise as to products, service, accidents, advertising and other matters typical of an extensive restaurant business such as that of the Company.

Intellectual Property

The Company has registered trademarks and service marks, some of which are of material importance to the Company's business. The Company also has certain patents on restaurant equipment, which while valuable, are not material to its business. From time to time, the Company may become involved in litigation to defend and protect its use of its intellectual property.

Government regulations

Local, state and federal governments have adopted laws and regulations involving various aspects of the restaurant business, including, but not limited to, franchising, health, safety, environment, zoning and employment. The Company does not believe that it is in violation of any existing statutory or administrative rules, but it cannot predict the effect on its operations from the issuance of additional requirements in the future.

Let's look at a couple of other examples of 10-K reports from companies that face a number of legal challenges. The first example is from the Philip Morris 10-K report, although we are including just a small portion of the legal section. It would be impossible to include it all, since it covers more than 8000 words (more than 20 pages). As the report points out, the company faces more than 1500 legal cases, primarily from cigarette smokers or the families of deceased smokers. The 10-K also includes another extensive section on "Taxes, Legislation, Regulation and Other Matters Regarding Tobacco and Smoking" that details additional legal battles the company faces in marketing its cigarettes in the United States and abroad. Here are some excerpts from the Philip Morris report:

Item 3. Legal Proceedings.

Legal proceedings covering a wide range of matters are pending or threatened in various United States and foreign jurisdictions against the Company, its subsidiaries and affiliates, including PM Inc. and Philip Morris International, as well as their respective indemnities. Various types of claims are raised in these proceedings, including product liability, consumer protection, antitrust, tax, patent infringement, employment matters, claims for contribution and claims of competitors and distributors.

Overview of Tobacco-Related Litigation

Types and Number of Cases

Pending claims related to tobacco products generally fall within the following categories: (i) smoking and health cases alleging personal injury brought on behalf of individual plaintiffs, (ii) smoking and health cases primarily alleging personal injury and purporting to be brought on behalf of a class of individual plaintiffs, (iii) health care cost recovery cases brought by governmental (both domestic and foreign) and non-governmental plaintiffs seeking reimbursement for health care expenditures allegedly caused by cigarette smoking and/or disgorgement of profits, and (iv) other tobacco-related litigation. Other tobacco-related litigation includes class action suits alleging that the use of the terms "Lights" and "Ultra Lights" constitutes deceptive and unfair trade practices, suits by foreign governments seeking to recover damages for taxes lost as a result of the allegedly illegal importation of cigarettes into their jurisdictions, suits by former asbestos manufacturers seeking contribution or reimbursement for amounts expended in connection with the defense and payment of asbestos claims that were allegedly caused in whole or in part by cigarette smoking, and various antitrust suits. Damages claimed in some of the smoking and health class actions, health care cost recovery cases and other tobacco-related litigation range into the billions of dollars. . .

As of February 15, 2002 there were approximately 1,500 smoking and health cases filed and served on behalf of individual plaintiffs in the United States against PM Inc. and, in some instances, the Company, compared with approximately 1,500 such cases on December 31, 2000, and approximately 380 such cases on December 31, 1999. In certain jurisdictions, individual smoking and health cases have been aggregated for trial in a single proceeding; the largest such proceeding aggregates 1,250 cases in West Virginia and is currently scheduled for trial in September 2002. An estimated ten of the individual cases involve allegations of various personal injuries allegedly related to exposure to ETS. In addition, approximately 2,835 additional individual cases are pending in Florida by current and former flight attendants claiming personal injuries allegedly related to ETS. The flight attendants allege that they are members of an ETS smoking and health class action, which was settled in 1997. The terms of the court-approved settlement in that case allow class members to file individual lawsuits seeking compensatory damages, but prohibit them from seeking punitive damages.

As of February 15, 2002, there were an estimated 25 smoking and health purported class actions pending in the United States against PM Inc. and, in some cases, the Company (including four that involve allegations of various personal injuries related to exposure to ETS), compared with approximately 36 such cases on December 31, 2000, and approximately 50 such cases on December 31, 1999. . .

As of February 15, 2002, there were an estimated 47 health care cost recovery actions, including the suit discussed below under "Federal Government's Lawsuit," filed by the United States government, pending in the United States against PM Inc. and, in some instances, the Company, compared with approximately 52 such cases pending on December 31, 2000, and 60 such cases on December 31, 1999. In addition, health care cost recovery actions are pending in Israel, the Marshall Islands, the Province of British Columbia, Canada, France (in a case brought by a local agency of the French social security health insurance system), and Spain.

There are also a number of other tobacco-related actions pending outside the United States against Philip Morris International and its affiliates and subsidiaries, including an estimated 65 smoking and health cases brought on behalf of individuals (Argentina (40), Brazil (15), Czech Republic (1), Ireland (1), Israel (2), Italy (1), Japan (1), the Philippines (1), Scotland (1), and Spain (2). . .

Smoking and Health Litigation

Plaintiffs' allegations of liability in smoking and health cases are based on various theories of recovery, including negligence, gross negligence, strict liability, fraud, misrepresentation, design defect, failure to warn, breach of express and implied warranties, breach of special duty, conspiracy, concert of action, violations of deceptive trade practice laws and consumer protection statutes, and claims under the federal and state RICO statutes. In certain of these cases, plaintiffs claim that cigarette smoking exacerbated the injuries caused by their exposure to asbestos. Plaintiffs in the smoking and health actions seek various forms of relief, including compensatory and punitive damages, treble/multiple damages and other statutory damages and penalties, creation of medical monitoring and smoking cessation funds, disgorgement of profits, and injunctive and equitable relief. Defenses raised in these cases include lack of proximate cause, assumption of the risk, comparative fault and/or contributory negligence, statutes of limitations and preemption by the Federal Cigarette Labeling and Advertising Act.

Health Care Cost Recovery Litigation

Overview

In certain pending proceedings, domestic and foreign governmental entities and non-governmental plaintiffs, including union health and welfare funds ("unions"), Native American tribes, insurers and self-insurers such as Blue Cross and Blue Shield plans, hospitals, taxpayers and others, are seeking reimbursement of health care cost expenditures allegedly caused by tobacco products and, in some cases, of future expenditures and damages as well. Relief sought by some but not all plaintiffs includes punitive damages, multiple damages and other statutory damages and penalties, injunctions prohibiting alleged marketing and sales to minors, disclosure of research, disgorgement of profits, funding of anti-smoking programs, additional disclosure of nicotine yields, and payment of attorney and expert witness fees. Certain of the health care cost recovery cases purport to be brought on behalf of a class of plaintiffs. . . .

Settlements of Health Care Cost Recovery Litigation

In November 1998, PM Inc. and certain other United States tobacco product manufacturers entered into the Master Settlement Agreement (the "MSA") with 46 states, the District of Columbia, Puerto Rico, Guam, the United States Virgin Islands, American Samoa and the Northern Marianas to settle asserted and unasserted health care cost recovery and other claims. PM Inc. and certain other United States tobacco product manufacturers had previously settled similar claims brought by Mississippi, Florida, Texas andMinnesota (together with the MSA, the "State Settlement Agreements"). The MSA has received final judicial approval in all 52 settling jurisdictions. . .

Federal Government's Lawsuit

In 1999, the United States government filed a lawsuit in the United States District Court for the District of Columbia against various cigarette manufacturers and others, including PM Inc. and the Company, asserting claims under three federal statutes, the Medical Care Recovery Act ("MCRA"), the Medicare Secondary Payer ("MSP") provisions of the Social Security Act and the Racketeer Influenced and Corrupt Organizations Act ("RICO"). The lawsuit seeks to recover an unspecified amount of health care costs for tobacco-related illnesses allegedly caused by defendants' fraudulent and tortious conduct and paid for by the government under various federal health care programs, including Medicare, military and veterans' health benefits programs, and the Federal Employees Health Benefits Program. The complaint alleges that such costs total more than $20 billion annually. It also seeks various types of what it alleges to be equitable and declaratory relief, including disgorgement, an injunction prohibiting certain actions by the defendants, and a declaration that the defendants are liable for the federal government's future costs of providing health care resulting from defendants' alleged past tortious and wrongful conduct. PM Inc. and the Company moved to dismiss this lawsuit on numerous grounds, including that the statutes invoked by the government do not provide a basis for the relief sought. . .

As the world's leading cigarette manufacturer, Philip Morris will always be involved in a number of legal proceedings. It's business as usual for all tobacco companies, and probably always will be. How important is that information in deciding whether or not to buy the stock? Perhaps not as important as you might believe, for two reasons. For one thing, tobacco is an extremely profitable product. Profit margins are incredibly high, so the company will continue to make money. The other reason the continuing legal challenges will have minimal effect is because it is already accounted for in the price of the stock. Investors know the tobacco industry has been under siege and have bid down the price of the stock. Tobacco stocks typically have very low price-earnings ratios. So while the legal information is of interest, and certainly of some concern, in this case, it's not necessarily going to lead to a falling stock price. The price is already depressed.

But with most companies, it's well worth your time and effort to look over the legal proceedings section of the 10-K to determine whether the company would be a good bet for your investment dollars.

Here's one final sample from the Qwest 10-K report "Legal Proceedings" section. The company doesn't face the legal obstacles of Philip Morris, but it does have some legal concerns:

Item 3. Legal proceedings

For a discussion of legal proceedings arising before December 31, 2001, see Note 9 to the consolidated financial statements. The following describes certain legal proceedings and claims that have arisen since December 31, 2001.

On February 14, 2002, the Minnesota Department of Commerce filed a formal complaint against us with the Minnesota Public Utilities Commission alleging that we, in contravention of federal and state law, failed to file interconnection agreements with the Minnesota Public Utilities Commission relating to certain of our wholesale customers, and thereby allegedly discriminating against other CLECs. The complaint seeks civil penalties related to such alleged violations between $50 million and $200 million. This proceeding is at an early stage. Other states in the local service area are looking into similar matters and further proceedings may ensue in those states.

You'll notice the first sentence refers you to "Note 9 to the consolidated financial statements" for further information on the company's legal proceedings. The consolidated financial statements are included further back in the 10-K report. By scanning down through the report, you can find the consolidated financial statements, and the footnotes accompanying them. In Note 9 (which follows), the company discusses the legal action it is taking against other parties:

Contingencies

Litigation. On July 23, 2001, we filed a demand for arbitration against Citizens alleging that it breached Agreements for Purchase and Sale of Telephone Exchanges dated as of June 16, 1999, between Citizens and U S WEST Communications, Inc., with respect to the purchase and sale of exchanges in Arizona, Colorado, Idaho, Iowa, Minnesota, Montana, Nebraska and Wyoming. The demand for arbitration was filed after Citizens failed to close the exchange sales in violation of the terms of the purchase agreements. Citizens, in turn, filed a demand for arbitration alleging counter claims against us in connection with the sale of those same exchanges, as well as exchanges located in North Dakota that we did sell to Citizens. In the arbitration, we seek a determination that Citizens breached the agreements and, as a result, we are entitled to draw down on a series of letters of credit Citizens provided in connection with the transactions and other damages. Citizens seeks a determination that we breached the agreements and, as a result, Citizens is entitled to damages. This arbitration is still at a preliminary stage.

In August 2001, we filed a complaint in state court in Colorado against Touch America, Inc. ("Touch America"). In response, also in August 2001, Touch America filed a complaint against us in a federal district court in Montana and removed the Colorado court complaint to federal district court in Colorado. Touch America has also filed answers and counterclaims in the Colorado lawsuit. Touch America's complaint in Montana was dismissed on November 5, 2001, and Touch America's motion for reconsideration was denied on December 17, 2001. The disputes between us and Touch America relate to various billing issues for services provided to Touch America under Qwest tariffs or wholesale interconnection agreements. Each party seeks damages against the other for amounts billed and unpaid and for other disputes. The court case is in a preliminary state, discovery has begun but no trial date has been set. Touch America also asserts that we violated the Telecommunications Act of 1996 (the "Act") and our tariffs, and has filed related complaints at the FCC.

Various other litigation matters have been filed against us. We intend to vigorously defend these outstanding claims.

In the corporate world, law suits and legal challenges are part of the business. Nearly all companies face some challenges in court from time to time. And companies in certain types of industries—such as Philip Morris—are bound to face more legal challenges than others. In reviewing a company's 10-K report, you must try to make a judgment as to whether those legal challenges would have a substantial impact on the stock's performance in a worst-case scenario. In most cases, lawsuits are settled with little long-term impact on shareholders, but major lawsuits and legal action by federal regulators can sometimes have a dramatic impact on a company's operations and profitability. That's why it is well worth your time to take a close look at the "Legal Proceedings" section of a company's 10-K report.

TYING IT ALL TOGETHER

There's not any single section of the 10-K report that is going to paint the entire picture for you of a company's operations and prospects for future growth. That's why it's important to comb through the entire report to get a taste of the wide range of factors that can influence the company's success.

From basic business operations to key officers to legal proceedings to competition, marketing, and distribution, the 10-K report gives you a wealth of valuable information in assessing the history and potential of a company. It's the best place to look to evaluate the strengths, weaknesses, and prospects of a particular stock.

In this chapter we focus on the first section of the 10-K—the narrative portion on the company's operations. But that's just part of the picture. In the next chapter we'll focus on the second part of the report, which covers the company's financial matters in great detail.

6

THE 10-K FINANCIALS: THE ACID TEST

IF YOU WANT TO GET TO THE HEART of a company's financial performance, you'll find it in the 10-K. The first section offers a detailed narrative description of the company's operations, as we learned in the previous chapter, and the second part lays out a wealth of financial statistics. By reviewing the financial section of the 10-K, you can get an idea of the company's strengths and weaknesses, and determine whether the company is growing, shrinking, or standing still.

In this section, we guide you through the financial elements of the 10-K report, reviewing each key table and section you're likely to encounter in reviewing a company's 10-K report.

We hope to answer several important questions in the financial section of the report:

• Is the company profitable?

• Are its earnings and revenue growing?

• How solid is its cash flow?

• Is the company's earnings growth genuine, or has the company used some questionable accounting practices to pump them up?

You can probe deeply into a company's financial fortunes in the 10-K report, but first you need to know what you're looking for. The financial section of every 10-K report includes the same key elements:

1. market for the registrant's common equity and related shareowner matters
2. selected financial data
3. management's discussion and analysis of financial condition and results of operations
4. quantitative and qualitative disclosures about market risk
5. consolidated financial statements and supplementary data
6. changes in and disagreements on accounting and financial disclosure

ANALYZING THE FINANCIAL TABLES

Let's review some of the key financial tables from Colgate-Palmolive to illustrate the type of information you should be able to find in the financial section, and the types of questions you should be asking. First, we make a cursory review of the income statement in Table 6-1 (and refer back to it later for more in-depth analysis):

TABLE 6-1

COLGATE-PALMOLIVE COMPANY

Consolidated Statements of Income

(Dollars in Millions Except Per Share Amounts)

	2001	2000	1999
Net sales	$9,427.8	$9,357.9	$9,118.2
Cost of sales	4,236.9	4,265.5	4,224.0
Gross profit	5,190.9	5,092.4	4,894.2
Selling, general and administrative expenses	3,261.6	3,299.6	3,254.4
Other expense, net	94.5	52.3	73.6
Interest expense, net	166.1	173.3	171.6
Income before income taxes	1,668.7	1,567.2	1,394.6
Provision for income taxes	522.1	503.4	457.3
Net income	$1,146.6	$1,063.8	$ 937.3
Earnings per common share, basic	$ 2.02	$ 1.81	$ 1.57
Earnings per common share, diluted	$ 1.89	$ 1.70	$ 1.47

This looks like a fairly healthy statement of income. Revenue and gross profit have gone up each year—although not by much—and net income and income per share had very solid gains from 1999 to 2001.

Now let's take a quick look at the consolidated balance sheets in Table 6-2 to see if we can learn anything else about the company's financial position:

TABLE 6-2

COLGATE-PALMOLIVE COMPANY

Consolidated Balance Sheets

(Dollars in Millions Except Per Share Amounts)

	2001	2000
Assets		
Current Assets		
Cash and cash equivalents	$ 172.7	$ 206.6
Receivables (less allowances of $45.6 and $39.8, respectively)	1,124.9	1,195.4
Inventories	677.0	686.6
Other current assets.	228.8	258.6
Total current assets	2,203.4	2,347.2
Property, plant and equipment, net	2,513.5	2,528.3
Goodwill and other intangibles, net	1,904.0	2,096.4
Other assets.	363.9	280.4
	$ 6,984.8	$ 7,252.3
Liabilities and Shareholders' Equity		
Current Liabilities		
Notes and loans payable	$ 101.6	$ 121.1
Current portion of long-term debt	325.5	320.2
Accounts payable	678.1	738.9
Accrued income taxes	195.0	163.7
Other accruals	823.3	900.2
Total current liabilities	2,123.5	2,244.1
Long-term debt	2,812.0	2,536.9
Deferred income taxes	480.6	447.3
Other liabilities	722.3	555.9
Shareholders' Equity		
Preferred stock	341.3	354.1
Common stock, $1 par value (1,000,000,000 shares authorized, 732,853,180 shares issued)	732.9	732.9
Additional paid-in capital	1,168.7	1,144.9

	2001	2000
Retained earnings	5,643.6	4,893.7
Accumulated other comprehensive income	(1,491.2)	(1,269.7)
....	6,395.3	5,855.9
Unearned compensation	(345.4)	(344.4)
Treasury stock, at cost	(5,203.5)	(4,043.4)
Total shareholders' equity	846.4	1,468.1
	$ 6,984.8	$ 7,252.3

In this table, we see that total shareholder equity has dropped slightly, which is a reason for some concern. What contributed to that drop? It's hard to reach any conclusions from this data, but there are other footnotes and tables in the report that shed some light on that as well. The company has been involved in an aggressive share repurchase program to buy back millions of shares of its own stock. That has contributed to the decline in shareholders' equity, but it hasn't affected the true value of the company.

Now let's take a longer-term view of the company's growth by looking at the historical financial table. (See Table 6-3 on pages 104-105.)

The historical performance looks very consistent, with six consecutive years of record income and earnings per share, and increased revenue for six of the past seven years.

However, we see that book value per common share has declined steadily to its lowest level in years. That is not a healthy sign, but the increasing revenues, income, and earnings per share do offer some hope of continuing success. To get a better picture of the company's financial position, let's dissect Colgate's financials with some other important ratios and formulas.

GOT CASH?

How solid is the company's cash position? Let's find out. The cash flow statement gives you a window on the company's short-term financial health.

The cash position of a company can be analyzed from several perspectives—its solvency (ability to meet its short-term cash needs), capital structure (its financial makeup), and its cash flow.

Let's analyze Colgate's statements of cash flows in Table 6-4 on page 106.

How healthy is the company's short-term financial condition? We see that cash and cash equivalents were lower in 2001 than they were in 1999 or 2000, but that is just a small part of the picture.

Let's use the ratios we reviewed in Chapter 4 to analyze the data in Colgate-Palmolive's statements of cash flow (and other financial tables). We calculate the key ratios that pertain to a company's short-term financial position—the cash flow, cash flow per share, the current ratio, the quick ratio, and the working capital. We also calculate the debt-to-equity ratio, the debt-to-assets ratio, inventory turnover ratio, operating margin, return on equity, gross profit margin ratio, and the price-to-book value ratio in order to get a full picture of the company's financial strength.

Cash flow.   To calculate cash flow, take net income after taxes and add back depreciation, amortization, and other noncash charges. Colgate's cash flow statement (Table 6-4) lists "net cash provided by operations" as $1599.6 million in 2001, $1536.2 million in 2000, and $1292.7 million in 1999—so net cash from operations went up each year, which is a good sign. But the cash from operations in the table also includes income taxes, which should not be included in cash flow. Subtract the income tax each year, and the picture changes a little—$1.43 billion in 2001, $1.47 billion in 2000, and $1.17 billion in 1999—so the cash flow actually went down a little in 2001 because the company paid more income taxes.

$1,599.6 million (Operational earnings)
−   168.6 (Income taxes)
$1,431 (Cash flow)

Cash flow per share.   To calculate this, divide cash flow by the number of shares outstanding. Usually, you can find an accurate figure for shares outstanding on the balance sheet, but not in this case. The balance sheet shows 732,853,180 common shares outstanding, but two other sources in the 10-K tell a different story. The historical financial summary (Table 6-3) reports 550 million shares. How do you explain the discrepancy? For the answer, check one more table, "Consolidated Statements of Retained Earnings, Comprehensive Income and Changes in Capital Accounts" (Table 6-5 on page 107).

The previous table shows that the number of shares outstanding has been declining annually (from 585 million in 1999 to 550 million in 2001). Why? According to the table, the company has been acquiring several million shares each year (shown on the table as "Treasury stock acquired"). So the company issued 732 million shares initially, but after a long corporate stock purchase program, the shares outstanding are down to 550 million. The number of shares outstanding is the figure you would use to determine cash flow per share. Divide the cash flow ($1.43 billion) by shares outstanding (550 million). That gives you a cash-flow-per-share total of about 2.6.

$1.43 billion (Cash flow) ÷ 550 million (Shares) = 2.6 (Cash flow per share)

To compare that to the previous year, divide the cash flow from 2000 ($1.47) by the number of shares outstanding (listed as 566 million in Table 6-5).

TABLE 6-3

COLGATE-PALMOLIVE COMPANY

Historical Financial Summary/(1)/

Dollars in Millions Except Per Share Amounts

	2001	2000	1999	1998	1997	1996	1995	1994
Continuing Operations								
Net sales	$9,427.8	$9,357.9	$9,118.2	$8,971.6	$9,056.7	$8,749.0	$8,358.2	$7,587.9
Results of operations:								
Net income	1,146.6	1,063.8	937.3	848.6	740.4	635.0	172.0/(2)/	580.2/(3)/
Per share, basic	2.02	1.81	1.57	1.40	1.22	1.05	.26/(2)/	.96/(3)/
Per share, diluted	1.89	1.70	1.47	1.30	1.13	.98	.25/(2)/	.89/(3)/
Depreciation and amortization expense	336.2	337.8	340.2	330.3	319.9	316.3	300.3	235.1
Financial Position								
Current ratio	1.0	1.0	1.0	1.1	1.1	1.2	1.3	1.4

104

Property, plant and equipment, net.	2,513.5	2,528.3	2,551.1	2,589.2	2,441.0	2,428.9	2,155.2	1,988.1
Capital expenditures.	340.2	366.6	372.8	389.6	478.5	459.0	431.8	400.8
Total assets.	6,984.8	7,252.3	7,423.1	7,685.2	7,538.7	7,901.5	7,642.3	6,142.4
Long-term debt.	2,812.0	2,536.9	2,243.3	2,300.6	2,340.3	2,786.8	2,992.0	1,751.5
Shareholders' equity.	846.4	1,468.1	1,833.7	2,085.6	2,178.6	2,034.1	1,679.8	1,822.9
Share and Other								
Book value per common share	1.54	2.57	3.14	3.53	3.65	3.42	2.84	3.12
Cash dividends declared and paid per common share.	.675	.63	.59	.55	.53	.47	.44	.39
Closing price.	57.75	64.55	65.00	46.44	36.75	23.06	17.56	15.84
Number of common shares outstanding (in millions).	550.7	566.7	578.9	585.4	590.8	588.6	583.4	577.6
Number of shareholders of record:								
$4.25 Preferred.	224	247	275	296	320	350	380	400
Common	40,900	42,300	44,600	45,800	46,800	45,500	46,600	44,100
Average number of employees	38,500	38,300	37,200	38,300	37,800	37,900	38,400	32,800

TABLE 6-4

COLGATE-PALMOLIVE COMPANY

Consolidated Statements of Cash Flows

(Dollars in Millions Except Per Share Amounts)

	2001	2000	1999
Operating Activities			
Net income	$ 1,146.6	$ 1,063.8	$ 937.3
Adjustments to reconcile net income to net cash provided by operations:			
Restructured operations	(8.9)	(14.9)	(35.6)
Depreciation and amortization	336.2	337.8	340.2
Income taxes and other, net	168.6	69.7	122.3
Cash effects of changes in:			
Receivables	19.4	(91.9)	(81.3)
Inventories	(18.7)	59.0	(82.8)
Payables and accruals	(43.6)	112.7	92.6
Net cash provided by operations	1,599.6	1,536.2	1,292.7
Investing Activities			
Capital expenditures	(340.2)	(366.6)	(372.8)
Payment for acquisitions, net of cash acquired.	(10.2)	(64.9)	(44.1)
Sale of noncore product lines	12.5	102.5	89.9
Sale of marketable securities and investments	9.3	137.4	22.7
Other	(90.6)	(17.0)	(27.2)
Net cash used for investing activities	(419.2)	(208.6)	(331.5)
Financing Activities			
Principal payments on debt	(595.9)	(739.4)	(491.0)
Proceeds from issuance of debt	887.9	925.4	555.5
Payments from (to) outside investors	89.7	(113.9)	—
Dividends paid	(396.7)	(382.4)	(366.0)
Purchase of common stock	(1,230.2)	(1,040.6)	(624.4)
Other	34.5	34.9	(14.2)
Net cash used for financing activities	(1,210.7)	(1,316.0)	(940.1)
Effect of exchange rate changes on cash and cash equivalents	(3.6)	(4.6)	(3.2)
Net (decrease) increase in cash and cash equivalents	(33.9)	7.0	17.9
Cash and cash equivalents at beginning of year	206.6	199.6	181.7
Cash and cash equivalents at end of year	$ 172.7	$ 206.6	$ 199.6
Supplemental Cash Flow Information			
Income taxes paid	$ 346.8	$ 306.3	$ 292.4
Interest paid	221.5	203.0	210.9
Principal payments on ESOP debt, guaranteed by the Company	12.9	8.8	6.7

TABLE 6-5

COLGATE-PALMOLIVE COMPANY

Consolidated Statements of Retained Earnings, Comprehensive Income and Changes in Capital Accounts

(Dollars in Millions Except Per Share Amounts)

	Common Shares		Additional Paid-in Capital	Treasury Shares		Retained Earnings	Accumulated Other Comprehensive Income	Comprehensive Income
	Shares	Amount		Shares	Amount			
Balance, January 1, 1999	585,419,480	$732.9	$ 824.6	147,433,700	$2,333.8	$3,641.0	$ (799.8)	
Shares issued for stock options	6,894,907		128.0	(6,894,907)	132.5			
Treasury stock acquired	(12,849,744)			12,849,744	624.4			
Other	(601,597)		110.6	611,087	(34.3)			
Balance, December 31, 1999	578,863,046	$732.9	$1,063.2	153,999,624	$3,056.4	$4,212.3	$(1,136.2)	
Shares issued for stock options	4,796,186		96.7	(4,796,186)	54.3			
Treasury stock acquired	(19,099,681)			19,099,681	1,040.6			
Other	2,096,323		(15.0)	(2,084,163)	(107.9)			
Balance, December 31, 2000	566,655,874	$732.9	$1,144.9	166,218,956	$4,043.4	$4,893.7	$(1,269.7)	
Shares issued for stock options	2,705,887		62.4	(2,705,887)	20.5			
Treasury stock acquired	(21,662,879)			21,662,879	1,230.2			
Other	3,023,451		(38.6)	(3,023,261)	(90.6)			
Balance, December 31, 2001	550,722,333	$732.9	$1,168.7	182,152,687	$5,203.5	$5,643.6	$(1,491.2)	

That equals a cash flow of about 2.6—identical to the 2001 cash flow per share. So the cash flow is holding steady, which is a healthy sign for the company.

Price-to-cash-flow-per-share ratio.   A popular measure of a stock's relative value, you can calculate this by dividing the current stock price by the cash flow per share. You can find the annual closing stock prices in the historical financial summary (Table 6-3) under "Closing price." It was as $64.55 in 2000 and $57.75 in 2001. Divide the stock price by cash flow per share (2.6 both years). That would come to a 24.8 ratio in 2000, and 22.2 in 2001.

$57.75 (Stock price) ÷ 2.6 (Cash flow per share) = 22.2 (Price-to-cash-flow)

For value investors, that's a positive sign. The price-to-cash-flow ratio is like the price-earnings ratio—the lower the better. It means you're getting more for your money. It means you're paying $22.20 for every dollar in cash flow in 2001 compared to $24.80 for each dollar of cash flow in 2000.

What else can we learn about the company's short-term financial condition? Let's calculate several other measures that will give us a little more perspective:

Current ratio.   To calculate current ratio, divide total current assets by total current liabilities. You'll find assets and liabilities in the consolidated balance sheets (Table 6-2). The company had current assets of $2.2 billion in 2001 and $2.35 billion in 2000. It had total current liabilities that were almost identical—$2.1 billion in 2001 and 2.2 billion in 2000. By dividing assets by liabilities, that comes to a current ratio of about 1.0 each year. A ratio of 1.0 is acceptable, although many companies have current ratios of 1.5 to 2.0. A current ratio of 2.0 would mean the company's current assets are twice as much as its current liabilities. Here is the calculation:

$2.2 billion (Current assets) ÷ $2.1 billion
                               (Current liabilities) = 1.0 (Current ratio)

Quick ratio.   To calculate the quick ratio, divide the company's current assets (not including inventory) by current liabilities. The difference between the quick ratio and the current ratio is the inventory factor—it's included in the current ratio but not in the quick ratio. Inventory is left out of the quick ratio because it's not liquid enough—it can take time to move inventory. Since the quick ratio measures the company's short-term financial strength, inventory wouldn't apply.

In Colgate's consolidated balance sheets (Table 6-2), you see that the company had current assets of $2.203 billion in 2001 and $2.347 billion in 2000. Subtract the inventories ($677 million in 2001 and $687 million in 2000) for a total of $1.53 billion in 2001 and $1.66 in 2000. Divide those figures by current liabilities ($2.1 billion in 2001 and $2.2 in 2000), and that comes to a quick ratio of 0.72 in 2001 and 0.75 in 2000. Here is the calculation:

$2,203 million (Current assets)
–   677 million (Inventory)
$1,526 million ÷ 2,124 (Current liabilities) = 0.72 (Quick ratio)

A quick ratio of 0.5 to 1.0 is fairly normal. Over 1.0 is even better because it means that the company is in a stronger position with its short-term assets. A quick ratio of under 0.5 means that the company is more at risk of facing problems meeting its short-term obligations. (It could also mean that the company is being more aggressive with its assets to try to pump up profits.) A declining quick ratio is an indication that the company's short-term financial strength is slipping.

Working capital.   A measure of a company's cash flow, calculate working capital by subtracting current liabilities from current assets. Find current assets and liabilities in the balance sheets (Table 6-2). Colgate-Palmolive had current assets of $2.203 billion in 2001. Subtract current liabilities of $2.124 billion, and that leaves a slim $79 million in working capital.

$2.2903 billion (Current assets)
–   2.124 billion (Current liabilities)
$79 million (Working capital)

The previous year, the company had $103 million in working capital, so there was a decline from one year to the next.

The higher a company's working capital, the more easily it can meet its short-term obligations.

All in all, Colgate-Palmolive's short-term position seems adequate, but not as strong as it could be. The company seems light on working capital, and its quick ratio and current ratio were just satisfactory—and well below the level of many other blue chip companies. On the bright side, its cash flow per share was holding steady, and its stock price-to-cash flow actually improved somewhat from the previous year—although that was due, in part, to a drop in the company's stock price.

The company offered some additional insight into its cash flow situation in a note in the financial section of the 10-K. Here is the company's assessment of its cash flow position:

> Internally generated cash flows are adequate to support currently planned business operations, acquisitions and capital expenditures. Free cash flow (defined as cash generated by the business after capital expenditures and dividend payments but before acquisitions, divestitures and share repurchases) was $862.7 and $787.2 in 2001 and 2000, respectively, and provides the Company with flexibility for further investments and/or financing. The Company has additional sources of liquidity available in the form of lines of credit maintained with various banks and access to financial markets worldwide. At December 31, 2001, unused lines of credit amounted to $1,370.5 and the Company had $1,351.4 available under a shelf registration filed in 2001. Significant acquisitions would require external financing.

The free cash generated by the company and its $1.37 billion line of credit should be more than enough to cover short-term expenses. That's one reason that Colgate is able to maintain a strong credit rating despite its relatively low measures for working capital, the quick ratio, and the current ratio.

The short-term position is just one part of the picture in assessing a company's financial condition. Let's look now at some other ratios that should give us a better picture of the company's long-term financial condition and its value as a stock.

MEASURING FINANCIAL STRENGTH

There are several ratios that can help us measure Colgate's long-term financial strength. Let's calculate the return on equity, operating margin, gross profit margin ratio, debt-to-equity ratio, the debt-to-assets ratio, inventory turnover ratio, and the price-to-book value ratio.

Return on Equity.   Are the shareholders getting a good return on their investment? The return on equity (ROE) can help answer that question. In fact, some analysts consider return on equity to be the most important ratio in assessing the performance of a company.

To calculate, divide net income for the year (after taxes) by shareholders' equity (from the start of the year). For instance, to calculate Colgate's ROE, we will use the net income for 2001 and the closing shareholder's equity for 2000. You can find net income on the income statement (Table 6-1), and shareholders' equity on the balance sheets (Table 6-2)—or you can find them both on the historical financial summary (Table 6-3).

$1,146.6 (Net income) ÷ $1,468 (Shareholders' equity) = 0.781 (78.1%)
(Return on Equity)

A return on equity of 78 percent is outstanding. In fact, anything over 25 percent is considered good. How did the company do the previous year, 2000? Colgate posted net income of $1,064 million on stockholders' equity of $1,834 million. Divide 1,064 by 1,834 for a return on equity of 58 percent, which is also a very high ROE.

Operating margin.   The operating margin helps show a company's profitability by measuring the percent of revenues remaining after paying all operating expenses. It is calculated by dividing operating income by total revenue. Let's calculate Colgate's operating margin. You find operating income in the cash flow statement (Table 6-4) by the line, "Net cash provided by operations." It showed the company had operating income of $1,599.6 million in 2001. Total revenue, from the income statement (Table 6-1), under "net sales" came to $9,427.8 million. Here's the calculation:

$1,599.6 million (Operating income) ÷ $9,427.8 million (Revenue) = 0.17
(17%) operating margin

A 17-percent operating margin would be considered only mediocre. Operating margins tend to vary by industry, but for a very rough guideline, over 50 percent would be considered excellent, 20 to 40 percent would be good, and under 10 percent would be poor.

Gross profit margin ratio.   This gives you an idea of the company's profitability by dividing gross profit margin by total sales. But first, you have to find the profit margin by subtracting cost of goods sold from total sales.

For Colgate-Palmolive, you can find both in the income statement (Table 6-1). In fact, the company lists gross profit on its income statement as $5.191 billion. Here's the calculation:

$9.428 billion (Sales)
− 4.237 billion (Cost of sales)

$5.191 billion (Gross profit margin) ÷ $9.428 billion (Sales) = 0.551
(55.1%) (Gross profit margin ratio)

A gross profit margin of 55 percent is very respectable for a consumer goods manufacturing company. The gross profit margin ratio can vary dramatically from one industry to another, so it's best to compare Colgate's ratio to other companies in its sector and to its previous ratios to get a better perspective. As a rule of thumb for companies like Colgate, a gross profit margin ratio of over 30 percent is considered very solid, over 50 percent is excellent, and over 70 percent is exceptional.

How do you explain the excellent gross profit margin ratio? The company offered its own explanation in a subsection of the 10-K:

Gross Profit

Gross profit margin increased to 55.1%, above both the 2000 level of 54.4% and the 1999 level of 53.7%. This favorable trend reflects the Company's financial strategy to improve all aspects of its supply chain through global sourcing and other cost-reduction initiatives, as well as its emphasis on higher margin products.

The company has apparently made gross profit margin a priority, using outsourcing of manufacturing to other countries, an emphasis on higher-margin products, and other cost-cutting measures to squeeze more profit out of every dollar of sales.

Debt-to-equity ratio. This helps to measure the company's financial strength by comparing its debt financing to equity ownership. To calculate, divide long-term debt for the most recent fiscal period by total shareholder equity for the same period. Lower is better. For Colgate, find long-term debt and shareholders' equity in both the balance sheets (Table 6-2) and the historical financial summary (Table 6-3).

Here's the calculation:

$2,812 million (Long-term debt) ÷ $846 million (Shareholders' equity) = 3.3
(Debt-to-equity ratio)

For a loose reference, less than 0.1 would be considered excellent, 0.1 to 0.9 would be considered good, 1.0 to 2.0 would be considered fair, 2.1 to 4.0 would be considered below average, and more than 4 would be considered poor. So Colgate's debt-to-equity ratio of 3.3 appears to be well below average.

However, the company included one paragraph among its many financial footnotes that should ease any concerns over its debt load:

During 2001, long-term debt increased to $3,137.5 from $2,857.1 and total debt increased to $3,239.1 from $2,978.2 primarily due to increased share repurchases. The Company's long-term debt rating was upgraded in 2001 to AA- by Standard & Poor's and Aa3 by Moody's.

As the paragraph mentions, the company is adding to its debt by repurchasing stock, which is a fairly healthy way to add the debt. On top of that, the report states that the company's debt rating has been raised, giving it an out-standing rating by the leading credit rating companies in the business. In other words, debt is not a problem for Colgate.

Debt-to-assets ratio.   Also known as the "debt ratio," it is used to help mea-sure a company's reliance on leveraging. The debt ratio is calculated by divid-ing total long-term and short-term liabilities by total assets. The lower the better (the more conservative the company). Higher leveraging can increase a company's returns, but it also puts the company at higher risk in bad times. Find liabilities and assets on Colgate's balance sheets (Table 6-2). Assets were $6985 million. To calculate total liabilities, the section from the balance sheet below represents all the company's liabilities:

Total current liabilities	2,123.5
Long-term debt	2,812.0
Deferred income taxes	480.6
Other liabilities	722.3
Total liabilities	$6,138 million

Here's the calculation:

$6,138 million (Total liabilities) ÷ $6,985 million (Total assets) = 0.88 (88%) (Debt-to-assets ratio)

A debt-to-assets ratio of 88 percent is higher than most blue chip companies. While the ratio level tends to vary by the industry, the debt should make up no more than about two-thirds of the company's assets—a debt-to-assets ratio of about 66 percent. But in Colgate's case, with its high debt rating and its ongoing stock repurchase program, the higher debt-to-assets ratio should not be a concern.

Inventory turnover ratio.   How quickly does Colgate turn over its prod-ucts? The inventory turnover ratio measures the number of times inventory is sold over the course of a year. Use it to compare companies in the same indus-try, or compare a company's current turnover rate to its historic rate.

Calculate by dividing cost of goods sold by inventory. You can find "Cost of sales" on the income statement (Table 6-1), and inventory on the balance sheet (Table 6-2) under assets. Here's the calculation:

$4,237 million (Cost of goods sold) ÷ $677 million (Inventory) = 6.26 (Inventory turnover ratio)

A high ratio is preferable, and indicates that the company is selling out its goods quickly, while a low ratio means that products are not moving. But there are vast differences in inventory turnover ratios from one industry to another. With an inventory turnover ratio of 6.26, it looks like Colgate is turning over the toothpaste and other consumer products at a pretty brisk pace.

Price-to-book value ratio.   You calculate this by dividing stock price by the book value per share. There are two ways to find book value per share: 1) You could subtract intangible assets from total shareholders' equity, and then divide the balance by the number of shares outstanding, or 2) you could do it the easy way and just look at the historical financial summary statement (Table 6-3) under the line "Book value per common share." You can also find the year-end stock price in the same table.

Here is the calculation for price-to-book value for Colgate:

$57.75 (Stock price) ÷ $1.54 (Book value) = 37.5 (Price-to-book value ratio)

This ratio helps you compare the stock price to the worth of the company's assets (its book value). The higher the price-to-book value ratio, the more expensive the stock. A price-to-book value of over 20 is considered very high, so Colgate's price-to-book of 37.5 is definitely higher than normal, and should be a cause of some concern for potential investors.

Return on assets.   Used to determine how much profit the company is churning out of its assets, the ratio is calculated by dividing income after taxes by total assets. Here's the calculation for Colgate:

$1,146.6 million (Net income after taxes) ÷ $6,985 million (Total assets) =
0.16 (16.4%) (Return on assets)

An ROA of 16.4 indicates a pretty solid level of profitability for Colgate. Generally speaking, over 30 percent is considered excellent, 15 to 25 percent is very good, 10 to 15 percent is about average, 5 to 10 percent is a little below average, and under 5 percent is generally considered very poor.

Price earnings ratio.   This is the leading ratio that Wall Street uses to determine whether a stock is trading at a fair price. To calculate, divide stock price by diluted earnings per share. You can find both the 2001 closing stock price ($57.75) and the earnings per share ($1.89) for Colgate in the historical financial summary (Table 6-3). Here's the calculation:

$57.75 (Stock price) ÷ $1.89 (Diluted earnings per share) = 30.6
(Price earnings ratio)

For a company that is growing at 10 to 15 percent per year, a PE of 30 is a little steep. Because of its established brand and long history of growth, Colgate can command a premium for its stock, which helps explain the high PE. But a PE of 15 to 25 would make the stock much more attractive.

Price-to-sales ratio.   One more measure of the stock's relative value, the price-to-sales ratio, is calculated by dividing the stock price ($57.75) by the revenue per share. To calculate revenue per share, divide revenue ($9.428 billion) by shares outstanding (551 million). All three figures (stock price, revenue, and shares outstanding) can be found in the historical financial summary (Table 6-3). Here's the calculation:

$9,428 million (Revenue) ÷ 551 million (Shares outstanding) = $17.11
Revenue per share

$57.75 (Stock price) ÷ $17.11 (Revenue per share) = 3.4
(Price-to-sales ratio)

A price-to-sales ratio of 3.4 is considered excellent. Like PEs, the lower the price-sales ratio the better. Anything under 5 is considered very good.

Stock price movement.   One more area that should be of interest to anyone considering buying the stock would be a little history on the stock's performance. You can find that in the 10-K, as well. Here is a section on Colgate's stock price history:

TABLE 6-6

The Company's common stock and $4.25 Preferred Stock are listed on the New York Stock Exchange. The trading symbol for the common stock is CL. Dividends on the common stock have been paid every year since 1895 and the amount of dividends paid per share has increased for 39 consecutive years.

Market Price Quarter Ended	Common Stock				$4.25 Preferred Stock			
	2001		2000		2001		2000	
	High	Low	High	Low	High	Low	High	Low
March 31 ...$	$62.50	$51.00	$64.81	$42.75	$89.00	$86.85	$89.00	$86.00
June 30	.61.00	51.26	62.63	52.63	89.75	85.93	88.00	86.00
September 30.	60.25	52.64	59.88	43.06	88.00	85.50	88.00	85.75
December 31.	59.41	56.15	64.56	46.50	88.00	85.00	88.50	86.50
Closing Price	$57.75		$64.55		$87.50		$87.75	

The table shows that the company's stock price—both common and preferred—have stayed fairly stable during the two-year period, with slight declines. (Preferred stock pays a fixed dividend rate set at the time of issue—much like a bond—but the stock price tends to show very little deviation. Preferred stocks trade based on their dividend yield rather than capital growth.)

All in all, Colgate's financials have weathered the analysis with a fairly solid bill of health. Its short- and long-term debt positions are higher than average, but its outstanding credit rating should ease any concerns about solvency. The biggest concern might be the company's slow sales growth, its declining book value per share, and its high price earnings ratio.

But there are some positives as well. Its net income and earnings per share have been moving up consistently. The company also has very solid profitability numbers, with very strong showings in return on equity, return on assets, and gross profit margin ratio. And while its PE ratio was somewhat too high, its price-to-sales ratio was very reasonable.

Now let's put Colgate through one more test—core earnings growth.

IN SEARCH OF THE CORE EARNINGS

Company accountants have learned how to obscure their true earnings by using countless "nonrecurring items," such as restructuring charges, discontinued operations charges, and extraordinary items. To get to the core—the true sustainable earnings—sometimes you need to peel back all of the nonrecurring charges, and uncover the sustainable earnings from one year to the next.

There is a system for removing nonrecurring items that can help you get a truer picture of the company's earnings growth. But it's not easy, and it's not quick. Finding all the nonrecurring items in a company's financial section can take the patience, perception, and perseverance of a detective. It means scouring dozens of pages of financial tables and single-spaced footnotes in search of all nonrecurring items. But the effort may pay off. By finding core earnings for the past two or three years, you may get a truer picture of the company's growth—and see if it's in line with its reported earnings growth.

In the Colgate cash flow statement (Table 6-4), the company does provide a sense of core earnings with an item listed as "net cash provided by operations." The report showed that cash provided by operations has increased from $1.29 billion in 1999 to $1.54 billion in 2000 to $1.6 million in 2001.

But the core earnings search should give you a slightly different perspective.

It would help to put together a worksheet to do the job right. On one page you can list all the charges that you would add back to earnings, and on the other page you would list all the charges you would deduct from the final earnings total. As an example, we've put together core earnings worksheets from Colgate's financials, which follows.

In order to find all the nonrecurring charges, you will need to examine the cash flow statement, the income statement, and pages upon pages of footnotes and related financial tables. It is a colossal task.

Here is a step-by-step approach to determining core earnings:

1. **Make a list of nonrecurring deductions to add back to earnings.** What types of nonrecurring items should be included? You should include such items as losses on sales of fixed assets and other assets, losses on sales of investments, investment write-downs, restructuring charges, foreign currency losses, inventory write-downs, litigation charges, exceptional bad-debt provisions, and pretax LIFO liquidation losses.

2. **Deduct estimated taxes.** It gets a little complicated here, but to get the truest possible picture of core earnings, this is a step you need to include. Once you've added up all the pretax, nonrecurring deductions, multiply that by the company's combined state and federal tax rate, and subtract the taxes from the total.

3. **Add after-tax deductions.** You may find a few after-tax, nonrecurring items to add to the list, such as increases in deferred tax valuation allowances, nonrecurring tax charges, losses on discontinued operations, extraordinary losses, losses due to cumulative effect of accounting changes, and other after-tax charges.

4. **Add together the taxed and after-tax items to come up with total additions.** That completes the first worksheet.

5. **On the second worksheet, list all nonrecurring deductions.** That might include such items as gains on the sale of investments, gains on the sale of fixed assets and other assets, foreign currency gains, gains on litigation, temporary expense decreases, temporary revenue increases, and pretax LIFO liquidation gains.

6. **Multiply the total by the tax rate, and subtract taxes from the total.**

7. **Add together after-tax items.** That might include items such as reduction in deferred tax valuation allowances, gains on discontinued operations, extraordinary gains, research and development tax credits, loss carry-forward benefits from prior periods, and after-tax LIFO liquidation gains.

8. **Add together the taxed and after-tax items.** That gives you the total deductions, and completes the second worksheet.

9. **Add the company's reported net income (or loss) for the year to the total additions (the first worksheet), and then subtract from that total the deductions from the second worksheet.** That will give you the company's total core earnings for the year.

One more tip: If in doubt, leave the item off your list. In other words, if you can't determine whether or not a specific line item is a nonrecurring item that would affect earnings, err on the safe side, and don't include it on your list. This is a very inexact science. No two financial reports are the same. Every company's financial situation is different, and so is the way they report the results, as you will learn when you do your own analysis. You will see numbers and references that you wouldn't understand without an M.B.A. in finance—and even the M.B.A.s would have a hard time deciphering parts of many company reports.

However, you can aid your own effort if you understand one more thing about the search for core earnings. Most, if not all, of the relevant nonrecurring items will be on either the income statement or the cash flow statement— or in a footnote or secondary table that relates to the income or cash flow statements.

Let's comb Colgate-Palmolive's financial section in search of nonrecurring items. (Unfortunately, after much scouring of tables and footnotes, I could find only a few examples of applicable nonrecurring items. Chances are, you will have a similar experience with most of the companies you analyze.)

In the cash flow statement (Table 6-4), you should focus primarily on the "Operating Activities" section. There is one line in Colgate's report that qualifies as a nonrecurring item, "Restructured operations."

(Dollars in Millions Except Per Share Amounts)

	2001	2000	1999
Operating Activities			
Restructured operations	(8.9)	(14.9)	(35.6)

In the income statement (Table 6-1), the one suspicious line in the table is "other expense, net:"

	2001	2000	1999
Other expense, net	94.5	52.3	73.6

But before we can begin our list of nonrecurring items, we need more details. A thorough reading of the footnotes and associated tables provides some more information. This footnote provides some elaboration on the "Other expense, net" line in the income statement:

Other Expense, Net

Other expense, net, consists principally of amortization of goodwill and other intangible assets, minority interest in earnings of less-than-

100%-owned consolidated subsidiaries, earnings from equity investments, gains on sale of noncore product lines, and other miscellaneous
gains and losses. Other expense, net, increased in 2001 from $52.3 to
$94.5 with $27.0 of the increase resulting from unrealized losses on foreign currency contracts in 2001 of $11.6 as compared with unrealized
gains of $15.4 in 2000. These contracts are an economic hedge of certain
foreign currency debt but do not qualify for hedge accounting.

   During 2000, the Company incurred charges of $92.7 ($61.2 after-
tax), including a restructuring charge related to the realignment of certain
manufacturing operations and the exiting of our business in Nigeria. Also
included were gains of $102.0 ($60.9 aftertax) recorded on the sale of real
estate and the sale of the Viva detergent brand in Mexico.

This section offers a few possible entries for the worksheet. Those would
include:

- Unrealized loss on foreign currency contracts of $27 million in 2001,
  and a gain on foreign currency contracts of $11.6 million in 2000.

- A charge of $92.7 million in 2000 that related, in part, to a restructuring
  charge for the realignment of certain manufacturing operations and its
  business in Nigeria.

- A gain of $102 million on the sales of real estate and the Viva detergent
  brand in Mexico.

A later footnote offers more elaboration on the restructuring charge:

Restructured Operations

   In December 2000, the Company recorded a charge of $63.9 ($42.5
aftertax) associated with the realignment of three manufacturing locations in Latin America and the exiting of our business in Nigeria. The
charge, recorded in Other expense, net, included $14.2 for termination
costs and $49.7 for exiting of manufacturing operations. The restructur-
ing was completed in 2001 with a final payment of $7.2 representing ter-
mination costs for 979 employees.

That paragraph helps us narrow down the restructuring charge to $63.9
million for 2000, and it adds another charge for 2001 of $7.2 million in termi-
nation costs. Unfortunately, there is no mention of 1999. So I went to the 1999
report and looked up the "Other Expenses" footnote. Here is what it said:
"Other expense, net, increased in 1999 from $61.2 to $73.6, primarily due to
one-time charges."

Based on the information we collected in the tables and footnotes, the
core earnings worksheets would look like this:

Losses to add back (dollars in millions)

	2001	2000	1999
Reported net income (from Income Statement)	$1,146.6	$1,063.8	$ 937.3
Add			
Restructuring charges for Latin American operations and other one-time charges in 1999	7.2	63.9	73.6
Unrealized loss on foreign currency contracts	$27		
Restructured operations from the cash flow statement	8.9	14.9	35.6
Total	$43.1	78.8	109.2
Taxes calculated at the company's average of 31 percent	13.4	24.4	33.9
Tax-adjusted additions	29.7	54.4	75.3
Gains to deduct			
Gains on sale of real estate and the Viva brand in Mexico	12.5	102.5	
Gains on foreign currency contracts		15.4	
Total	12.5	117.9	
Tax calculated at the company's average of 31 percent	3.9	36.5	
Tax-adjusted deductions	8.6	81.4	0
Balance from both tables	+ 21.1	− 27	+75.3
Reported net income	1,146.6	1,063.8	$ 937.3
Adjusted core earnings	1,167.7	$1036.8	$1022.6

You can see from the previous table that the core earnings increased from one year to the next (1999 to 2001). That is a positive sign for Colgate, and it reconfirms the general trend of the reported net income, which also showed gains each year from 1999 to 2001.

PENSION FUND LIABILITIES

Recently, investors have focused on pension fund liabilities, which could weaken a company's financial strength. Gains and losses from company pension funds can directly affect the company's bottom line. Some companies include pension fund gains and losses on the annual income statement. In the late 1990s, as stocks were climbing, the gains in the pension funds helped boost the bottom line of many companies. But from 2000 through 2002, as stocks tumbled, market losses for pension fund holdings cut into corporate earnings. Major losses from pension fund could affect the company's ability to make pension payments. In fact, some companies have had to dip into corporate earnings to meet pension fund liabilities.

Not all companies account for pension funds in the same way. You can find out more about a company's pension funds in the footnotes of the 10-K financial section. The following excerpt is from the McDonald's 10-K report:

Employee benefit palns

The Company's Profit Sharing and Savings Plan for U.S.-based employees include profit sharing, 401 (k) and leveraged employee stock ownership (ESOP) features. . . In addition, the Company maintains a non-quailified unfunded Supplemental Plan that allows participants to make tax-deferred contributions and receive Company-provided allocations that cannot be made under the Profit Sharing and Savings Plan because of Internal Revenue Service limitations. The investment alternatives in the Supplemental Plan include certain of the same investment as the Profit Sharing and Savings Plan. Total liabilities under the supplemental Plan were $301.1 million at December 31, 20001 and $288.8 million at December 31, 2000, and were included in other long-term liabilities in the Consolidated balance sheet.

The Company has entered into derivative contracts to hedge the changes in these liabilities. At December 31, 2001, derivatives with a fair value of $68.2 million indexed to the Company's stock and $18.5 million indexed to certain market indices were included in miscellaneous other assets in the Consolidated balance sheet. All changes in Plan liabilities and in the fair value of the derivatives are recorded in selling, general and administrative expenses. Changes in fair value of the derivatives indexed to the Company's stock are recorded in the income statement because the contracts provide the counterparty with a choice of cash settlement or settlement in shares.

This section gives details of the company's contributions to the plan and mentions where the pension fund is listed in its financial filings. Total liabilities from the supplemental plan were included in the long-term liabilities in the consolidated balance sheet, while the derivative contracts used to hedge against changes in liabilities were listed in "selling, general & administrative expenses," and changes in the value of the derivatives are included in the income statement.

SUBSIDIARIES

There's one more attachment to the 10-K that may also be worth a look. That is the attachment that covers "subsidiaries of the registrant." The section gives you a good idea of how large, complex, and globally positioned the company is. Colgate's list of subsidiaries covers about two pages. We won't show the full list, but here is a sample from the list:

SUBSIDIARIES OF THE REGISTRANT

Name of Company	State in which Incorporated or Country in which Organized
Colgate (Guangzhou) Co. Ltd.	China
Colgate Oral Pharmaceuticals, Inc.	Delaware
Colgate-Palmolive A.B.	Sweden
Colgate-Palmolive Argentina S.A.	Argentina
Colgate-Palmolive A/S	Denmark
Colgate-Palmolive Belgium S.A.	Belgium
Colgate-Palmolive (B) Sdn. Bhd.	Brunei
Colgate-Palmolive Canada, Inc.	Canada
Colgate-Palmolive (Central America), Inc.	Delaware
Colgate-Palmolive (Centro America) S.A.	Guatemala
Colgate-Palmolive Cia.	Delaware
Colgate-Palmolive Compania Anonima	Venezuela
Colgate-Palmolive Company, Distr.	Puerto Rico
Colgate-Palmolive do Brasil Ltda.	Brasil
Colgate-Palmolive (Dominican Republic), Inc.	Delaware
Colgate-Palmolive (Eastern) Pte. Ltd	Singapore
Colgate-Palmolive Espana, S.A.	Spain
Colgate-Palmolive Europe S.A.	Belgium
Colgate-Palmolive Europe SARL	France
Colgate-Palmolive France, S.A.	France
Colgate-Palmolive G.m.b.H.	Germany
Colgate-Palmolive Gesellschaft G.m.b.H.	Austria
Colgate-Palmolive (Guangzhou) Co., Ltd.	China
Colgate-Palmolive (H.K.) Limited	Hong Kong
Colgate-Palmolive, Inc.	Delaware
Colgate-Palmolive (India) Limited	India
Colgate-Palmolive International Incorporated	Delaware
Colgate-Palmolive Italia S.r.l.	Italy
Colgate-Palmolive Limited	New Zealand
Colgate-Palmolive (Malaysia) Sdn Bhd	Malaysia

This list constitutes about half of the company's subsidiaries. As you can see, Colgate has subsidiaries all over the world. In all, it listed nearly 50 subsidiaries throughout the United States and the world.

ENRON'S RED FLAG

Colgate's long list of subsidiaries pales by comparison to Enron's. In Enron's 10-K report, it listed thousands of subsidiaries and limited partnerships. In fact, just to print the company's list of subsidiaries would take 65 single-spaced pages. Clearly that would seem to be an unreasonable number of subsidiaries to track and manage—and should raise a red flag for anyone analyzing the company's operations. There is yet another red flag in the subsidiaries list as well. Maybe you can figure it out. Here is the very top part of Enron's list:

ENRON CORP.
AND SUBSIDIARY COMPANIES
Subsidiary and Limited Partnership Interests as of 12/31/00

Subsidiary, Place of Incorporation
ATLANTIC COMMERCIAL FINANCE B.V., i.l., (Cayman Islands)
ATLANTIC COMMERCIAL FINANCE, INC , (Delaware)
  Compression Projects Finance Ltd., (Cayman Islands)
  EDC Atlantic Ltd., (Cayman Islands)
  Enron Equity Corp., (Delaware)
    Enron Dominican Republic Ltd., (Cayman Islands)
      Smith/Enron Cogeneration Limited Partnership,
      (Turks & Caicos Isles)
      Smith/Enron O&M Limited Partnership,
      (Turks & Caicos Isles)
    Enron Dominican Republic Operations Ltd.,
    (Cayman Islands)
      Smith/Enron Cogeneration Limited Partnership,
      (Turks & Caicos Isles)
      Smith/Enron O&M Limited Partnership,
      (Turks & Caicos Isles)
    Enron Global Power & Pipelines LLC, (Delaware)
      Enron Dominicana Holding Limited,
      (Cayman Islands)
        Enron Dominicana Limited Partnership,
        (Cayman Islands)
          Smith/Enron Cogeneration Limited
          Partnership, (Turks & Caicos Isles)
    Enron Holding Company L.L.C., (Delaware)
      Enron Dominican Republic Ltd., (Cayman Islands)
        Smith/Enron Cogeneration Limited Partnership,
        (Turks & Caicos Isles)
        Smith/Enron O&M Limited Partnership,
        (Turks & Caicos Isles)
      Enron Dominican Republic Operations Ltd.,
      (Cayman Islands)

> Smith/Enron Cogeneration Limited
> Partnership, (Turks & Caicos Isles)
> Smith/Enron O&M Limited Partnership,
>   (Turks & Caicos Isles)
> Enron Global Power & Pipelines LLC, (Delaware)
> Enron Dominicana Holding Limited,
>   (Cayman Islands)
>   Enron Dominicana Limited Partnership,
>   (Cayman Islands)

Many of the listed subsidiaries in this excerpt and throughout the entire list are based in the Cayman Islands. Corporations base their subsidiaries there not because there's that much business to do in the Caymans, but because they can protect assets from U.S. taxes, and they can conceal information on operations that investors and analysts can never uncover. When a company has hundreds of Cayman subsidiaries and limited partnerships, that is a strong indication that they may have some things to hide. And, indeed, Enron had plenty to hide.

ENRON'S COLLAPSE

One of Enron's largest stumbling blocks related directly to its vast empire of subsidiaries and limited partnerships. The company used a variety of complex accounting tricks to disguise its huge and growing debt. The debt was a major concern for Enron because a rising debt load can adversely affect a company's credit rating. And a lower credit rating would mean that the company would have to pay higher interest on new loans, which would restrict its aggressive expansion plans.

Enron was able to hide its debt through an ingenious-yet-corrupt limited partnership strategy. If one of its plants or subsidiaries was losing money, the company would look for an investor who could afford to buy at least 3 percent of that company, and then Enron would help the investor get a bank loan for the remaining amount by putting up stock as collateral to cover the bank's risk. Enron created hundreds of such limited partnerships through this technique. But in doing so, the company also put up billions of dollars in stock as collateral for the loans.

Once the company's financials began to crack, all those bank loans tied to Enron stock quickly brought down its house of cards. The beginning of the end came when one of Enron's partnerships defaulted on its $560 million loan. The bank demanded that Enron make good on the loan by compensating it with $560 million in stock. But that was just the beginning. News of the default caused Enron's stock price to nose-dive. As it did, the banks behind Enron's many limited partnerships demanded more shares of stock to make up for the loss in value. That diluted its share value even further and led to the eventual collapse of the company.

Enron's massive list of subsidiaries and limited partnerships—including hundreds of Cayman companies—was not an absolute indication of a high-risk company, but it should have raised some serious concerns among analysts and investors. For future reference, if you see a company with the type of subsidiary holdings that Enron had, you might want to move on to another stock prospect.

As an investor, you have many choices. There are thousands of stocks to choose from in building your own portfolio. One of the reasons you comb through a company's SEC reports is to get a feel for the company's operations, its financials, and its approach to business. If you find any significant reason for concern with any of those issues, do yourself a favor and pass on that stock.

7

CHECKING UP ON THE DIRECTORS AND EXECUTIVES

WANT TO LEARN ABOUT THE FINANCIAL ARRANGEMENTS that companies have with their top executives and boards of directors? You can find it at EDGAR. Want to learn more details on the backgrounds, ages, and previous employment of the company's officers? That's also available at EDGAR—if you know where to look.

You can also find out about the stock holdings of a company chairman or leading executive. In fact, in this chapter, we dig up the stock holdings of the founders of four of America's most prominent high tech businesses— Microsoft's Bill Gates, Dell's Michael Dell, Amazon's Jeff Bezos, and Oracle's Larry Ellison.

You can find executive compensation and insider share ownership in the proxy statement and additional information on share ownership (and changes in ownership) through Forms 3, 4, 5, or 13G. To dig up the information on a specific individual, you can do a search at EDGAR either for that person's company or for the specific individual.

For instance, let's look up William Gates, the chairman of Microsoft and the nation's richest person. At the "Company Search" box, you could type in either "Microsoft" or "Gates," but since we're interested specifically in Gates, we type in "Gates." The search comes up with several options, including the

FIGURE 7-1 William Gates files.

GATES WILLIAM H III (0000902012)

State location: <u>WA</u>

To limit filing results, enter
form type or date (as 2002/05/23).

Business Address	Mailing Address
ONE MICROSOFT WAY	ONE MICROSOFT WAY
REDMOND WA 98052	REDMOND WA 98052
4258828080	

Form Type

Prior to

Retrieve Filings

Items 1 - 14

Form	Formats	Description	Filing Date	Text size
SC 13G	[html][text]	Statement of acquisition of beneficial ownership by individuals	2002-03-01	29 KB
SC 13G/A	[html][text]	[Amend]Statement of acquisition of beneficial ownership by individuals	2002-02-14	28 KB
SC 13G/A	[html][text]	[Amend]Statement of acquisition of beneficial ownership by individuals	2001-02-14	29 KB
SC 13D	[text]	General statement of acquisition of beneficial ownership	1998-11-19	18 KB
SC 13G/A	[text]	[Amend]Statement of acquisition of beneficial ownership by individuals	1996-02-07	8 KB

one we're looking for, William H. Gates, III. Click on the name, and a short list of options appears. (See Figure 7-1.)

Click on the top entry (Schedule 13G), and you learn that Gates owns about nine million shares of Nextel Partners, which represents 5.5 percent of the company's total shares.

Click on the second entry (Schedule 13G/A), and you find out how incredibly rich Gates really is. That second entry gives details of the Microsoft shares owned by Gates. Here is an excerpt from that form:

Item 1.

    (a) *Name of Issuer:* Microsoft Corporation (the "Issuer")

    (b) *Address of principal executive offices of the Issuer:* One Microsoft Way, Redmond, Washington 98052

Item 2.

    (a) *Name of Persons Filing:* William H. Gates III

    (b) *Address of Principal Business Office:* One Microsoft Way, Redmond, Washington 98052

    (c) *Citizenship:* United States of America

    (d) *Title of Class of Securities:* Common Stock, $0.0000125 par value per share

    (e) *CUSIP Number:* 594918104

Item 3.   Not Applicable

Item 4.   *Ownership.*

    (a) *Amount beneficially owned:* 651,749,668

(b) *Percent of class:* 12.0%

(c) *Number of shares as to which the person has:*

(i) Sole power to vote or to direct the vote 651,749,668

(ii) Shared power to vote or to direct the vote -0-

(iii) Sole power to dispose or to direct the disposition of 651,749,668

(iv) Shared power to dispose or to direct the disposition of -0-

You can see under "Item 4," that Gates owns just over 650 million shares of Microsoft stock—which represents about 12 percent of the company's total shares. How much are those 651,749,668 shares worth? If Microsoft shares were trading at $50 a share, that would put the value of Gates' shares at nearly $33 billion.

Let's look at a couple of the holdings of Jeff Bezos, founder and chairman of Amazon.com. Enter his name in the company search. (See Figure 7-2.)

That leads you to a short list of choices for Jeffrey P. Bezos, one 13G filing for each of the past five years. When you click on the current year's filing, you see that it lists these facts about Bezos' ownership of Amazon.com stock:

Item 4.   Ownership.

The following describes the ownership of Common Stock by Mr. Bezos as of December 31, 2001:

(a) Amount beneficially owned: 114,716,666

(b) Percent of class: 30.7%

(c) Number of shares as to which such person has:

FIGURE 7-2 Bezos search.

    (i)   Sole power to vote or direct the vote: 114,709,844

    (ii) Shared power to vote or to direct the vote: 6,822 /1/

    (iii) Sole power to dispose or to direct the disposition of: 114,709,844

    (iv) Shared power to dispose or to direct the disposition of: 6,822 /1/

/1/ These shares are held with Mr. Bezos' wife in a joint brokerage account.

In this filing, we learn that Bezos holds 30.7 percent of all Amazon.com common stock, with a total of 114,709,844 shares with full voting rights, and another 6822 shares with "shared power." In footnote /1/, we learn that the 6822 shared-power shares are "held with Mr. Bezos' wife in a joint brokerage account."

Now let's check out Larry Ellison, founder and chairman of Oracle. Here's an excerpt from the 13G filing from Ellison:

Item 4. Ownership.

    (a) Amount beneficially owned: 1,378,171,324 (includes options to purchase 59,375,000 shares exercisable within 60 days of December 31, 2001).

    (b) Percent of class: 24.8%.

    (c) Number of shares as to which the person has:

        (i)   Sole power to vote or to direct the vote: 1,378,171,324 (includes options to purchase 59,375,000 shares exercisable within 60 days of December 31, 2001).

        (ii) Shared power to vote or to direct the vote: 0.

        (iii) Sole power to dispose or to direct the disposition of: 1,378,171,324 (includes options to purchase 59,375,000 shares exercisable within 60 days of December 31, 2001).

        (iv) Shared power to dispose or to direct the disposition of: 0.

As the report details, Ellison owns 24.8 percent of all Oracle common shares—nearly 1.4 billion shares in all (with an option to buy another 59,375,000 shares). When the stock was at its peak of about $45 a share in 2000, Ellison's 1.4 billion shares would have been worth about $63 billion. But after the tech market crash, Oracle's stock dropped to just under $10 a share. In all, he saw the value of his shares drop about $50 billion. Ouch! But shed no tears for Ellison. Even at $9 a share, his 1.4 billion shares would be worth more than $10 billion.

FORMS 3, 4, AND 5

Schedule 13G is not the only place to look for stock holdings of company officers. Forms 3, 4, and 5 also contain information about stock purchases and ownership by the officers or directors of a company. Although these filings are fairly rare at EDGAR, when you do see them, they can give you some good information about the officers' financial maneuverings.

Let's look at the filings for Michael Dell, founder and chairman of Dell Computer. Dell was very active in acquiring stock in recent years. He filed more than 30 Form 4 and Form 5 reports from 1999 through 2002. He also filed several Schedule 13G forms. Let's take a look first at the 13G form:

1.   NAMES OF REPORTING PERSON: Michael S. Dell
     I.R.S. IDENTIFICATION NOS. OF ABOVE PERSONS (Entities Only):

----

2.   CHECK THE APPROPRIATE BOX IF A MEMBER OF A GROUP
     (See Instructions):
(a) [ ]

(b) [ ]

----

3.   SEC USE ONLY

----

4.   CITIZENSHIP OR PLACE OF ORGANIZATION: United States
     of America

Number of Shares	5. SOLE VOTING POWER 301,274,605 (a)
Beneficially Owned By Each	6. SHARED VOTING POWER 11,658,000 (b)
Reporting Person With	7. SOLE DISPOSITIVE POWER 304,794,605 (a)

----

8. SHARED DISPOSITIVE POWER
    11,658,000 (b)

---

9. AGGREGATE AMOUNT BENEFICIALLY OWNED BY EACH
    REPORTING PERSON
    312,932,605 (a)(b)

----

10. CHECK BOX IF THE AGGREGATE AMOUNT IN ROW (9)
     EXCLUDES CERTAIN SHARES
     (SEE INSTRUCTIONS) ....[X]
     40,889,112 (c)

----

11. PERCENT OF CLASS REPRESENTED BY AMOUNT IN ROW (9):
     12%

----

12. TYPE OF REPORTING PERSON (SEE INSTRUCTIONS): IN

(a) Includes 673,626 shares subject to options that were exercisable at or within 60 days of December 31, 2001.

(b) Includes 3,520,000 shares subject to options that were exercisable at or within 60 days of December 31, 2001 and are being held in trusts of which the reporting person or his spouse is the trustee for the benefit of their children.

(c) Includes 34,809,112 shares held in a separate property trust for the reporting person's spouse and 6,080,000 shares held in trusts of which either the reporting person or his spouse is the trustee for the benefit of their children.

As the filing and footnotes detail, Dell owns more than 300 million shares of Dell stock outright, which accounts for about 12 percent of all outstanding shares. He also holds another 35 million shares in a trust for his wife, and about 6 million more shares in trusts for his wife and children. The stock was trading at about $25 in 2002—which means that his 300 million shares would be worth about $7.5 billion.

EXECUTIVE COMPENSATION: FIND IT IN THE PROXY

If you want to find salary and other compensation information for a company's officers, the place to look is in the proxy statement.

At the EDGAR site, the proxy is usually listed as Form 14 (although it may be listed in the company's search page as "DEF 14A," or "DEFM 14A," or a similar title). The key is to find a listing with "14" or "14A" in the title.

For example, if you look up the filings from Dell Computer, "DEF 14A" is among the listings for 2002. Click on that, and you find the full proxy with a wealth of information about the company's key people and their compensation.

The following table (Figure 7-3) from Dell's proxy provides details of the compensation for the company's leading officers:

As you might notice, Michael Dell made a paltry $925,962 in 2002, along with a bonus of $347,236, options on one million shares of Dell stock, and other compensation totaling $34,499. The table indicates that Dell's bonus of $347,236 was considerably below his bonus of the previous two years, when it exceeded $1.6 million. A note in the same section of the proxy explains the drop in bonus money:

Compensation of the Chief Executive Officer

In fiscal 2002, Mr. Dell's annualized base salary was increased to $950,000. Mr. Dell's salary remains below the median base salary earnings for chief executive officers of the peer group of companies. The committee continues to focus on the performance-based elements of Mr. Dell's compensation package, with less emphasis on fixed base pay.

As a result of the Company's performance in fiscal 2002, Mr. Dell received an incentive bonus equal to 25% of his target bonus. Although the Company per-

FIGURE 7-3. Dell compensation table.

Summary Compensation Table

The following table summarizes the total compensation, for each of the last three fiscal years, for Mr. Dell and the four other most highly compensated executive officers who were serving as executive officers at the end of fiscal 2002. These persons are referred to as the "Named Executive Officers."

| Name and Principal Position | Fiscal Year | Annual Compensation | | | Restricted Stock Awards[c] | Long-Term Compensation Awards — Shares Underlying Options[d] | All Other Compensation[e] |
		Salary	Bonus[a]	Other[b]			
Michael S. Dell	2002	$925,962	$ 347,236	—	—	1,000,000	$ 34,499
Chairman of the Board,	2001	892,308	1,668,462	—	—	1,250,000	27,264
Chief Executive Officer	2000	850,000	1,670,250	—	—	805,595	107,966
Kevin B. Rollins	2002	721,154	243,389	—	—	5,350,000	11,904
President and Chief	2001	688,462	1,158,923	—	—	1,250,000	6,423
Operating Officer	2000	613,461	1,087,000	—	—	290,910	9,577
James T. Vanderslice	2002	718,269	242,416	—	—	2,850,000	29,088
Vice Chairman	2001	663,462	1,116,865	$120,395	—	1,250,000	10,738
	2000	69,231	1,000,000	—	$37,575,000	1,500,000	906
Paul D. Bell	2002	444,231	188,798	—	—	1,400,000	7,513
Senior Vice President,	2001	390,769	448,800	233,713	—	600,000	5,821
Europe, Middle East and Africa	2000	301,539	375,000	—	—	100,700	4,925
Joseph A. Marengi	2002	439,040	193,539	—	—	1,400,000	8,974
Senior Vice President,	2001	426,931	496,770	—	—	375,000	25,565
Americas	2000	410,008	410,294	—	—	89,510	16,405

formed very well against its peers in fiscal 2002, the Company's revenue growth performance fell short of some of the aggressive internal goals established at the beginning of the year. The Company managed to increase unit volume sales in the midst of the first year-over-year decline in the personal computer market. Mr. Dell elected to forego this bonus in lieu of a discounted stock option grant under Dell's Executive Stock Ownership Incentive Plan, as described above.

What else does the proxy tell us about the officers and directors? Plenty. Dig around through the proxy, and you find more tables on compensation, and more background information on each of the company's key people. The following table from the proxy details the stock options paid to Dell executives:

OPTION GRANTS IN LAST FISCAL YEAR

Name	Number of Shares Underlying Options Granted	Percentage of Total Options Granted to Employees In Fiscal Year	Exercise Price Per Share	Fair Market Value on Grant Date	Grant Date	Expiration Date	Grant Date Present Value[a]
Mr. Dell	500,000	0.41%	$22.94	$22.94	2/12/01	2/12/11	$ 4,878,750
	307,285[c]	0.25%	21.72	27.15	3/23/01	3/23/11	4,704,533
	500,000[d]	0.41%	24.09	24.09	6/18/01	6/18/11	5,032,500
Mr. Rollins	350,000[b]	0.29%	22.94	22.94	2/12/01	2/12/11	3,415,125
	213,442[c]	0.17%	21.72	27.15	3/23/01	3/23/11	3,267,797
	5,000,000[d]	4.07%	24.09	24.09	6/18/01	6/18/11	50,325,000
Dr. Vanderslice	350,000[b]	0.29%	22.94	22.94	2/12/01	2/12/11	3,415,125
	205,696[c]	0.17%	21.72	27.15	3/23/01	3/23/11	3,149,206
	2,500,000[d]	2.04%	24.09	24.09	6/18/01	6/18/11	33,550,000
Mr. Bell	200,000[b]	0.16%	22.94	22.94	2/12/01	2/12/11	1,951,500
	82,656[c]	0.07%	21.72	27.15	3/23/01	3/23/11	1,265,463
	1,000,000[b]	0.81%	24.09	24.09	6/18/01	6/18/11	10,065,000
	200,000[b]	0.16%	22.10	22.10	9/6/01	9/6/11	1,858,500

We've seen the tables that detail the compensation for the company's top executives. But what about the board of directors—how much are they paid by the company to sit on the board? That information is also available in the proxy. The following excerpt from Dell's proxy lays out the company's director compensation policy and lists the payments to each director:

Director Compensation

Mr. Dell and Mr. Topfer, who are the only directors that were also Dell employees during fiscal 2002, did not receive any additional compensation for serving on the Board of Directors in fiscal year 2002. Mr. Topfer retired as an employee of the Company at the end of fiscal 2002 and will begin receiving compensation as a nonemployee director for fiscal 2003. *www.dell.com/investor*

Annual Retainer Fee. Each nonemployee director receives an annual retainer fee, which was $40,000 during fiscal 2002. The director can receive that amount in cash, can defer all or a portion of it into a deferred compensation plan or can receive fair market value stock options instead. Amounts deferred into the deferred compensation plan are payable in a lump sum or in installments beginning upon termination of service as a director. The number of options received in lieu of the annual retainer fee (or the method of computing the number) and the terms and conditions of those options are determined from time to time by the Compensation Committee.

Option or Stock Awards. The nonemployee directors are also eligible for stock option and restricted stock awards. The number of options or shares awarded, as well as the other terms and conditions of the awards (such as vesting and exercisability schedules and termination provisions) are generally within the discretion of the Compensation Committee, except that (1) no non-employee director may receive awards covering more than 40,000 shares of stock in any year (other than the year the director joins the Board, when the limit is three times the normal annual limit), (2) no more than 20% of the awards granted to a nonemployee director during a year may consist of restricted stock, (3) the exercise price of any option cannot be less than the fair market value of the stock on the date of grant, (4) no option can become exercisable, and no share of restricted stock can become transferable, earlier than six months from the date of grant and (5) no option can be "repriced" if the effect would be to reduce the exercise price per share.

Other Benefits. Dell reimburses directors for the reasonable expenses associated with attending Board meetings and provides them with liability insurance coverage for their activities as directors of Dell.

Compensation During Fiscal 2002. The following table describes the compensation paid to the nonemployee directors for the last fiscal year.

Name	Cash Payments	Options Granted[a]
Mr. Carty	$40,000	24,080
Mr. Gray	40,000	24,080
Mr. Jordan	40,000	24,080
Ms. Lewent[b,c]	0	76,488
Mr. Luce[c]	0	28,330
Mr. Luft[c]	0	28,330
Mr. Mandl[c]	0	28,330
Mr. Miles	40,000	24,080
Mr. Nunn[c]	0	28,330

a—Effective July 19, 2001, each nonemployee director (other than Ms. Lewent) received options to purchase 24,080 shares of common stock with an exercise price of $28.24 per share. The options vest and become exercisable ratably over five years (20% per year), so long as the director remains a member of the Board. The options terminate when the director ceases to be a member of the Board (if the Board demands or requests the director's resignation), 90 days after the director ceases to be a member of the Board (if the director resigns for any other reason) or one year after the director ceases to be a member of the Board because of death or permanent disability. In any event, the options terminate ten years from the date of grant. The options are transferable to family members under specified conditions.

As the table shows, Dell's directors are well compensated for their efforts. In addition to a $40,000 payment, they also received options to purchase 24,080 shares of Dell stock. The options would be of little value if the stock does poorly, but if it does well, those options could be worth hundreds of thousands of dollars.

What else can we learn about the finances of Dell's key people? The following table from the proxy shows the stock and options holdings by the company's executives and directors:

The following table sets forth certain information, as of April 30, 2002, about the ownership of Dell common stock by the directors and executive officers. The Company knows of no person, other than Mr. Dell, who owns more than 5% of the total number of shares outstanding. Unless otherwise indicated, each person named below holds sole investment and voting power over the shares shown.

Beneficial Owner	Number of Shares Owned	Options Exercisable Within 60 Days	Total Beneficial Ownership	Total as a Percentage of Shares Outstanding (if 1% or more)[a]
Michael S. Dell 807 Las Cimas Parkway Austin, Texas 78746	300,574,296[b]	7,863,657	308,437,953	11.8%
Donald J. Carty	0	1,328,867	1,328,867	—
William H. Gray, III	1,000	16,287	17,287	—
Michael H. Jordan	8,841	664,067	672,908	—
Judy C. Lewent	0	0	0	—
Thomas W. Luce, III	0	57,491	57,491	—
Klaus S. Luft	499,200	141,089	640,289	—
Alex J. Mandl	400[c]	26,558	26,958	—
Michael A. Miles	538,438	1,636,068	2,174,506	—
Samuel A. Nunn, Jr.	2,366	23,471	25,837	—
Morton L. Topfer	227,395	627,986	855,381	—
Kevin B. Rollins	14,698	6,860,517	6,875,215	—
James T. Vanderslice	614,800	1,622,848	2,237,648	—
Paul D. Bell	4,547	703,299	707,846	—
Joseph A. Marengi	136,960	466,356	603,316	—
Directors and executive officers as a group (19 persons)	303,884,025	25,799,464	329,683,489	12.6%

You can even find out about the status of the stock options exercised by the company's top brass. (See page 136.)

Interested in background information on the directors and executives? You can find detailed information on most of them in the proxy. This excerpt from the Dell proxy offers a close look at some of the company's

**AGGREGATED OPTION EXERCISES IN LAST FISCAL YEAR
AND FISCAL YEAR-END OPTION VALUES**

Name	Shares Acquired On Exercise	Value Realized[a]	Number of Shares Underlying Unexercised Options at Fiscal Year-End		Value of Unexercised In-the-Money Options at Fiscal Year-End[b]	
			Exercisable	Unexercisable	Exercisable	Unexercisable
Mr. Dell	4,160,000	$80,998,080	4,093,626	12,534,809	$ 33,046,400	$89,572,408
Mr. Rollins	1,550,000	39,020,075	5,409,325	7,587,455	111,015,551	21,382,085
Dr. Vanderslice	0	0	800,000	5,005,686	0	9,170,885
Mr. Bell	642,384	13,102,250	292,573	2,388,779	0	5,730,424
Mr. Marengi	500,000	9,940,000	149,732	2,284,546	0	12,254,000

a If the shares were sold immediately upon exercise, the value realized was calculated using the difference between the actual sales price and the exercise price. Otherwise, the value realized was calculated using the difference between the closing price of the common stock on the date of exercise and the exercise price.

b–Amounts were calculated using the closing price of the common stock in the last trading day of fiscal year ($26.80).

officers (We've only included about half of the officer's bios here due to space considerations):

> Set forth below is biographical and other information about the persons who will make up the Board following the annual meeting, assuming election of the nominees named above.

Donald J. Carty
Class I
Age: 55
Director since December 1992
Board committees: Audit

Mr. Carty is Chairman of the Board and Chief Executive Officer of AMR Corporation, positions he has held since 1998. From 1998 to 2002, Mr. Carty also held the position of President of AMR Corporation. From 1995 to 1998, he was President AMR Airline Group/AA for for American Airlines, Inc., a subsidiary of AMR Corporation. Mr. Carty has held other executive level positions with American Airlines, Inc. or its subsidiaries since 1978. Mr. Carty is also a director of Sears, Roebuck and Co.

Michael S. Dell
Class II
Age: 37
Director since May 1984
No Board committees

Mr. Dell has been Chairman of the Board and Chief Executive Officer since founding the Company in 1984. He serves as Vice Chairman of the U.S. Business Council, a member of the Executive Committee of the World Business Council, chairman of the Computer Systems Policy Project and as a member of the U.S. President's Committee of Advisers on Science and Technology. Mr. Dell is Chief Executive Magazine's 2001 CEO of the Year.

William H. Gray, III
Class I

Mr. Gray is the President and Chief Executive Officer of The College Fund/ UNCF, positions

Age: 60
Director since November 2000
Board committees: Audit,
Nominating

Michael H. Jordan
Class II
Age: 65
Director since December 1992
Board committees:
Compensation, Finance

Judy C. Lewent
Class I
Age: 53
Director since May 2001
Board committees: Finance

he has held since September 1991. Mr. Gray has also served as the Senior Minister of the Bright Hope Baptist Church in Philadelphia since 1972. From 1979 to 1991, Mr. Gray served as a United States Congressman from Pennsylvania. During his tenure, he was Chairman of the House Budget Committee, a member of the Appropriations Committee, Chairman of the House Democratic Caucus and Majority Whip. Mr. Gray is also a director of Viacom Inc., J.P. Morgan Chase & Co., Electronic Data Systems Corporation, Municipal Bond Investors Assurance Corporation, Prudential Financial, Rockwell International Corporation, Visteon Corporation and Pfizer Corporation.

Currently, Mr. Jordan is a general partner of Global Asset Capital, LLC, a partner of Beta Capital Group, LLC and chairman of the board of directors of eOriginal, Inc. (electronic document service). Mr. Jordan is the former Chairman and Chief Executive Officer of CBS Corporation (formerly Westinghouse Electric Corporation), positions he held from July 1993 until December 1998. Prior to joining Westinghouse, he was a principal with the investment firm of Clayton, Dubilier and Rice from September 1992 through June 1993, Chairman of PepsiCo International from December 1990 through July 1992 and Chairman of PepsiCo World-Wide Foods from December 1986 to December 1990. Mr. Jordan serves as a director of Aetna Inc., i2 Technologies Inc., WPP Group Plc., ScreamingMedia, Inc. and several small, privately held companies.

Ms. Lewent is Executive Vice President and Chief Financial Officer of Merck & Co., Inc. She has served as Chief Financial Officer of Merck since 1990 and has also held various other financial and management positions since joining Merck in 1980. Ms. Lewent is a director of Johnson & Johnson Merck Consumer Pharmaceuticals Company, Motorola, Inc. and Merial Limited. Ms. Lewent is also a

Thomas W. Luce, III
Class I
Age: 61
Director since November 1991
Board committees: Audit

Klaus S. Luft
Class II
Age: 60
Director since March 1995
Board committees:
Compensation

trustee of the Rockefeller Family Trust, a Massachusetts Institute of Technology Corporation life member and a member of the Penn Medicine Executive Committee and the RAND Health Board of Advisors.

Mr. Luce is Of Counsel with the law firm Hughes & Luce, L.L.P., Dallas, Texas, having co-founded the firm in 1973. He is also a partner with Luce & Williams, Ltd., a business advisory firm. From October 1991 through April 1992, Mr. Luce was Chairman of the Board and Chief Executive Officer of First Southwest Company, a Dallas-based investment firm that is a member of the National Association of Securities Dealers, Inc.

Mr. Luft is the founder, owner and President of MATCH — Market Access for Technology Services GmbH, a private company established in 1994 and headquartered in Munich, Germany. MATCH provides sales and marketing services to high technology companies. Since August 1990, Mr. Luft has served and continues to serve as Vice Chairman and International Advisor to Goldman Sachs Europe Limited. From March 1986 to November 1989, he was Chief Executive Officer of Nixdorf Computer AG, where he served for more than 17 years in a variety of executive positions in marketing, manufacturing and finance.

What else can you find in a proxy statement? The following table of contents on page 139 from the Dell proxy provides some insight into the types of issues covered in the proxy.

As with most proxies, this one was used to announce the upcoming annual meeting of shareholders and to solicit votes for the board of directors. The proxy also asked shareholders to vote on a company proposal regarding a a long-term incentive plan, and provided details of that plan. The proxy also included other information about shareholders' voting rights, and provided a review of the company's five-year stock performance.

Proxies also usually include a letter to shareholders inviting them to the annual meeting and requesting their votes on corporate issues. The following letter on page 140 comes from the Microsoft proxy statement.

MONEY MATTERS AT MICROSOFT

Let's look at some other information from the Microsoft proxy. If you happen to be a Microsoft shareholder, you might be interested in the executive compensation for Bill Gates, Steve Ballmer, and other top brass in the company. The following table on page 140 from the Microsoft proxy provides details of their compensation.

September 27, 2001

Dear Shareholder:

You are cordially invited to attend the annual meeting of shareholders of Microsoft Corporation which will be held at the Washington State Convention and Trade Center, 800 Convention Place, Seattle, Washington, on November 7, 2001, at 8:00 a.m. Parking validation coupons for the Convention Center and the Freeway Park garages will be available at the meeting. Driving directions to the Convention Center and parking garages can be found on the inside front cover of this document. Please note that parking is limited, so plan ahead if you are driving to the meeting.

Details of the business to be conducted at the annual meeting are given in the attached Notice of Annual Meeting and Proxy Statement.

Whether or not you attend the annual meeting, it is important that your shares be represented and voted at the meeting. Therefore, I urge you to promptly vote and submit your proxy by phone, via the Internet or by signing, dating, and returning the enclosed proxy card in the enclosed postage-paid envelope. If you decide to attend the annual meeting, you will be able to vote in person, even if you have previously submitted your proxy.

We will provide live coverage of the annual meeting from the Microsoft Investor Relations website at www.microsoft.com/msft. Additionally, the transcript along with video and audio of the entire annual meeting of shareholders will be available on the Investor Relations website after the meeting. We hope this will allow those of you who are unable to attend the meeting to hear Microsoft executives discuss the year's results.

On behalf of the Board of Directors, I would like to express our appreciation for your continued interest in the affairs of the Company. I look forward to greeting as many of our shareholders as possible.

Sincerely,

Rick Belluzzo
President and Chief Operating Officer

Summary Compensation Table

| | | Annual Compensation | | Long-Term Compensation Awards | |
| | | | | Securities Underlying | All Other |
	Year	Salary	Bonus (1)	Options (#)	Compensation (2)
Steven A. Ballmer	2001	$494,076	$171,444	—	$5,100
Chief Executive Officer;	2000	428,414	200,000	—	5,100
Director	1999	388,392	272,181	—	4,800
William H. Gates	2001	494,992	171,762	—	—
Chairman of the Board;	2000	439,401	200,000	—	—
Chief Software Architect	1999	400,213	223,160	—	—
Robert J. Herbold (3)	2001	626,250	400,000	—	57,512
Executive Vice President	2000	585,802	425,000	2,900,000	57,512
	1999	562,465	363,693	—	50,997
Richard E. Belluzzo (4)	2001	468,758	350,000	1,500,000	2,194,366
President; Chief Operating Officer	2000	335,835	293,000	—	4,447,619
	1999	n/a	n/a	n/a	n/a
James E. Allchin	2001	419,576	275,000	1,000,000	3,200
Group Vice President,	2000	355,263	275,000	3,000,000	3,925
Platforms	1999	288,364	217,785	—	3,415
Jeffrey S. Raikes	2001	420,826	275,000	1,000,000	5,100
Group Vice President,	2000	370,991	258,500	3,000,000	5,250
Productivity and Business	1999	309,629	211,820	—	5,119
Services					

(1) The amounts disclosed in the Bonus column were all awarded under the Company's Executive Bonus Plan.

As the following table shows, Gates and Ballmer make less than $1 million a year in salary and bonuses. But shed no tears for the two top guys at Microsoft. As the following table shows, both hold billions of dollars in Microsoft stock. Gates has nearly 662 million shares, and Ballmer has nearly 240 million. Microsoft stock was recently trading around $50 a share. Do the math, and you see that these guys are both richer than a Saudi oil prince.

Information Regarding Beneficial Ownership of Principal Shareholders, Directors, and Management

The following table sets forth information regarding the beneficial ownership of the Company's common shares by the nominees for directors, the Company's Chief Executive Officer and the five other highest paid executive officers (the "Named Executive Officers"), and the directors and executive officers as a group.

Names	Amount and Nature of Beneficial Ownership of Common Shares as of 9/10/2001 (1)	Percent of Class
William H. Gates	661,749,300(2)(3)	12.3%
Steven A. Ballmer	239,375,740	4.4%
Ann McLaughlin Korologos	6,000(4)	*
David F. Marquardt	2,132,698(5)	*
Raymond V. Gilmartin	0	*
Wm. G. Reed, Jr.	616,872(6)	*
Jon A. Shirley	7,856,351(7)	*
James I. Cash	7,300	*
Robert J. Herbold	1,060,912(8) *	
Richard E. Belluzzo	821,555(9)	*
James E. Allchin	930,903(10) *	
Jeffrey S. Raikes	6,802,844(11)	*
Executive Officers and Directors as a group (30 persons)	936,438,253(12)	17.3%

* Less than 1%.

COMPENSATION AT ENRON

Let's look at a couple of other examples. First, let's see how much the executives at Enron charged for their services in running the company into the ground. The following table on page 142 comes from Enron's 2000 proxy statement.

The table shows that the top two Enron officers, Chairman Kenneth Lay and company president Jeffrey Skilling, were well compensated for their efforts. Lay received a salary of $1.3 million and a bonus of $3.9 million. In addition to that, he received $206,716 in "other annual compensation" and $560,000 in "all other compensation." That's more than $5 million—plus stock options on 1.3 million shares.

Lay's partner in crime, Jeffrey Skilling, earned a salary of $850,000, a bonus of $3 million, other annual compensation of $51,700, and $116,000 in "all other compensation." That's about $4 million in all—plus a million in stock options.

Not bad for a year's work—$4 million for Skilling and $5 million for Lay. But look further through the proxy, and you'll see that that was really just a drop in the bucket compared to their REAL earnings for the year. The following table on page 143 from the proxy statement shows how much they made by cashing out their earlier stock options.

The table shows that in addition to his $5 million dollars cash, bonus, and other compensation, Lay also cashed out nearly $44 million in stock options for the year, and still had options worth about $175 million ($130.2 exercisable and $44.3 unexercisable) still available to cash out.

According to the table, Skilling collected $46.4 million in stock options, and still had another $29 million in options yet to be exercised. And that was just for starters. As we'll see, the stakes continued to rise for the Enron execs.

EXECUTIVE COMPENSATION

The following table summarizes certain information regarding compensation paid or accrued during each of Enron's last three fiscal years to Enron's Chief Executive Officer and each of Enron's four other most highly compensated executive officers (the "Named Officers"):

SUMMARY COMPENSATION TABLE

NAME & PRINCIPAL POSITION	YEAR	ANNUAL COMPENSATION			LONG-TERM COMPENSATION			ALL OTHER COMPENSATION
		SALARY $	BONUS $	OTHER ANNUAL COMPENSATION ($) (1)	RESTRICTED STOCK AWARDS ($) (2)	SECURITIES UNDERLYING OPTIONS/ SARS(#)	LTIP PAYOUTS ($) (3)	($) (4)
Kenneth L. Lay Chairman of the Board and Chief Executive Officer, Enron	1999	$1,300,000	$3,900,000	$ 206,716	$ —	1,300,000	$ —	$560,046
	1998	$1,266,667	$3,150,000	$ 160,292	$ 3,883,503(5)	749,630(12)	$ —	$554,904
	1997	$1,200,000	$ 475,000	$ 228,847	$ —	1,900,920(13)	$ —	$545,264
Jeffrey K. Skilling President and Chief Operating Officer, Enron	1999	$ 850,000	$3,000,000	$ 51,701	$ —	1,000,000	$ —	$116,342
	1998	$ 816,667	$2,250,000	$ 23,949	$ 1,764,544(5)	586,330(12)	$ —	$114,055
	1997	$ 750,000	$ 450,000	$ 22,525	$10,230,268(6)	2,000,000(13)	$ —	$107,673
Joseph W. Sutton Vice Chairman, Enron	1999	$ 626,942	$2,100,000	$ 43,044	$ 7,586,284(7)	597,580	$1,537,767	$762,168
	1998	$ 512,084	$1,212,250	$ 13,500	$ —	548,780(14)	$2,940,860	$116,088
	1997	$ 442,709	$1,089,500	$ 8,100	$ 4,354,423(8)	570,966(8)	$1,303,479	$ 47,415
Mark A. Frevert Chairman and Chief Executive Officer, Enron Europe, Ltd	1999	$ 513,333	$1,300,000	$1,670,356	$ —	201,905	$ —	$198,203
	1998	$ 458,337	$1,000,000	$ 612,258	$ 2,390,004(9)	697,550(9)	$ —	$390,917
	1997	$ 400,008	$1,000,000	$ 651,942	$ 2,057,545(10)	492,516(10)	$ —	$289,267
Stanley C. Horton Chairman and Chie Executive Officer, Enron Gas Pipeline Group	1999	$ 513,333	$1,000,000	$ 15,000	$ 1,002,548(5, 11)	—	$ —	$ 7,078
	1998	$ 491,667	$ 700,000	$ 14,300	$ —	91,260(12)	$ —	$ 13,362
	1997	$ 461,667	$ 250,000	$ 19,537	$ —	291,790(15)	$ —	$ 1,103

142

AGGREGATED STOCK OPTION/SAR EXERCISES DURING 1999 AND STOCK OPTION/SAR VALUES AS OF DECEMBER 31, 1999

(SAR stands for "Stock Appreciation Rights")

The following table sets forth information with respect to the Named Officers concerning the exercise of SARs (stock appreciation rights) and options during the last fiscal year and unexercised options and SARs held as of the end of the fiscal year:

NAME	SHARES AQUIRED ON EXERCISE(#)	VALUE REALIZED	NUMBER OF SECURITIES UNDERLYING UNEXERCISED OPTIONS/SARS AT DECEMBER 31, 1999		VALUE OF UNEXERCISED IN-THE-MONEY OPTIONS/SARS AT DECEMBER 31, 1999	
			EXERCISABLE	UNEXERCISABLE	EXERCISABLE	UNEXERCISABLE
\<S>	\<C>	\<C>	\<C>	\<C>	\<C>	\<C>
Kenneth L. Lay......	1,926,770	$43,845,331	5,486,528	2,725,712	$130,228,958	$44,308,458
Jeffrey K. Skilling...	2,359,448	$46,359,937	1,081,662	1,074,960	$ 20,154,469	$ 9,256,280
Joseph W. Sutton......	100,000	$ 1,726,803	770,213	1,070,451	$ 15,788,963	$13,243,811
Mark A. Frevert........	305,970	$ 5,517,450	865,133	632,678	$ 18,078,732	$ 9,337,383
Stanley C. Horton......	290,080	$ 5,784,104	441,344	202,296	$ 10,115,077	$ 4,512,113

THE STOCK OPTION SWINDLE

The use of stock options has been a popular method of rewarding executives for solid performance. When initially awarded, stock options have no immediate value. They can only be claimed if the company's stock climbs to a target level, or "strike price." So if the stock doesn't climb to that target price by a specified target date, the options awarded to the executives would become worthless.

But if the stock price hits the target, the execs could exercise their options and cash in on millions of dollars in gains. The reason that companies use stock option awards is to encourage the executives to manage the company effectively and boost the profits, which, in turn, would push up the price of the stock. That would seem to make perfect sense—shareholders see their stock price climb, and executives get an extra reward for enhancing the company's value.

But that stock option incentive actually worked against the shareholders in Enron's case. In order to help push up the stock price, Enron executives cooked the books, lied about their earnings, and hid billions of dollars in debt. Through false financial reporting, they managed to keep the stock price climbing so that they could continue to exercise their options and claim millions of dollars in stock gains. In doing so, they ran the company into the ground—and into bankruptcy—while enriching themselves with a level of executive compensation nearly unprecedented in corporate America.

The following table on page 145 offers some more details regarding the options awarded to Lay, Skilling, and the other Enron executives. For Lay, you see that he received options for 1.3 million shares with a strike price of $37.1875 per share, and an expiration date of 12/13/09. In other words, if Enron stock reached a price of about $37.19 a share by the end of 2009, Lay could exercise his options, sell out the stock and collect tens of millions of dollars in gains.

According to the following table, the stock options Lay received in 1999 had a projected value of $30 to $77 million, depending on the growth of the stock. (The figures displayed were based on 5-percent stock growth, and 10-percent stock growth over the length of the option term.) Skilling's stock options had a projected value of $25 to $65 million.

But of course, that still wouldn't be enough if Lay were to lose his job. How could you get by on less than a hundred million dollars? So as the company continued to build its house of cards, Lay got the board to amend his golden parachute so that he would be covered if anything were to happen to his job. In a Schedule DEFA-14A filing by Enron in late 2001, you learn about the agreement that Lay had pushed through a year and half earlier:

STOCK OPTION GRANTS DURING 1999

The following table sets forth information with respect to grants of stock options pursuant to the Enron Corp. 1991 Stock Plan to the Named Officers reflected in the Summary Compensation Table. No stock appreciation rights("SARs") were granted during 1999.

INDIVIDUAL GRANTS'

NAME	NUMBER OF SECURITIES UNDERLYING OPTIONS/ SARS GRANTED (#)(2)	% OF TOTAL OPTIONS/SARS GRANTED TO EMPLOYEES IN FISCAL YEAR	EXERCISE OR BASE PRICE ($/SH)	EXPIRATION DATE	POTENTIAL REALIZABLE VALUE AT ASSUMED ANNUAL RATES OF STOCK PRICE APPRECIATION FOR OPTION TERM(1)		
					0 %(3)	5%	10%
Kenneth L. Lay........	1,300,000(4)	3.77%	$37.1875	12/13/09	$0	$ 30,403,125	$ 77,047,487
Jeffrey K. Skilling......	1,000,000(4)	2.90%	$41.0625	11/16/09	$0	$ 25,823,986	$ 65,443,050
Joseph W. Sutton........	123,290(5)	0.36%	$44.0625	8/9/06	$0	$ 2,211,559	$ 5,153,873
	173,335(4)	0.50%	$38.8750	10/11/06	$0	$ 2,743,205	$ 6,392,834
	200,000(4)	0.58%	$39.0000	11/19/06	$0	$ 3,175,383	$ 7,399,993
	100,955(4)	0.29%	$44.3750	12/31/09	$0	$ 2,817,371	$ 7,139,772
Mark A. Frevert........	201,905(6)	0.59%	$44.3750	12/31/09	$0	$ 5,634,603	$ 14,279,190
All Employee and Director Optionees..............	34,446,667(7)	100%	$38.1638(8)	N/A	$0	$ 2,141,370,466(9)	$ 3,409,774,586(9)
All Shareholders......	N/A	N/A	N/A	N/A	$0	$44,480,621,930(9)	$70,827,956,490(9)
Optionee Gain as % of Gain................	N/A	N/A	N/A	N/A	N/A	4.81%	4.81%

Mr. Lay entered into an employment agreement with Enron which was amended in February 2000. As so amended, Mr. Lay's employment agreement provided for a term through December 31, 2003 and provided that, among other things, in the event Mr. Lay terminated his employment within 60 days of a change of control, Mr. Lay would receive a lump sum payment equal to the number of full calendar years remaining under the term of the agreement multiplied by $20.2 million, plus an amount for any related tax penalties if the payment was held to constitute an "excess parachute payment."

As impending doom fell over the company, Lay and Skilling cashed out their options as fast as possible. And their salaries and bonuses continued to grow. If you thought the $49 million in cash and exercised options that Lay collected in 1999 was a bit excessive, check out his 2000 returns. The first table that follows on page 147, from the 2001 proxy statement, shows his salary, and the second shows options he (and others) exercised:

Including salary, bonus, stock awards, and other compensation (including $857,000 not shown on this table) Lay received about $18.3 million in total compensation. But of course, how can you keep food on the table with such a scant amount? That's why he had to exercise his options on the Enron stock that he and his cohorts had so cunningly inflated. And as every sage CEO knows, it's crucial to cash out those options while the stock price is still high when you're falsely inflating the financials. The following table on page 148 shows the money Lay and others received in exercising their stock options.

The table shows that Lay collected $123 million in stock options in 2000—and left another $361 million on the table for later in case of a rainy day (in "exercisable" and "unexercisable" options).

But Jeffrey Skilling had to settle for just $62.5 million in exercised options, while the other three key officers, were left with a piddling $65 million in exercised options between the three of them.

For Lay, with a mere $123 million in exercised options, $18.5 million in salary and other compensations, and $361 million in unexercised options (and less for his board underlings), he could not afford to face the future on such precarious financial footing. That's why he also persuaded the board to set aside even more options for himself and his cohorts. This table on page 149 lays out their stock option awards for 2000.

All in all, not a bad year for a group of guys running the company into the ground.

To provide just a little more perspective on the issue, by mid-2002, Enron stock was trading at about 12 cents a share. The company's total capitalization (the total cost of the company if someone bought every share of stock) would have been about $91 million—less than half of Lay's two-year haul of $187

SUMMARY COMPENSATION TABLE

NAME & PRINCIPAL POSITION	YEAR	ANNUAL COMPENSATION			LONG-TERM COMPENSATION		
		SALARY $	BONUS $	OTHER ANNUAL COMPENSATION ($) (1)	RESTRICTED STOCK AWARDS ($) (2)	SECURITIES UNDERLYING OPTIONS/ SARS(#)	LTIP PAYOUTS ($)
Kenneth L. Lay........... Chairman of the Board	2000	$1,300,000	$7,000,000	$ 381,551	$7,500,025(4)	782,83	$1,218,750(13)
	1999	$1,300,000	$3,900,000	$ 206,716	$ —	1,300,000	$ —
	1998	$1,266,667	$3,150,000	$ 160,292	$3,883,503(5)	749,630(9)	$ —
Jeffrey K. Skilling....... President and Chief Executive Officer	2000	$ 850,000	$5,600,000	$ 47,403	$3,500,037(4)	867,880(10)	$ —
	1999	$ 850,000	$3,000,000	$ 51,701	$ —	1,000,000	$ —
	1998	$ 816,667	$2,250,000	$ 23,949	$1,764,544(5)	586,330(9)	$ —
Mark A. Frevert........... Chairman and Chief Executive Officer, Enron Wholesale Services	2000	$ 520,000	$2,000,000	$2,603,541	$1,500,043(4)	1,147,820(11)	$ —
	1999	$ 513,333	$1,300,000	$1,670,356	$ —	201,905(6)	$ —
	1998	$ 458,337	$1,000,000	$ 512,258	$2,390,004(6)	697,550(6)	$ —
Kenneth D. Rice........... Chairman and Chief Executive Officer, Enron Broadband Services, Inc.	2000	$ 420,000	$1,750,000	$ 81,333	$ —	1,796,733(12)	$3,953,820(14)
	1999	$ 413,333	$1,100,000	$ 63,681	$ —	201,905	$ —
	1998	$ 362,500	$1,100,000	$ 9,000	$2,503,766(7)	497,550	$ —
Stanley C. Horton........ Chairman and Chief Executive Officer, Enron Transportation Services	2000	$ 520,000	$1,200,000	$ 15,600	$1,000,044(4)	108,035	$ 300,000(13)
	1999	$ 513,333	$1,000,000	$ 15,000	—	—	$ —
	1998	$ 491,667	$ 700,000	$ 14,300	$1,002,548(8)	91,260(9)	$ —

AGGREGATED STOCK OPTION/SAR EXERCISES DURING 2000 AND STOCK OPTION/SAR VALUES AS OF DECEMBER 31, 2000

The following table sets forth information with respect to the Named Officers concerning the exercise of SARs and options during the last fiscal year and unexercised options and SARs held as of the end of the fiscal year:

NAME	SHARES AQUIRED ON EXERCISE(#)	VALUE REALIZED	NUMBER OF SECURITIES UNDERLYING UNEXERCISED OPTIONS/SARS AT DECEMBER 31, 2000		VALUE OF UNEXERCISED IN-THE-MONEY OPTIONS/SARS AT DECEMBER 31, 2000	
			EXERCISABLE	UNEXERCISABLE	EXERCISABLE	UNEXERCISABLE
<S>	<C>	<C>	<C>	<C>	<C>	<C>
Kenneth L. Lay.......	2,288,724	$123,399,478	5,145,963	1,451,763	$257,483,342	$104,094,272
Jeffrey K. Skilling...	1,193,370	$ 62,484,460	483,732	1,347,400	$ 20,596,905	$ 48,737,354
Joseph W. Sutton.....	490,000	$ 28,732,712	1,010,139	1,220,492	$ 41,030,788	$ 32,180,218
Mark A. Frevert........	282,402	$ 16,226,027	869,395	1,824,213	$ 34,516,748	$ 41,480,119
Stanley C. Horton......	360,002	$ 20,601,248	233,146	158,527	$ 13,238,096	$ 7,362,286

INDIVIDUAL GRANTS

NAME	NUMBER OF SECURITIES UNDERLYING OPTIONS/SARS GRANTED (#)(2)	% OF TOTAL OPTIONS/SARS GRANTED TO EMPLOYEES IN FISCAL YEAR	EXERCISE OR BASE PRICE ($/SH)	EXPIRATION DATE	POTENTIAL REALIZABLE VALUE AT ASSUMED ANNUAL RATES OF STOCK PRICE APPRECIATION FOR OPTION TERM(1)		
					0%(3)	5%	10%
<S>	<C>	<C>	<C>	<C>	<C>	<C>	<C>
Kenneth L. Lay............	769,235(4)	1.96%	$47.3125	01/10/07	$ 0	$ 14,816,188	$ 34,528,019
	50(5)	0.00%	$62.5000	02/07/07	$ 0	$ 1,272	$ 2,965
	13,545(6)	0.03%	$83.1250	12/29/07	$ 0	$ 458,366	$ 1,068,187
Jeffrey K. Skilling.......	358,975(4)	0.92%	$47.3125	01/10/07	$ 0	$ 6,914,195	$ 16,113,016
	50(5)	0.00%	$62.5000	02/07/07	$ 0	$ 1,272	$ 2,965
	8,855(6)	0.02%	$83.1250	12/29/07	$ 0	$ 299,655	$ 698,324
	500,000(7)	1.28%	$66.1250	02/08/07	$ 0	$ 13,459,758	$ 31,366,959
Mark A. Frevert..........	153,850(4)	0.39%	$47.3125	01/10/07	$ 0	$ 2,963,295	$ 6,905,738
	50(5)	0.00%	$62.5000	02/07/07	$ 0	$ 1,272	$ 2,965
	5,420(6)	0.01%	$83.1250	12/29/07	$ 0	$ 183,414	$ 427,433
	75,000(8)	0.19%	$65.0000	01/24/07	$ 0	$ 1,984,615	$ 4,624,996
	525,000(9)	1.34%	$71.1250	06/01/02	$ 0	$ 3,827,414	$ 7,841,531
	463,500(10)	1.18%	$71.1250	06/01/03	$ 0	$ 5,196,335	$ 10,911,891
Kenneth D. Rice...........	50(5)	0.00%	$62.5000	02/07/07	$ 0	$ 1,272	$ 2,965
	4,375(6)	0.01%	$83.1250	12/29/07	$ 0	$ 148,051	$ 345,022
	692,308(11)	1.77%	$67.8125	02/14/02	$ 0	$ 4,812,081	$ 9,858,899
	600,000(12)	1.53%	$67.8125	02/14/03	$ 0	$ 6,413,367	$ 13,467,563
	500,000(12)	1.28%	$67.8125	02/14/05	$ 0	$ 9,367,672	$ 20,700,105
Stanley C. Horton........	102,565(4)	0.26%	$47.3125	01/10/07	$ 0	$ 1,975,498	$ 4,603,751
	50(5)	0.00%	$62.5000	02/07/07	$ 0	$ 1,272	$ 2,965
	5,420(6)	0.01%	$83.1250	12/29/07	$ 0	$ 183,414	$ 427,433

million in salary, bonuses, and exercised stock options. Lay, Skilling, and other well-compensated Enron brass helped drain the value right out of the company.

EXECUTIVE COMPENSATION SAMPLER

What is normal, acceptable executive compensation? There may be no such thing "as normal." Every company has a different scale. As a point of reference, let's look at the executive compensation tables from several other companies, both large and small. We start small. Here is the compensation table on page 151 for Daktronics, a manufacturer of scoreboards for sports stadiums:

The Daktronics officers won't have to pinch pennies, but they're not raking in the millions of dollars that some of the blue chip firms pay their executives. Let's look at the compensation table on page 152 for another smaller company, Embrex, which manufactures poultry vaccine injection systems.

Like the Daktronics executives, Embrex's managers won't have a problem keeping food on the table, but they're not raking in millions of dollars—unless their stock options really pay off.

As we see next, the larger companies are willing to pay more for their top officers. The table on page 153 details the executive compensation at Merck.

The big fish in the bigger ponds draw bigger stipends. The top executives at Merck are all making over $1 million a year (plus some options awards), but that's nowhere near the level of compensation Enron executives were hauling in.

Now let's look at the executive compensation for Exxon-Mobil to see how another energy company paid its officers (See page 154).

Clearly, it pays to be in the energy business. L.R. Raymond, the chairman and CEO of Exxon-Mobile, received more than $8 million in salary, bonuses, and other compensation, and another $9 million in restricted stock awards.

Finally, let's see what life at the top was like at WorldCom for those talented executives who managed to drive the company into bankruptcy. (See page 155.)

The table shows that Bernard Ebbers, the company's president and CEO, collected more than $8 million a year in salary and bonuses—including a $17 million bonus in 1997—plus options on nearly 2 million shares of WorldCom stock each year. Even with all that compensation, however, the footnote shows that Ebbers used another $54,000 a year of the company's money to cover his personal use of the company airplane.

DAKTRONICS COMPENSATION

| Name and Principal Position | Fiscal Year Ended | Annual Compensation(1) | | All Other Compensation(3) | Long-Term Compensation Awards |
		Salary	Bonus (2)		Securities Underlying Options (#)
Dr. Aelred J. Kurtenbach Chairman And Director	2002	$242,596	$0	$2,733	10,000
	2001	271,154	75,000	3,750	30,000
	2000	225,385	62,500	1,531	40,000
James B. Morgan President, Chief Executive Officer and Director	2002	$241,346	$0	$3,699	10,000
	2001	222,571	62,500	3,000	24,000
	2000	181,217	50,000	1,577	32,000
Frank J. Kurtenbach Vice President And Director	2002	$127,431	$0	$3,632	5,000
	2001	127,960	33,000	2,789	8,000
	2000	118,389	31,250	1,584	12,000

151

EMBREX COMPENSATION

| Name and Principal Position | Year | Annual Compensation(1)(2) | | Long-Term Compensation |
		Salary	Bonus (3)	Securities Underlying Options (#)
Randall L. Marcuson President and Chief Executive Officer	2001	$290,000	$170,800	50,000
	2000	$280,000	$130,000	50,000
	1999	$260,000	$ 60,000	20,000
Don T. Seaquist Vice President, Finance and Administration	2001	$205,000	$ 65,000	20,000
	2000	$190,000	$ 55,000	22,000
	1999	$164,000	$ 30,000	10,000
David M. Baines, Ph.D. Vice President, Global Marketing and Sales	2001	$176,000	$ 65,000	20,000
	1999	$168,000	$ 13,000	12,000
	1998	$144,450	-0-	12,000
Brian V. Cosgriff Vice President, Marketing and Sales, North America	2001	$182,000	$ 70,000	20,000
	2000	$170,000	$ 60,000	22,000
	1999	$155,000	$ 29,000	12,000
Catherine A. Ricks, Ph.D. Vice President, Research and Development	2001	$175,000	$ 60,000	15,000
	2000	$155,000	$ 35,000	13,000
	1999	$150,000	$ 21,600	10,000
Brian C. Hrudka Vice President, Global Product Development and Supply	2001	$185,000	$ 50,000	17,500
	2000	$160,700	$ 30,000	15,000
	1999(4)	$118,700	-0-	-0-

MERCK COMPENSATION

| | | Annual Compensation | | | Long-Term Compensation | | | |
| | | | | | Awards | | Payouts | |
Name and Principal Position	Year	Salary ($)	Bonus ($)	Other Annual Compensation ($)	Restricted Stock Awards ($)	Securities Underlying Options/SARs(a) (#)	LTIP Payouts(b) ($)	All Other Compensation ($)
Raymond V. Gilmartin Chairman of the Board, President and Chief Executive Officer	2001	$1,383,338	$1,500,000	—	—	500,000	—	$ 7,650(c)
	2000	1,283,340	1,700,000	—	—	400,000	—	7,650(c)
	1999	1,183,334	1,500,000	—	—	400,000	—	3,438,450(d)
Edward M. Scolnick Executive Vice President, Science and Technology and President, Merck Research Laboratories	2001	820,000	825,000	—	—	200,000	—	3,825(c)
	2000	790,000	860,000	—	—	200,000	—	3,825(c)
	1999	759,334	825,000	—	—	185,000	1,419,744	3,600(c)
Judy C. Lewent Executive Vice President and Chief Financial Officer	2001	563,334	600,000	—	—	150,000	—	7,650(c)
	2000	525,838	600,000	—	—	130,000	—	7,650(c)
	1999	500,840	505,000	—	—	160,000	757,134	7,200(c)
David W. Anstice President, The Americas and U.S. Human Health	2001	563,334	500,000	—	—	150,000	—	7,650(c)
	2000	526,670	600,000	—	—	130,000	—	7,650(c)
	1999	506,334	510,000	—	—	130,000	757,134	7,200(c)
Per Wold-Olsen President, Human Health-Europe, Middle East & Africa	2001	520,834	540,000	—	—	130,000	—	7,650(c)
	2000	495,838	515,000	—	—	130,000	—	7,650(c)
	1999	466,674	350,000	—	—	130,000	473,225	7,200(c)

153

EXXON-MOBIL COMPENSATION

| Name and Principal Position | Year | Annual Compensation | | | Long-Term Compensation | | Payouts | All Other Compensation ($)(i) |
| | | Salary ($) | Bonus ($)(b) | Other Annual Compensation ($) | Awards | | LTIP Payouts ($)(h) | |
					Restricted Stock Awards(s)($) (f)	Options (#)		
L. R. Raymond CHAIRMAN AND CEO	2000	2,500,000	2,700,000	91,643(c)	9,043,750	525,000	2,817,630	227,925
	1999	2,100,417	13,900,000	222,571	8,356,250	425,000	0	128,547
	1998	1,900,000	1,400,000	55,849	7,162,500	425,000	1,275,000	114,000
L. A. Noto (a) VICE CHAIRMAN (RETIRED 1/31/01)	2000	1,500,000	1,075,000	178,344(d)	0	375,000	1,603,872	180,366
	1999	1,048,334	8,598,300	0	2,089,063	564,029(g)	2,111,007	137,833
	1998	955,000	1,537,700	0	0	264,029	2,985,052	102,016
R. Dahan SENIOR VICE PRESIDENT AND DIRECTOR	2000	1,100,000	863,000	5,485	904,375	250,000	893,520	99,689
	1999	953,333	2,640,000	5,484	835,625	200,000	0	75,136
	1998	860,000	440,000	244,935	716,250	200,000	382,500	65,686
H. J. Longwell SENIOR VICE PRESIDENT AND DIRECTOR	2000	1,100,000	863,000	5,485	904,375	250,000	893,520	99,689
	1999	953,333	2,640,000	5,484	835,625	200,000	0	75,136
	1998	860,000	440,000	5,660	716,250	200,000	382,500	65,686
E. A. Renna (a) SENIOR VICE PRESIDENT AND DIRECTOR	2000	1,100,000	863,000	458,101(e)	904,375	250,000	878,111	105,420
	1999	828,750	2,880,500	0	835,625	351,816(g)	1,172,501	102,095
	1998	754,167	874,500	0	0	151,816	1,657,785	80,396

154

WORLDCOM COMPENSATION

Name and Principal Position	Year	Annual Compensation			Long-Term Compensation Awards		All Other Compensation ($)
		Salary ($)	Bonus ($)	Other Annual Compensation ($)	Restricted Stock Awards ($)	Securities Underlying Options/SARs (#)	
Bernard J. Ebbers	1999	935,000	7,500,000	52,624(3)	—	1,800,000/0	8,000(5)
President and Chief	1998	935,000	7,115,000	54,444(3)	—	1,800,000/0	4,800
Executive Officer	1997	935,000	17,031,250	—	—	1,800,000/0	4,800
Bert C. Roberts, Jr.	1999	1,050,000	800,000	81,943(3)	—	0/0	14,877(6)
Chairman of the Board	1998	1,050,000	9,651,188(1)	1,995,548(3)	1,785,883(4)	617,924/0	769,472
Timothy F. Price(2)	1999	600,000	1,180,000	20,454(3)	—	0/0	81,853(6)
Former President and Chief	1998	580,000	7,331,700(1)	306,643(3)	999,117(4)	737,287/0	6,231
Executive Officer MCI WorldCom Communications							
John W. Sidgmore	1999	600,000	2,760,000	—	—	900,000/0	8,000(5)
Vice Chairman of the	1998	500,000	2,000,000	—	—	900,000/0	4,800
Board	1997	500,000	0	—	—	1,500,000/0	962,050
Scott D. Sullivan	1999	600,000	2,760,000	—	—	900,000/0	8,000(5)
Chief Financial Officer	1998	500,000	2,000,000	—	—	900,000/0	4,800
and Secretary	1997	500,000	3,500,000	—	—	1,500,000/0	4,800

(3) Includes the imputed value of personal use of the Company airplane of $52,624 in 1999 and $54,444 in 1998 for Mr. Ebbers and $54,609 in 1999 and $21,650 in 1998 for Mr. Roberts; and the annuity premium and taxes paid of $1,937,355 in 1998 for Mr. Roberts and $306,643 in 1998 for Mr. Price as the result of the purchase of an annuity to discharge MCI's Supplemental Pension Plan's obligation. The amounts reduce dollar for dollar the actual amount of pension to be paid to the executive upon retirement. All other perquisites and other personal benefits are less than $50,000 in the aggregate.

Did WorldCom shareholders get their money's worth from Ebbers's high-paid management? WorldCom stock was trading at about $59 a share in 1999. By the end of 2002, it was trading at about 8 cents a share. You be the judge.

Proxy statements offer a wealth of revealing facts and figures about a company and its managers. With EDGAR, it's an easy task to find the proxies and look up detailed information about executive compensation and other important corporate matters.

In researching and analyzing a stock, the proxy statement is yet another important tool to help you make an educated decision on the investment potential of the company.

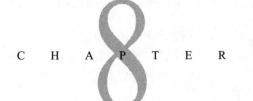

C H A P T E R

8

NEW OFFERING IN TOWN: THE REGISTRATION STATEMENT AND PROSPECTUS

W
HEN A COMPANY OFFERS STOCKS OR BONDS for sale to investors, it is required to file a registration statement with the SEC, including a prospectus. The prospectus is a lengthy document similar to the 10-K that reveals volumes about the company's operations and its financial history. You can review the registration statements and prospectus to decide if the new stock offering is something you would be interested in buying.

The registration statement includes two parts—the prospectus; and a report on the expenses of issuance and distribution, indemnification of directors and officers, recent sales of unregistered securities, and copies of material contracts.

The prospectus, which constitutes Part I of the registration statement, is very similar to a Form 10-K. It includes a vast range of information about the company's operations and financial performance. A prospectus in its preliminary form is frequently called a "red herring" prospectus and is subject to completion or amendment before the registration statement becomes effective. The red herring typically has a few facts missing, such as the cost of shares in the new offering, that are filled in later in the amended prospectus.

Companies sometimes file several amended registration statements before eventually filing the final version.

If you have an interest in a company's new offerings—whether it's a stock, bond, or convertible bond offering—it would be worth your while to go to EDGAR to review the prospectus (forms 424 or 425) or registration statement (form S-1).

In this chapter, we look at the registration forms filed by a pair of rather high-profile companies that had their initial public stock offerings in recent years—Martha Stewart and Krispy Kreme.

PROBING THE PROSPECTUS

A prospectus typically covers more than 100 pages of single-spaced copy—much like a 10-K. The prospectus discusses the investment offering, and provides a wealth of details on the company, its business history, products, markets, officers, any pending litigation, and its financial situation.

Businesses file forms 424 and 425 when they issue more shares of stock or bonds to raise additional capital.

There are several other types of registration forms. One of the most common is the S-1, which is a basic form used to register securities. The S-4 is another common form, used to register securities in connection with business combinations and exchange offers. Real estate investment trusts would use the Schedule S-11 to register, while small businesses would use the SB-1 to register a stock offering of up to $10 million. Foreign companies typically use registration beginning with the letter "F," including the F-1, F-2, F-3, etc.

U.S. companies that want to file a registration statement prior to a stock offering would typically use the S-1 form (which is the same as a prospectus).

Let's review the S-1 prospectus filed by Martha Stewart Living Omnimedia, Inc. in 1999, prior to its initial public offering.

PUTTING MARTHA UNDER THE MICROSCOPE

What should we learn by reviewing the prospectus? Here are several questions we hope to answer:

- What is the company's primary business?

- Who runs the company now, and how much control will that person have after the offering?

- How will management be compensated?

- What is the book value of the shares, and what is the IPO asking price?

- What are its plans and prospects for growth, and what are the risks?

- What is the company's financial position?

We should be able to find the answer to those questions and others with a thorough review of the prospectus. Let's take a close look at the Martha Stewart registration form.

Near the top of the filing is an announcement of the offering:

Issued September 24, 1999

7,200,000 Shares

[Martha Stewart Living Omnimedia Logo]

CLASS A COMMON STOCK

MARTHA STEWART LIVING OMNIMEDIA, INC. IS OFFERING SHARES OF ITS CLASS A COMMON STOCK. THIS IS OUR INITIAL PUBLIC OFFERING AND NO PUBLIC MARKET CURRENTLY EXISTS FOR OUR SHARES. WE ANTICIPATE THAT THE INITIAL PUBLIC OFFERING PRICE WILL BE BETWEEN $13 AND $15 PER SHARE.

FOLLOWING THIS OFFERING, WE WILL HAVE TWO CLASSES OF AUTHORIZED COMMON STOCK, CLASS A COMMON STOCK AND CLASS B COMMON STOCK. THE RIGHTS OF THE HOLDERS OF CLASS A COMMON STOCK AND CLASS B COMMON STOCK ARE IDENTICAL, EXCEPT WITH RESPECT TO VOTING AND CONVERSION. EACH SHARE OF CLASS A COMMON STOCK IS ENTITLED TO ONE VOTE PER SHARE. EACH SHARE OF CLASS B COMMON STOCK IS ENTITLED TO TEN VOTES PER SHARE AND IS CONVERTIBLE INTO ONE SHARE OF CLASS A COMMON STOCK.

OUR CLASS A COMMON STOCK HAS BEEN APPROVED FOR LISTING ON THE NEW YORK STOCK EXCHANGE, SUBJECT TO OFFICIAL NOTICE OF ISSUANCE, UNDER THE SYMBOL "MSO."

Here you learn that the company is offering 7.2 million shares at about $13 to $15 a share. You also learn that the stock symbol will be "MSO."

What else might you find in a registration statement? Initial stock offering registrations like Martha Stewart's can run over 100 pages, and cover much of the same type of material that the 10-K covers. There is information about the company's business, its competition, its corporate officers, and its financial history. There are also a number of details on the actual stock offering itself. The section offers more details on the offering on page 160.

CALCULATION OF REGISTRATION FEE

TITLE OF EACH CLASS OF SECURITIES TO BE REGISTERED	AMOUNT TO BE REGISTERED(1)	PROPOSED MAXIMUM OFFERING PRICE PER UNIT	PROPOSED MAXIMUM AGGREGATE OFFERING PRICE(2)	AMOUNT OF REGISTRATION FEE
Class A Common Stock, par value $.01 per share	8,280,000 shares	$15.00	$124,200,000	$34,528(3)

(1) Includes an aggregate of 1,080,000 shares which the Underwriters have the option to purchase from the Registrant solely to cover over-allotments.

(2) Estimated solely for the purpose of computing the amount of the registration fee pursuant to Rule 457(o) under the Securities Act of 1933, as amended.

(3) Of this amount, $27,800 has previously been paid.

In this table, we learn that the company could raise as much as $124.2 million in the offering. The table also reports the amount of shares being offered as 8,280,000—which is over a million more than the 7,200,000 shares mentioned in the other section. How do you explain the discrepancy? The first footnote explains that the additional 1,080,000 shares are being made available for the underwriters (Morgan Stanley) to purchase, if they wish.

What else might you find in the registration statement? The following table of contents from the Martha Stewart report provides a better glimpse of the type of information included in a registration statement:

TABLE OF CONTENTS

Let's look at some of the other sections of the registration statement to find out what else we might learn about Martha Stewart Living Omnimedia. The statement offers a detailed description of the company's operations. As an investor researching a new company, you should read these descriptions and try to evaluate whether the company's business model has the potential for solid, sustained, long-term growth—or if it's a one-hit wonder with limited prospects for the long term. Here is an excerpt from the S-1 registration statement describing Martha Stewart's operations:

MARTHA STEWART LIVING OMNIMEDIA, INC.

We are a leading creator of original "how to" content and related products for homemakers and other consumers. We leverage the well-known "Martha Stewart" brand name across a broad range of media and retail outlets, providing consumers with the "how to" ideas, products and other resources they need to raise the quality of living in and around their homes.

In each of our seven core content areas—Home, Cooking and Entertaining, Gardening, Crafts, Holidays, Keeping and Weddings—our creative experts continually seek to develop new ideas that support the high quality and look associated with our brand name. Our editors, art directors, designers, cooks, gardeners and craftspeople have developed an extensive library of "how to" articles, books, television programs, newspaper columns, radio segments and products relating to our seven core content areas. We have two primary strategic objectives:

— to provide our original "how to" content and information to as many consumers as possible

— to turn our consumers into "doers" by offering them the information and products they need for do-it-yourself ingenuity the "Martha Stewart way"

We accomplish this first objective by distributing our "how to" content over a broad range of different media outlets. These outlets comprise what we call our "omnimedia" platform, which currently includes:

— two magazines, Martha Stewart Living(R) and Martha Stewart Weddings(TM), together reaching an estimated 9.9 million readers per month

— the Emmy Award-winning and number-one-rated "how to" domestic arts television program in the United States, airing six episodes per week, plus a weekly segment on CBS This Morning

— From Martha's Kitchen(TM), a daily cable television program

— 27 books, which together have sold more than 8.5 million copies

— a weekly askMartha(R) newspaper column, syndicated in 233 newspapers

— the askMartha radio program, airing on 270 stations throughout the United States

— marthastewart.com, our website, with over 925,000 registered users

To accomplish our second business objective, we have created our "omnimerchandising" platform. Our omnimerchandising platform consists of products we design or select for production and sale. As of July 1999, our merchandise included more than 2,800 distinct variations of products, including bed and bath products, interior paints, craft kits, outdoor furniture and garden tools. Through this platform, we seek to offer our consumers quality, convenience and choice across a broad range of retail and direct to consumer channels. Retail sales of Martha Stewart branded merchandise by Kmart Corporation and our other merchandising partners reached $763 million in 1998, an increase of 96% over 1997.

So far, the company sounds like a solid, broad-based operation with several potential growth areas. It has books, magazines, newspaper columns, a TV show, a Web site, and 2800 products it sells through Kmart and other retailers.

How does the company gets its products to the public? The S-1 offers these details:

We distribute our products through:

— the mass market discount channel in the United States and Canada

— the national department store channel in the United States and Canada

— specialty paint stores and specialty craft and fabric stores across the United States

— our upscale catalog, Martha by Mail(R)

— our online Martha by Mail store

Our omnimedia and omnimerchandising platforms support four business segments: Publishing, Television, Merchandising and Internet/Direct Commerce. Our Internet/Direct Commerce business provides a unique opportunity for us to fulfill both of our strategic objectives by leveraging our content and our merchandising capabilities to create a one-stop online destination for consumers interested in the domestic arts.

DISTRIBUTION CHANNEL	PRODUCT LINE(S)	LAUNCH DATE	STRATEGIC PARTNER	RETAILER
Mass Market Discount..........	Martha Stewart Everyday Home	March 1997/ June 1998	Kmart/Zellers	Kmart/Zellers
	Martha Stewart Everyday Colors	May 1997	Sherwin-Williams	Kmart
	Martha Stewart Everyday Garden	January 1999	Kmart/Zellers	Kmart/Zellers
	Martha Stewart Everyday Baby baby	Fall 1999 (anticipated)	Kmart	Kmart
	Martha Stewart Everyday Housewares	Fall 2000 (anticipated)	Kmart	Kmart
National Department Stores............	Martha Stewart Everyday Colors	March 1998/ May 1999	Sherwin-Williams	Sears/Canadian Tire
Specialty Stores.....	Martha Stewart Home Collection	Fall 1999	P/Kaufmann	Specialty fabric stores
	Araucana Colors(R) and Colors of the Garden(R) fine paint collection	March 1995	Fine Paints of Europe, Inc.	Specialty paint dealers

Further in the report, the company displays a table (seen on the previous page) that offers a little more detail on its distribution network.

CORPORATE HISTORY

The S-1 report also included a history of the company. As the following excerpt shows, Martha Stewart has been big in the entertaining business since 1982, and Stewart launched her first magazine in 1991. So the company has established a fairly long track record—another sign of strength for this stock offering:

HISTORY

The Martha Stewart name first gained prominence in 1982 with the publication of Martha Stewart's first book, Entertaining, which is now in its 30th printing. Martha Stewart Living magazine was then launched by Martha Stewart and Time Publishing Ventures in 1991. We purchased the magazine and related businesses from Time Publishing Ventures and consolidated them with other businesses previously owned by Martha Stewart in February 1997. The following is a timeline of significant events in the development of our brands and our omnimedia and omnimerchandising platforms:

YEAR	EVENT
1991.....	Martha Stewart Living magazine launched as a quarterly publication
1993.....	Martha Stewart Living television program launched as a weekly half-hour syndicated show
1994.....	Martha Stewart Weddings magazine launched as an annual publication
1995.....	Martha by Mail catalog tested as an insert in Martha Stewart Living magazine askMartha syndicated newspaper column published in the United States and Canada Martha Stewart Living magazine expanded to ten issues per year
1997.....	Martha Stewart Living Omnimedia LLC acquires magazine and related businesses from Time Publishing Ventures in February Branded bed and bath and paint collections launched at Kmart Martha Stewart Living television program expanded to six days per week Weekly television segment on CBS This Morning debuted Martha Stewart Weddings expanded to semi-annual publication askMartha radio program launched marthastewart.com launched
1998.....	Martha Stewart Living weekday television program expanded to one hour

Branded bed and bath products launched at Zellers in Canada

Branded kitchen textiles, window treatments and bath acces-
sories launched at Kmart and Zellers

First special interest publication, Clotheskeeping, published

Branded paints launched at Sears in the United States at Canada

1999..... Branded garden products launched at Kmart and Zellers

Martha Stewart Weddings published as a quarterly publication

Seven dedicated subsites launched on marthastewart.com

From Martha's Kitchen television program begins to air daily
on the Food Network cable channel

Branded decorative fabrics launched

Branded baby bedding to launch in October at Kmart

The timeline shows a consistent pattern of growth in the size and diversity of the company's operations—another good sign for this offering.

Now let's take a look at the company's financial statements to see what kind of growth the company has managed over the previous few years. The registration statement—as well as the prospectus—contains a wealth of financial information on the company. Here is a copy of the balance sheet on pages 168-169.

What do we learn in this table? We learn that the company has four key divisions—publishing, television, merchandising, and Internet/direct commerce —although the publishing division is much larger than the other three divisions combined. We see that revenue for each division grew rapidly from 1996 through 1998 and again in the first six months of 1999.

That's a strong sign. But we also see that income from operations and net income grew rapidly from 1996 to 1998, but showed only a small gain in the first six months of 1999. That should give investors some reason for concern, but all in all, the consolidated statement of operations shows a pretty solid company. But let's look at some other financial tables in the report to see what else we might learn about the company's growth momentum:

MARTHA STEWART LIVING OMNIMEDIA LLC

NOTES TO CONSOLIDATED FINANCIAL STATEMENTS
(CONTINUED)

(IN THOUSANDS, EXCEPT SHARE DATA)

INTERIM FINANCIAL STATEMENTS

The interim consolidated financial statements of the Company are unaudited but in the opinion of management reflect all adjustments consisting of normal recurring accruals, necessary for a fair presentation of the results for the interim period.

3. ACCOUNTS RECEIVABLE

The components of accounts receivable are as follows:

	DECEMBER 31,	
	1997	1998
Advertising	$15,975	$23,123
Newsstand	715	1,698
Licensing	157	2,585
Other	3,657	3,859
	20,504	31,265
Less: reserve for credits and uncollectible accounts	2,557	6,005
	$17,947	$25,260

This first table shows that accounts receivable are up substantially—even though the company more than doubled its reserve for credits and uncollectible accounts. That's a good sign.

The following table on inventories shows that inventories have nearly doubled, which can be interpreted as a sign of the company's increasing value—unless, of course, the inventories are piling up because products aren't selling. But we saw in earlier tables that sales have been increasing, so the inventory increase is probably not a bad sign.

4. INVENTORIES

The components of inventories are as follows:

	DECEMBER 31,	
	1997	1998
Paper	$3,061	$4,621
Catalog products	366	1,901
	$3,427	$6,522

Next, let's look at the company's consolidated balance sheet on page 170.

The consolidated balance sheet reveals very little additional information. With results for only two and a half years, it's difficult to get any perspective on growth, consistency, and momentum. But you can see that from 1997 to 1999, total current assets and total assets increased, and long-term debt declined. Total liabilities and members' equity edged up from 1997 to 1998, but dipped down in 1999.

All in all, the financials seem solid, and the company's history and description of current operations seems positive. So far, the stock seems like a

MARTHA STEWART LIVING OMNIMEDIA LLC

CONSOLIDATED STATEMENTS OF OPERATIONS

FOR THE YEARS ENDED DECEMBER 31, 1996, 1997, AND 1998

AND FOR THE SIX MONTHS ENDED JUNE 30,

1998 AND 1999 (UNAUDITED)

(000'S OMITTED)

| | FOR THE YEAR ENDED DECEMBER 31, | | | FOR THE SIX MONTHS ENDED JUNE 30, | |
	1996	1997	1998	1998	1999
				(UNAUDITED)	
Revenues					
Publishing	$3,899	$108,694	$127,020	$64,701	$ 73,314
Television	—	12,396	23,351	10,587	12,787
Merchandising	—	6,919	15,004	6,622	11,509
Internet/Direct Commerce .	—	4,812	14,673	4,343	13,892
Total revenues	3,899	132,821	180,048	86,253	111,502

168

Operating costs and expenses					
Production, distribution and editorial	—	59,148	82,930	36,492	54,710
Selling and promotion	—	31,973	34,540	17,838	19,994
General and administrative	99	21,182	29,659	14,005	18,601
Depreciation and amortization	—	3,927	5,534	2,665	2,732
Total operating costs and expenses	99	116,230	152,663	71,000	96,037
Income from operations	3,800	16,591	27,385	15,253	15,465
Other expenses					
Interest expense, net	165	2,195	2,243	1,315	597
Income tax provision	—	467	1,336	750	702
Total other expenses	165	2,662	3,579	2,065	1,299
Net income	$3,635	$ 13,929	$ 23,806	$13,188	$ 14,166

MARTHA STEWART LIVING OMNIMEDIA LLC

CONSOLIDATED BALANCE SHEETS

DECEMBER 31, 1997 AND 1998 AND JUNE 30, 1999 (UNAUDITED)

(000'S OMITTED)

	DECEMBER 31,		JUNE 30,
	1997	1998	1999
			(UNAUDITED)
ASSETS			
CURRENT ASSETS			
Cash and cash equivalents	$ 9,971	$ 24,578	$ 22,269
Accounts receivable, net.	17,947	25,260	24,683
Inventories	3,427	6,522	7,977
Deferred television production costs.	3,805	3,038	3,190
Other current assets	606	275	1,329
Total current assets.	35,756	59,673	59,448
PROPERTY, PLANT AND EQUIPMENT, net	13,852	11,468	11,491
INTANGIBLE ASSETS, net	55,183	53,108	51,633
OTHER NONCURRENT ASSETS	915	1,123	1,273
Total assets.	$105,706	$125,372	$123,845
LIABILITIES AND MEMBERS' EQUITY			
CURRENT LIABILITIES:			
Accounts payable and accrued liabilities	$ 16,650	$ 21,242	$ 22,771
Accrued payroll and related costs	2,056	4,056	3,093
Accrued interest payable.	2,581	1,581	265
Current maturities of long-term debt	—	—	3,000
Current portion of deferred subscription income	23,444	26,756	26,483
Total current liabilities	44,731	53,635	55,612
DEFERRED ROYALTY INCOME	13,203	1,782	1,151
DEFERRED SUBSCRIPTION INCOME.	4,137	4,722	4,674
LONG-TERM DEBT, less current maturities.	30,000	27,650	12,000
OTHER NONCURRENT LIABILITIES	400	768	849
COMMITMENTS AND CONTINGENCIES			
MEMBERS' EQUITY.	13,235	36,815	49,559
Total liabilities and members' equity.	$105,706	$125,372	$123,845

solid bet. But there are more factors to consider in the report, and they are not all positive.

RED FLAGS

There's a section in nearly every prospectus and registration report that focuses on risks the company faces that prospective shareholders should know about. As an investor researching a new company, that's a section you should definitely read closely. In the Martha Stewart report, the "Risk Factors" section goes for many pages, so we can't print it all here, but here are some important highlights from that section:

RISK FACTORS

If any of the events described below were to occur, our business, prospects, financial condition, results of operations or cash flow could be materially adversely affected. When we say below that something could or will have a material adverse effect on us, we mean that it could or will have one or more of these effects.

* THE LOSS OF THE SERVICES OF MARTHA STEWART OR OTHER KEY EMPLOYEES WOULD MATERIALLY ADVERSELY AFFECT OUR REVENUES, RESULTS OF OPERATIONS AND PROSPECTS

We are highly dependent upon our founder, Chairman and Chief Executive Officer, Martha Stewart. Martha Stewart's talents, efforts, personality and leadership have been, and continue to be, critical to our success. The diminution or loss of the services of Martha Stewart, and any negative market or industry perception arising from that diminution or loss, would have a material adverse effect on our business. While our other key executives have substantial experience and have made significant contributions to our business, Martha Stewart remains the personification of our brands as well as our senior executive and primary creative force. See "Management— Key Executive Insurance" for a description of key executive life insurance policies we maintain with respect to Martha Stewart.

One of our business strategies is to reduce our dependence on Martha Stewart, but we may be unable to do so. If we are unsuccessful in accomplishing this strategy because, for example, we are unable to develop the public reputation of our other experts, and Martha Stewart's services become unavailable to us, our business and prospects would be materially adversely affected.

Effective as of the completion of this offering, we will enter into a five-year employment agreement with Martha Stewart. This agreement is important to the future of our business, and if we were to lose our rights under this agreement for any reason, including as a result of Martha Stewart's voluntary resignation or retirement, our business would be materially adversely affected. See "Management—Executive Employment Arrangements—Employment Agreement with Martha Stewart" for a description of this agreement.

> * Our success depends on our brands and their value. Our business would be adversely affected if...Martha Stewart's public image or reputation were to be tarnished

> Martha Stewart, as well as her name, her image and the trademarks and other intellectual property rights relating to these, are integral to our marketing efforts and form the core of our brand name. Our continued success and the value of our brand name therefore depends, to a large degree, on the reputation of Martha Stewart.

Those two considerations—the strong dependence on Martha Stewart's services and her ability to keep her reputation from being "tarnished"— should have given pause to anyone considering investing in the IPO. This is a company that is dependent not just on the leadership ability of its chief officer, but also on her personal marketability, health, and reputation in the public eye. As we saw in Stewart's insider trading scandal involving Imclone Systems stock, overdependence on one person can be a severe handicap. When the investigation into the insider trading charges began, Martha Stewart stock plunged by more than 50 percent—from a high of about $20 to a low of under $7. Stewart was accused of receiving insider information that enabled her to sell out her Imclone stock the day before it collapsed.

The "Risk Factors" section of the report also identified one other reason to worry about the company's dependence on Stewart:

MARTHA STEWART WILL CONTROL OUR COMPANY AND THIS CONTROL COULD INHIBIT POTENTIAL CHANGES OF CONTROL

> Following this offering, Martha Stewart will control all of our outstanding shares of Class B common stock, representing approximately 96% of our voting power. As a result, Martha Stewart will have the ability to control the outcome of all matters requiring stockholder approval, including the election and removal of our entire Board of Directors, any merger, consolidation or sale of all or substantially all of our assets, and the ability to control our management and affairs.

> The Class B common stock has ten votes per share, while Class A common stock, which is the stock we are offering in this prospectus, has one vote per share. Because of this dual-class structure, Martha Stewart will

continue to be able to control all matters submitted to our stockholders even if she comes to own significantly less than 50% of the equity of our company. This concentrated control could discourage others from initiating any potential merger, takeover or other change of control transaction that may otherwise be beneficial to our businesses. As a result, the market price of Class A common stock could be adversely affected.

Whenever one person controls the entire company, it gives the shareholders—and even the board of directors—no say in the decisions that affect the operation and growth of the company. Poor decisions by one person— unchecked by a board of directors—could affect the success of the company, and ultimately, the value of the shareholders' stock. Martha Stewart was essentially asking investors to trust that she could continue to run the company successfully, and transform it from an entrepreneurial start-up into a media conglomerate. That is not an easy task for anyone. Potential investors would have reason to be skeptical of her ability to do that, and of her unfettered control over the corporation.

The report also included a number of other risk factors, many of which would be relevant to nearly any young company going public:

OUR GROWTH IS DEPENDENT UPON THE CONTINUED ACCEPTANCE AND GROWTH OF THE INTERNET AND ELECTRONIC COMMERCE, AND IF SUCH GROWTH DOES NOT CONTINUE OUR PROSPECTS COULD BE MATERIALLY ADVERSELY AFFECTED

TERMINATION OR IMPAIRMENT OF OUR RELATIONSHIPS WITH A SMALL NUMBER OF KEY LICENSING AND STRATEGIC PARTNERS COULD ADVERSELY AFFECT OUR REVENUES AND RESULTS OF OPERATIONS

TERMINATION OF OUR LICENSING AGREEMENT WITH KMART RELATING TO BED AND BATH PRODUCTS COULD ADVERSELY AFFECT OUR REVENUES AND RESULTS OF OPERATIONS

OUR BUSINESS IS CURRENTLY HEAVILY DEPENDENT ON PUBLISHING, AND THE REVENUE AND INCOME WE DERIVE FROM PUBLISHING COULD DECREASE AS A RESULT OF INDUSTRY DOWNTURNS AND COST INCREASES

IF OUR TELEVISION SHOWS FAIL TO MAINTAIN A SUFFICIENT AUDIENCE, IF ADVERSE TRENDS DEVELOP IN THE TELEVISION PRODUCTION BUSINESS GENERALLY OR IF MARTHA STEWART WERE TO CEASE TO BE ABLE TO DEVOTE SUBSTANTIAL TIME TO OUR TELEVISION BUSINESS, THAT BUSINESS COULD BECOME UNPROFITABLE

FAILURE TO DEVELOP NEW OR EXPAND EXISTING RETAIL MERCHANDISING PROGRAMS WILL IMPAIR OUR ABILITY TO GROW AND ADVERSELY AFFECT OUR PROSPECTS

OUR REVENUES AND INCOME COULD DECLINE DUE TO GENERAL ECONOMIC TRENDS AND DECLINES IN CONSUMER SPENDING

FAILURE TO DEVELOP OUR INTERNET/DIRECT COMMERCE BUSINESS WILL IMPAIR OUR ABILITY TO GROW AND ADVERSELY AFFECT OUR PROSPECTS

WE COMPETE IN HIGHLY COMPETITIVE MARKETS AND ARE VULNERABLE TO LARGER AND MORE EXPERIENCED COMPETITORS

SINCE OUR STOCK HAS NOT BEEN PUBLICLY TRADED BEFORE THIS OFFERING, THE PRICE OF OUR STOCK MAY BE SUBJECT TO WIDE FLUCTUATIONS

WE HAVE A SHORT OPERATING HISTORY WITH RESPECT TO OUR CURRENT BUSINESSES; WE HAVE NEVER OPERATED AS A PUBLIC COMPANY, AND THE OBLIGATIONS INCIDENT TO BEING A PUBLIC COMPANY WILL REQUIRE ADDITIONAL EXPENDITURES

IF WE ARE NOT ABLE TO EFFECTIVELY MANAGE OUR GROWTH, OUR FINANCIAL CONDITION, RESULTS OF OPERATIONS AND PROSPECTS COULD DECLINE

Risk is part of the equation in the stock market, and when you invest in a new company, there will always be risk. What you want is a company that offers the highest reward potential for the lowest risk. Most of the risk factors listed above are the same ones faced by any company in the same business. The one risk factor that stands out, of course, is the dependence on Martha Stewart.

Here's one more risk factor worth considering. It is a factor in every IPO, but the risk can vary by the company:

YOU WILL EXPERIENCE IMMEDIATE AND SUBSTANTIAL DILUTION

The initial public offering price is substantially higher than the net tangible book value of each outstanding share of our common stock. Purchasers of Class A common stock in this offering will experience immediate and substantial dilution. The dilution will be $14.01 per share in net tangible book value of Class A common stock from the initial public offering price. If outstanding options to purchase shares of Class A common stock are exercised, there would be further dilution. See "Dilution" and "Management" for information regarding outstanding stock options and additional stock options which may be granted.

In other words, 1) you're paying a lot more for the shares than they are actually worth based on book value, and 2) the company could issue even more stock and stock options later, which would dilute the value of your shares even further. Both policies are fairly standard for IPOs. Companies tend to issue their stocks at prices that are well above book value (and most good stocks trade well above book value after they're issued, as we explain in Chapter 4). Companies also routinely hand out stock options to management as part of their compensation package. But some companies may give IPO investors a better value for their dollars. It is one more area worth investigating. The above paragraph from the Martha Stewart report refers readers to the sections on "Dilution" and "Management" for more details. As an interested investor, it would be worth your time to turn to those sections and find out more. Here is the section on "Dilution:"

DILUTION

Our net tangible book value (deficit) as of June 30, 1999 was approximately $(2.1) million or $(0.05) per share based on an aggregate of 39,175,714 shares of common stock outstanding. Net tangible book value per share is determined by dividing the number of outstanding shares of common stock into our net tangible book value, which is the total tangible assets less total liabilities.

After giving effect to

— the sale of 5% of Martha Stewart Living Omnimedia LLC in exchange for $24.75 million, and

— the sale of the 7,200,000 shares of Class A common stock offered in this prospectus,

before deducting estimated offering expenses and the underwriting discounts and commissions based on an assumed initial public offering price of $17.00 per share, our net tangible book value as of June 30, 1999 would have been $145.3 million, or $3.00 per share. This represents an immediate dilution of $14.01 per share to new investors purchasing shares of Class A common stock at the initial offering price.

To summarize, the company's current book value before the stock offering was minus 5 cents per share, but after raising $24.5 million by selling off 5 percent of the company, and another $121 million through the IPO, the book value of the shares would be about $3. That's about $14 less than the $17-per-share asking price of the IPO. Or to put it another way, the book value represents about 17 percent of $17-per-share asking price. That's a pretty steep asking price. In the Internet IPO heyday, many stocks carried an even higher price relative to the book value. (But we also saw what happened to many of those stocks—they collapsed to a fraction of the original asking price.)

Now let's take a look at the "Management" section to see what other dilution might occur. There are several sections that deal with options. Here are two that shed the most light on the option compensation plan:

Options

On the day of the pricing of this offering, each director will be granted options for 5,000 shares of Class A common stock with an exercise price per share equal to the initial public offering price. After each annual meeting of stockholders, each continuing director will be granted options for 2,000 shares of Class A common stock. Each new director will be granted options for 5,000 shares of Class A common stock upon being elected or appointed to our Board of Directors. The exercise price for all options will be 100% of the fair market value of a share of Class A common stock on the date of the grant of such option, except that options granted before or upon consummation of this offering will be granted at the initial public offering price. Each option will vest and become exercisable on the first anniversary of the date of grant of such option, if the director remains a member of our Board of Directors at that time. Each vested option will terminate one year after the director's service on our Board of Directors ceases for any reason, other than for cause. If a director is removed for cause, all vested and unvested options will be forfeited. However, the options will expire no later than the tenth anniversary of the date of grant. Any unvested options will terminate and be canceled as of the date a director's service on our Board of Directors ceases for any reason. All options become fully vested and exercisable upon a change in control.

General

The 1999 plan provides that the maximum number of shares of Class A common stock available for grant under the 1999 plan is 7,300,000.

The term of options granted under the 1999 plan may not exceed 10 years. Unless otherwise determined by our Compensation Committee, options will vest ratably on each of the first four anniversaries after the grant date and will have an exercise price equal to the fair market value of the Class A common stock on the date of grant.

At the time of this offering, we expect to grant options to purchase 4,582,220 shares of Class A common stock under the 1999 plan at an exercise price equal to the initial public offering price.

So in addition to the 7.2 million shares offered to the public—and the shares already owned by Martha Stewart and other investors in the company—the company says it will award options on about 4.6 million shares to various parties involved with the company and the administration of the IPO. The report also said that the maximum shares available for grant (to officers and directors) was 7.3 million—an amount roughly equal to all the shares offered to the public in the IPO. There's no question that the additional options grants could serve to dilute the value of the IPO shares. (However, the awarding of stock options is standard procedure for nearly all companies that are involved in an initial public offer.)

MANAGEMENT'S HOLDINGS
We've already seen that Martha Stewart had total control of the company because of her vast holdings of company stock. How much stock would she and other leading investors in the company control? A table on pages 178-179 from the report provides all the details.

The table shows that Stewart owned about 34 million shares of Class B stock (convertible to Class A stock), which represented 96 percent of the voting power. At the IPO asking price of $17 a share, her 34 million shares would have been worth about $578 million.

In all, the above table accounts for about 43 million shares, including those held by Stewart, the other officers, and two businesses. That means that the 7.2 million shares offered to the public in the IPO would represent just a small fraction of the total holdings of the company—just 16 percent in all.

That percentage would drop even further with further options grants to company insiders. The report said that the company expected to grant up to 7.3 million additional stock options, which could put the total holdings by company insiders to about 50 million shares compared with the 7.2 million shares issued to the public in the IPO. That would represent just 14 percent of all outstanding shares—and those are nonvoting shares, so outside investors would have little clout and no real legal voice in the operation. That's generally considered a red flag for investors, who are concerned that a board with dominant control would be more interested in its own welfare than that of the investing public. However, many companies that go public do so with the board members and leading principals holding much of the voting stock. But

PRINCIPAL STOCKHOLDERS

The following table sets forth information with respect to beneficial ownership of Class A and Class B common stock, including the percent of the total voting power, as of September 24, 1999, and as adjusted to reflect completion of this offering, by

— each of our five most highly compensated officers
— each director
— each holder of more than 5% of either class of common stock
— all current directors and executive officers as a group

	BENEFICIAL OWNERSHIP BEFORE OFFERING(1)							BENEFICIAL OWNERSHIP AFTER OFFERING						
	CLASS A COMMON STOCK		CLASS B COMMON STOCK		% TOTAL		CLASS A COMMON STOCK		CLASS B COMMON STOCK		% TOTAL
NAME	SHARES	%	SHARES	%	VOTING POWER		SHARES	%	SHARES	%	VOTING POWER
Martha Stewart(2)......	—	—	34,126,831	100	98.0		—	—	34,126,831	100	96.0
Time Inc.(3).......... 1271 Avenue of the Americas New York, New York 10020	2,585,597	36.4	—	—	*		2,585,597	18.0	—	—	*

178

Kleiner Perkins Caufield & Byers(4) 2750 Sand Hill Road Menlo Park, California 94025	2,061,880	29.0	—	*	2,061,880	14.3	—	—	*
L. John Doerr(4)	2,061,880	29.0	—	*	2,061,880	14.3	—	—	*
Charlotte Beers(5)	—	—	—	—	—	—	—	—	—
Sharon Patrick(6)	2,342,339	32.9	—	*	2,356,664	16.4	—	—	*
Naomi O. Seligman(7)	—	—	—	—	—	—	—	—	—
Gael Towey(8)	—	—	—	—	192,176	1.3	—	—	*
Stephen Drucker(9)	—	—	—	—	4,050	—	—	—	*
Suzanne Sobel(10)	—	—	—	—	7,315	—	—	—	*
All directors and executive officers as a group (15 persons)(11)	4,404,219	61.9%	34,126,831	100%	4,655,938	32.3%	34,126,831	100%	97.3%

the Martha Stewart offering—with 96 percent of the voting power in the hands of one person—would be considered an extreme example!

EXECUTIVE COMPENSATION: WHAT MARTHA MAKES

Let's look at one more aspect of management's financial situation—their salaries, bonuses, and other compensation. In other words, what did Martha decide to pay herself and her managers? This table from the report on page 181 gives the details.

As the table shows, Stewart received about $3 million in salary and $1.7 million in bonuses, with no other compensation, including stock options. The following paragraph gives a little more detail on her salary after the offering:

EMPLOYMENT AGREEMENT WITH MARTHA STEWART

Prior to completion of the offering, we will enter into an employment agreement with Martha Stewart. The employment agreement will replace Martha Stewart's existing employment agreement with Martha Stewart Living Omnimedia. The employment agreement provides for Martha Stewart's employment as our Chairman of the Board and Chief Executive Officer, and is for a term of five years, commencing upon completion of the offering. Under the employment agreement, Martha Stewart's annual base salary is $900,000, and she will receive annual bonus payments based upon our performance, with a minimum annual bonus of $300,000. Our Compensation Committee will determine the performance goals, which will include targets based on our operating income as well as other performance measures.

To summaraize, Stewart was to receive a salary of $900,000 and a bonus of at least $300,000, and probably more depending on the company's performance. The agreement also stipulates that if she leaves the company under favorable conditions, she would receive a golden parachute that would include three years' salary, and "the higher of $5,000,000 or three times the highest annual bonus paid."

PENNY WISE, POUND FOOLISH

You may recall that when Stewart was embroiled in an insider trading scandal involving ImClone Systems stock, she was accused of selling out all of her holdings the day before ImClone announced that the U.S. Food and Drug Administration had rejected approval of the company's leading drug. The rejection was a devastating blow to the company, and caused the stock to plunge more than $20 the first day—and much more in subsequent days

EXECUTIVE COMPENSATION

The following table sets forth the cash compensation paid to our Chief Executive Officer and our other four most highly compensated executive officers for the fiscal year ended December 31, 1998:

SUMMARY COMPENSATION TABLE

NAME AND PRINCIPAL POSITION	ANNUAL COMPENSATION			ALL OTHER COMPENSATION ($)
	1998 SALARY ($)	1998 BONUS ($)	OTHER ANNUAL COMPENSATION ($)	
Martha Stewart.................... Chairman and Chief Executive Officer	$2,975,000	$1,695,717	—	—
Sharon Patrick.................... President and Chief Operating Officer	493,755	518,443	—	—
Gael Towey.......................... Executive Vice President—Art and Style Creative Director	300,000	305,000	—	—
Stephen Drucker.................. Executive Vice President—Editorial Core and Editor-in-Chief	265,000	198,750	—	—
Suzanne Sobel.................... Executive Vice President—Advertising Sales and Marketing, Publisher	239,000	225,855	—	—

and weeks. From a high of about $75, the stock sunk to under $6 a share. Stewart, a friend of the founder of ImClone, owned about 4000 shares of the stock, which she sold for about $60 a share the day before the stock began its free fall.

If Stewart had sold her ImClone stock after the announcement of the FDA ruling, the value of her shares would have been about $100,000 less. So she saved $100,000 by selling in advance. But the sale raised suspicions of insider trading—that she was tipped off in advance by her broker or contacts at ImClone.

The scandal reflected directly on Martha Stewart's image, her business, and her company's stock price. Martha Stewart stock, which had reached a high of about $20 a share, dropped steadily in the wake of the scandal to a low of about $7. That $13-per-share drop had a devastating effect on Stewart's own personal holdings. In all, the value of her 34 million shares declined about $440 million during the insider trading scandal. So that $100,000 in losses she saved on her ImClone stock cost her nearly half a billion dollars in lost value on her own company's stock. Penny wise, pound foolish.

SLICING AND DICING KRISPY KREME

Another prominent IPO of recent years was Krispy Kreme Doughnuts. In this section, we review the Krispy Kreme prospectus, and compare it with the Martha Stewart offering.

I will admit a bit of bias here. After the company went public, I had the opportunity to taste Krispy Kreme donuts straight off the assembly line. Hot, gooey, and delicious, they melt in your mouth. I quickly became one of the millions of Krispy Kreme fanatics—though, much to the benefit of my physique, I happen to live in a city that has no Krispy Kremes. But I can certainly understand the buzz surrounding the company and its doughnuts.

Krispy Kreme went public in 2000, filing its prospectus with the SEC in April of 2000. Let's review and analyze some of the key elements of that prospectus to get a feel for the company's long-term prospects.

We learned some valuable information in the Martha Stewart report that should also be of interest in the Krispy Kreme prospectus. Here are some of the key questions we hope to answer:

- What's the company's history?

- Who owns the company now?

- How much voting control will the current managers have after the offering?

- How will management be compensated?
- What is the book value of the shares and what is the IPO asking price?
- How much dilution might occur in the stock price due to option awards and other factors?
- What is the makeup of the company?
- How does it market its products?
- What are its plans and prospects for growth?
- What are the risk factors?
- Does it face any significant litigation?
- How solid are the financials?
- Has the company shown a history of consistent growth, and does it still show solid growth momentum in all the key categories?

The prospectus will help us answer all of those questions. Krispy Kreme's prospectus covers well over 100 pages—much too long to print here—but we go over the sections that shed light on our key questions. First, let's find out a little about the company and its history:

KRISPY KREME DOUGHNUTS, INC.

Krispy Kreme is a leading branded specialty retailer of premium quality doughnuts which are made throughout the day in our stores. We opened our first store in 1937 and there were 144 Krispy Kreme stores nationwide, consisting of 58 company-owned and 86 franchised stores, as of January 30, 2000. Our principal business is the high volume production and sale of over 20 varieties of premium quality doughnuts, including our signature Hot Original Glazed. We have established Krispy Kreme as a leading consumer brand with a loyal customer base through our longstanding commitment to quality and consistency. Our place in American society was recognized in 1997 with the induction of Krispy Kreme artifacts into the Smithsonian Institution's National Museum of American History. We differentiate ourselves by combining quality ingredients, vertical integration and a unique retail experience featuring our stores' fully displayed production process, or doughnutmaking theater.

The combination of our well-established brand, our one-of-a-kind doughnuts and our strong franchise system creates significant opportunities for continued growth. Our sales growth has been driven by new store openings, as well as systemwide comparable store sales growth of 12.7% in fiscal 1998, 9.7% in fiscal 1999 and 14.1% in fiscal 2000.

Not many IPOs can claim, as Krispy Kreme did in the opening paragraph, that artifacts from the company have been inducted into the Smithsonian. Krispy Kreme has a long history, dating back to 1937, and is well entrenched, with 144 stores nationwide. We also learn here that not only is the company increasing its store count, it has also improved store sales by about 10 to 14 percent annually the past three years. Those are all very positive factors for a prospective investor.

FUTURE GROWTH

How does the company expect to expand, and what are its expectations. The next section form the prospectus answers those questions:

GROWTH STRATEGY

We believe there are significant opportunities to expand our business by further penetrating existing markets and entering new markets. After establishing our brand in a new market through our retail stores, we attempt to maximize store productivity by selling off-premises to grocery and convenience stores, institutional customers and select co-branding customers. Key elements of our growth strategy include:

– OPEN NEW STORES. We plan to expand primarily through franchising with area developers and have existing agreements with franchisees to open approximately 22 new stores in fiscal 2001 and over 100 new stores between fiscal 2002 and fiscal 2005. This represents 15% store growth in fiscal 2001 and an increase in our store base to over 260 stores by the end of fiscal 2005. We depend upon our franchisees to execute our store expansion strategy. If they cannot finance new stores, build them on suitable sites or open them on schedule, our growth strategy may be impeded.

– IMPROVE OUR EXISTING STORES' ON-PREMISES SALES. To improve our on-premises sales, we plan to remodel and, in certain instances, close and relocate selected older company-owned stores to emulate the format of our new, highly successful stores in new markets.

– INCREASE OUR OFF-PREMISES SALES. We intend to expand our off-premises customer base, as well as increase sales to our existing off-premises customers by continuing to offer premium quality products, category management and superior customer service.

The company's expansion plans look to be well designed, with intentions to open 22 stores in 2001 and over 100 more in the following four years. They are also working to increase same-store sales, and to increase sales to off-premises customers.

But there must also be some downside to the business. What are the risk factors that Krispy Kreme investors face?

RED FLAGS?

Most of the concerns listed in the "Risk Factors" section of the prospectus would be considered boilerplate-type risks that any retailer or food services operation would face. This section covers many pages, so we've just included the highlights:

RISK FACTORS

OUR GROWTH STRATEGY DEPENDS ON OPENING NEW KRISPY KREME STORES. OUR ABILITY TO EXPAND OUR STORE BASE IS INFLUENCED BY FACTORS BEYOND OUR CONTROL, WHICH MAY SLOW STORE DEVELOPMENT AND IMPAIR OUR STRATEGY.

IF OUR FRANCHISEES CANNOT DEVELOP OR FINANCE NEW STORES OR BUILD THEM ON SUITABLE SITES, OUR GROWTH AND SUCCESS WILL BE IMPEDED.

IF OUR FRANCHISEES CANNOT OPEN NEW STORES ON SCHEDULE, OUR GROWTH AND SUCCESS WILL BE IMPEDED.

WE MAY BE HARMED BY ACTIONS TAKEN BY OUR FRANCHISEES THAT ARE OUTSIDE OF OUR CONTROL.

WE ARE THE EXCLUSIVE SUPPLIER OF DOUGHNUT MIXES, OTHER KEY INGREDIENTS AND FLAVORS TO ALL KRISPY KREME STORES. IF WE HAVE ANY PROBLEMS SUPPLYING THESE INGREDIENTS, OUR STORES' ABILITY TO MAKE DOUGHNUTS WILL BE NEGATIVELY AFFECTED.

WE ARE THE ONLY MANUFACTURER OF OUR DOUGHNUT-MAKING EQUIPMENT. IF WE HAVE ANY PROBLEMS PRODUCING THIS EQUIPMENT, OUR STORES' ABILITY TO MAKE DOUGHNUTS WILL BE NEGATIVELY AFFECTED.

ANY INTERRUPTION IN THE DELIVERY OF GLAZE FLAVORING FROM OUR ONLY SUPPLIER COULD IMPAIR OUR ABILITY TO MAKE OUR TOP PRODUCT.

A NUMBER OF OUR DIRECTORS OWN AND SOME OFFICERS HAVE A FINANCIAL INTEREST IN SOME OF OUR FRANCHISES.

THE INTERESTS OF THESE INDIVIDUALS MAY THEREFORE BE POTENTIALLY IN CONFLICT WITH OUR INTERESTS.

OUR FAILURE OR INABILITY TO ENFORCE OUR TRADEMARKS COULD ADVERSELY AFFECT THE VALUE OF OUR BRAND.

THE FOOD SERVICE INDUSTRY IS AFFECTED BY CONSUMER PREFERENCES AND PERCEPTIONS. CHANGES IN THESE PREFERENCES AND PERCEPTIONS MAY LESSEN THE DEMAND FOR OUR DOUGHNUTS, WHICH WOULD REDUCE SALES AND HARM OUR BUSINESS.

OUR SUCCESS DEPENDS ON OUR ABILITY TO COMPETE WITH MANY FOOD SERVICE BUSINESSES.

There is really nothing in the above section that stands out as a viable reason for concern about this specific company. Any company in the same type of business would face the same issues.

The report also included some risk factors concerning the stock offering itself. These concerns are typical of nearly all companies involved in initial stock offerings, but the information is still worth analyzing:

RISKS RELATING TO THE OFFERING

9.3 MILLION, OR 74.8%, OF OUR TOTAL OUTSTANDING SHARES ARE RESTRICTED FROM IMMEDIATE RESALE BUT MAY BE SOLD INTO THE MARKET IN THE FUTURE, WHICH COULD DEPRESS THE MARKET PRICE OF OUR COMMON STOCK.

After this offering, we will have outstanding approximately 12.5 million shares of common stock, or 12.9 million shares if the underwriters fully exercise their over-allotment option. This includes the 3 million shares that we are selling in this offering, which may be resold in the public market immediately, unless held by one of our affiliates or purchased by certain participants in our directed share program, and the 144,737 shares to be contributed to our stock bonus plans. The remaining 74.8%, or 9.3 million shares, of our total outstanding shares will become available for resale in the public market one year after this offering. However, it is possible that these shares may be sold sooner if they are registered under the Securities Act of 1933. For a more detailed description, see "Shares Eligible for Future Sale."

As restrictions on resale end, the prevailing market price of our common stock could drop significantly if the holders of these restricted shares sell them or are perceived by the market as intending to sell them. Our ability to raise additional capital through future issuances of equity securities could also be impaired.

As soon as practicable after this offering, we intend to register for resale 2,153,000 shares of common stock reserved under our stock option plan, of which options exercisable into 1,821,000 shares of common stock were outstanding as of January 30, 2000. Options for 91,000 shares were exercisable as of that date.

It is typical of companies involved in an IPO to issue stock and options to officers, directors, and the underwriters. Every IPO faces the same concern. Many of the dot-com companies of the 1990s ultimately drowned in stock options. As officers and investors cashed in their options and sold out their stock, other shareholders saw the value of their shares drop dramatically. What other concerns might you have about the offering? Here is another risk factor:

OUR EXISTING SHAREHOLDERS WILL CONTINUE TO CONTROL US AFTER THIS OFFERING, AND THEY MAY MAKE DECISIONS WITH WHICH YOU MAY DISAGREE.

After this offering, our existing shareholders will beneficially hold approximately 74.8% of our outstanding common stock, or approximately 72.2% if the underwriters' over-allotment option is exercised in full. Our executive officers and directors as a group—currently 16 persons — will beneficially hold approximately 41.7% of our outstanding common stock after this offering, including currently exercisable stock options, or 40.2% if the over-allotment option is fully exercised. Consequently, our existing shareholders will continue to control us after this offering is completed, and our officers and directors will continue to be significant holders. Through their voting power, these persons may make decisions regarding Krispy Kreme with which you may disagree.

Again, this is a situation that is typical of an IPO. The officers and directors often control the company, and you and other outside shareholders would have no real say in the operation of the company.

The good news is that the company is apparently controlled by 16 officers and directors who hold about 41 percent of the stock—and not by a single person, such as Martha Stewart, who holds 96 percent of the voting rights of her company. The company is not controlled by one person, nor is it dependent on one person for its public image and commercial success.

Finally, the issue of dilution is addressed:

YOU WILL EXPERIENCE AN IMMEDIATE AND SUBSTANTIAL DILUTION IF YOU PURCHASE COMMON STOCK IN THIS OFFERING.

The initial public offering price is substantially higher than the net tangible book value per share of the outstanding common stock will be immediately after this offering. Any common stock you purchase in this offering will have a post-offering net tangible book value per share of $13.05 less than the initial public offering price of $21.00 per share. Future issuances of our common stock including issuances in connection with stock option exercises, could cause further dilution.

This is yet another boilerplate concern for any IPO, and is not unique to Krispy Kreme. Of all the risk factors raised in the company's prospectus, none pose any specific concern to Krispy Kreme that would not be an issue for any company in the same type of business.

ANALYZING THE OFFERING

Let's take a closer look at the offering itself. A table near the front of the prospectus lays out some of the details:

3,000,000 Shares
Common Stock

This is the initial public offering of Krispy Kreme Doughnuts, Inc. and we are offering 3,000,000 shares of our common stock at an initial public offering price of $21.00 per share.

Our common stock is quoted on the Nasdaq National Market under the symbol KREM.

	Public Offering Price	Underwriting Discounts and Commissions	Proceeds to Krispy Kreme
Per Share	$21.00	$1.47	$19.53
Total	$63,000,000	$4,410,000	$58,590,000

We have granted the underwriters the right to purchase up to an additional 450,000 shares to cover any over-allotments.

Here we learn that the company is using the offering to raise $63 million by issuing 3 million shares at $21 a piece. After paying $4.4 million in stocks and fees to the underwriters, Krispy Kreme would end up with about $58.6 million from the sale.

What does the company plan to do with that money? This table near the front of the report summarizes the offering and its purpose:

THE OFFERING

Common Stock Offered by Krispy Kreme	3,000,000 shares
Common Stock to be Outstanding after the Offering	12,484,957 shares
Use of Proceeds	– Repayment of borrowings under our loan agreement
	– A distribution to our existing shareholders as part of our pre-offering corporate reorganization
	– Remodeling and relocation of selected older company-owned stores
	– Additional mix production capacity to support expansion
	– Joint venture investments in area developer stores
	– General corporate purposes, including working capital needs
Dividend Policy.	We do not anticipate paying any cash dividends in the foreseeable future.
Proposed Nasdaq National Market Symbol	KREM

The table above excludes 1,821,000 shares of common stock issuable upon exercise of stock options outstanding under our stock option plan on January 30, 2000, of which 91,000 were exercisable, and includes 144,737 shares to be contributed to our stock bonus plans contemporaneously with this offering.

In all, the company would have up to 14 million shares outstanding, including 1.8 million shares available through stock options. That means that the 3 million shares offered to the public would represent about 21 percent of all shares outstanding—and 21 percent of the voting rights. By comparison, Martha Stewart's outside shareholders held just 14 percent of the shares, and had no voting rights. So from the perspective of shareholder power, the Krispy Kreme offering is clearly preferable, but not ideal. I would rather see more power in the hands of outside shareholders. Unfortunately, with many IPOs, the insiders maintain dominant control of the company.

FINDING THE BOOK VALUE

What else can we learn about the offering? Let's look at the "Dilution" section to see what the shares are really worth in terms of book value:

The following tables give us several good bits of information:

- The book value of the shares after the offering will be $7.95. That represents 37 percent of the $21 asking price. That may not sound like a great value, but it's more that double the value of the Martha Stewart offering, which had a book value that represented only 17 percent of the asking price of the stock.

DILUTION

Our net tangible book value as of January 30, 2000 was $47,755,000, or $5.11 per share of common stock. Net tangible book value per share is the amount by which total tangible assets exceeds total liabilities, divided by the total number of shares of common stock outstanding. Our adjusted net tangible book value as of January 30, 2000 would have been $98,140,000, or $7.95 per share, after giving effect to the sale of 3,000,000 shares of common stock offered by this prospectus at the initial offering price of $21.00 per share and after deducting underwriting discounts and estimated offering expenses and the distribution to be paid to existing shareholders as part of the corporate reorganization in connection with this offering. This represents an immediate increase in the net tangible book value of $2.84 per share to existing shareholders, in addition to the cash distribution they will receive, and an immediate dilution of $13.05 per share to new investors. The following table illustrates the per share dilution:

Initial public offering price		$21.00
Net tangible book value per share as of January 30, 2000	$5.11	
Increase attributable to the sale of shares offered hereby	2.84	
Adjusted net tangible book value after this offering		7.95
Dilution in the net tangible book value to new investors		$13.05

The following table shows, as of January 30, 2000, the number of shares of common stock purchased from us, the total consideration paid to us and the average price per share paid to us by existing shareholders, reduced to reflect the cash distribution the existing shareholders will receive, and by new investors in this offering at the initial offering price of $21.00 per share:

	SHARES PURCHASED		TOTAL CONSIDERATION		AVERAGE PRICE
	NUMBER	PERCENT	AMOUNT	PERCENT	PER SHARE
Existing shareholders...	9,340,220	75.7%	$15,474,673	19.7%	$ 1.66
New investors...	3,000,000	24.3	63,000,000	80.3	$21.00
Total........	12,340,220	100.0%	$78,474,673	100.0%	

- Existing shareholders will own 9.3 million shares of the 12.3 million total shares. On average, they paid about $1.66 per share for their holdings, while new shareholders will pay $21.

- Existing shareholders will control about 80 percent of the stock versus new investors, who will control about 20 percent.

WHO RUNS THE SHOW?
Now let's find out a little bit about these existing shareholders. Who currently owns the company? A paragraph near the front of the report offers some insight:

> Currently, all of the stock of Krispy Kreme Doughnuts, Inc. is owned by Krispy Kreme Doughnut Corporation, which was incorporated in 1982. Krispy Kreme Doughnuts, Inc., the issuer of the common stock offered by this prospectus, was incorporated in North Carolina in 1999 to be the holding company for Krispy Kreme Doughnut Corporation and its other subsidiaries.

We learn here that Krispy Kreme is owned by a corporation, but who are the individuals behind that corporation? The table on page 192 lists the principal stock holders:

Apparently, based on the chart and footnote, the late Joseph A. McAleer, Sr., was the leading shareholder of the company. His two sons, John and Joseph, Jr., continue to be leading shareholders in the company. Does either son have a role in running the company?

Another table from the prospectus, on pages 194-195, lays out the management team. We see that John McAleer is the second in command as vice chairman of the board, and his brother is a director.

The prospectus included bios of each officer and director. As you see in the bio portion, Scott Livengood, the chairman, president and CEO, and

NAME	NUMBER OF SHARES BENEFICIALLY OWNED	PERCENT BENEFICIALLY OWNED	
		BEFORE OFFERING	AFTER OFFERING
John N. McAleer (1)	2,680,200	28.7%	21.5%
Robert L. McCoy (2)(3)(4)	705,380	7.5	5.6
Bonnie Silvey Vandegrift (4)(5)	625,000	6.7	5.0
Carolyn McCoy (4)(6)	550,000	5.9	4.4
Joseph A. McAleer, Jr. (2)	455,720	4.9	3.6
J. Paul Breitbach (7)	324,560	3.5	2.6
Scott A. Livengood	307,860	3.3	2.5
Steven D. Smith (2)(8)	213,580	2.3	1.7
Frank E. Guthrie (2)(9)	180,380	1.9	1.4
Robert J. Simmons (2)(10)	113,000	1.2	*
L. Stephen Hendrix	73,460	*	*
William T. Lynch (2)(11)	33,000	*	*
Robert L. Strickland (2)(12)	33,000	*	*
Robert H. Vaughn, Jr	20,000	*	*
All directors and executive officers as a group (16 persons)	5,239,180	55.6	41.7

(1) Includes 2,344,060 shares owned by the estate of Joseph A. McAleer, Sr., of which Mr. John N. McAleer is the executor. Mr. McAleer's address is 370 Knollwood Street, Winston-Salem, North Carolina 27103.

John McAleer have been with the company for about 20 years, and have played a prominent role in the growth of the company.

What else can we find out about management? Let's look at the executive compensation table from the report, on page 196.

Compared with some of the compensation packages we've seen from other companies, Krispy Kreme's executives seem to be at the lower end of the scale. The highest-paid officer, Scott Livengood, received about $1 million in salary, bonuses, and other compensation. The table also shows that he received options on about 580,000 shares of stock. The value of those options was listed in a separate table as about $9.1 million. I wouldn't necessarily call this a red flag, but it would certainly be a concern. On the other hand, if an executive has spent 20 years at a company expanding the business and creating a loyal customer base, there should be a reward. That's what drives the capitalist system.

But as we learned with Enron, a generous award of options can also encourage management to cook the books to give the impression that the company is doing better than it really is in order to bump up the stock price, and the value of their options.

Cash bonuses for executives, with less emphasis on options, would seem to be a more honest way to reward good performance. And it would do less to dilute the company's stock value. Why not pay the executive well, and if he or she does a good job of running the company and fostering its growth, he or she could be rewarded with a bonus, a raise, and an opportunity to keep his or her job. If not, out the executive goes. The reliance on huge stock option awards for executives has robbed shareholders of billions of dollars in value, encouraged dishonesty in company accounting practices, and created enormous financial problems for the companies involved.

In this case, an award of $9.1 million seems pretty steep for a company the size of Krispy Kreme. As we see in the consolidated statement of operations (in the next section), the company only had income of $5.96 million in 2000. So with his options, salary, and bonuses, Livengood earned almost twice as much as the entire company. That's certainly not unheard-of, but it does seem a little out of whack.

THE FINANCIALS
We've learned a lot about the company, and so far it looks promising. Now for the acid test. Let's take a quick look at the financials to see how the company has done. The consolidated statements of operations is on pages 198-199.

What can we learn from this table? We see that total revenue had a healthy jump both years, and that income from operations, earnings per share, and diluted earnings per share were all up substantially from 1998 to 2000.

EXECUTIVE OFFICERS AND DIRECTORS

NAME	AGE	POSITION	DIRECTOR TERM EXPIRES
Scott A. Livengood.......	47	Chairman of the Board of Directors, President and Chief Executive Officer	2001
John N. McAleer..........	41	Vice Chairman of the Board of Directors and Executive Vice President, Concept Development	2002
J. Paul Breitbach.........	62	Executive Vice President, Finance, Administration and Support Operations	—
Margaret M. Urquhart...	50	Executive Vice President and Chief Operating Officer	—
Randy S. Casstevens......	34	Senior Vice President, Finance and Secretary	—
L. Stephen Hendrix.......	50	Senior Vice President, Company Store and Associate Operations	—
Michelle P. Parman.......	37	Senior Vice President, Corporate Development	—
Robert H. Vaughn, Jr.....	43	Senior Vice President, Area Developer Operations	—
Philip R.S. Waugh, Jr...	39	Senior Vice President, Franchise Development	—
Frank E. Guthrie..........	60	Director	2000

William T. Lynch, Jr....	57	Director	2002
Joseph A. McAleer, Jr....	49	Director	2001
Robert L. McCoy..........	50	Director	2000
Robert J. Simmons........	76	Director	2000
Steven D. Smith..........	46	Director	2001
Robert L. Strickland.....	68	Director	2002

SCOTT A. LIVENGOOD has been employed by Krispy Kreme since 1978. He was appointed Chairman of the board of directors in October 1999. He has served as Chief Executive Officer since February 1998 and as President since August 1992. From August 1992 to January 1998, Mr. Livengood was also Chief Operating Officer. He has served as a director since February 1994.

JOHN N. MCALEER has been employed by Krispy Kreme since 1981. Mr. McAleer has served as Executive Vice President, Concept Development and as Vice Chairman of the board of directors since October 1999. He has also served as Executive Vice President, Brand Development from March 1998 until October 1999, Executive Vice President, Marketing from August 1992 until March 1998 and as Senior Vice President, Marketing, Real Estate and Construction from September 1990 until August 1992. Mr. McAleer has served as a director since September 1990 and served as Chairman of the board of directors from February 1998 until October 1999. Mr. McAleer is the brother of Mr. Joseph A. McAleer, Jr., another member of the board of directors.

Fiscal 2000 Summary Compensation Table

| | ANNUAL COMPENSATION | | | LONG-TERM COMPENSATION | | | |
| | | | | COMMON SHARES | | | |
NAMED OFFICER	SALARY	BONUS	OTHER ANNUAL COMPENSATION	UNDERLYING OPTIONS	LTIP PAYOUTS	ALL OTHER COMPENSATION
Scott A. Livengood........ Chairman of the Board, President and Chief Executive Officer	$332,446	$450,339	$66,751	580,000	$151,098	$ 46,331
J. Paul Breitbach.......... Executive Vice President, Finance, Administration and Support Operations	234,731	298,611	57,547	150,000	162,434	33,169
John N. McAleer............ Vice Chairman of the Board and Executive Vice President, Concept Development	199,845	254,232	52,903	150,000	80,636	28,240
L. Stephen Hendrix........ Senior Vice President, Company Store and Associate Operations	130,091	125,877	31,824	60,000	35,729	16,534
Robert H. Vaughn, Jr...... Senior Vice President, Area Developer Operations	139,792	133,377	3,372	60,000	—	16,425

196

The biggest cause for concern would be the 1999 returns. The company showed a $3.7 million "loss from operations" for that year—which contributed to a loss of 38 cents per share.

What happened? The table on pages 200–201 from the notes to consolidated financial statements breaks down the revenue and income by business segments. The table shows solid growth in every area, but again we see that $3.7 million loss in operating income for 1999. But unlike the first table, this one gives a little more detail about the loss. Under "operating income" is a "provision for restructuring." It appears that the company wrote off $9.46 million for restructuring—all of it in 1999. That would help explain the loss for 1999.

What else can we learn about that $9.5 million provision for restructuring? By poking around in the footnotes, one can find an explanation of that charge:

Fiscal 1999:

On January 13, 1999, the Board of Directors of the Company approved a restructuring plan for assets and operations included in the Company Store Operations segment determined either to be inconsistent with the Company's strategy or whose carrying value may not be fully recoverable. Of the total restructuring and impairment charge of $9.5 million, $7.8 million related to the closing of five double drive-through stores and the write-down of five other inactive double drive-through stores and sites including provisions to write-down associated land, building and equipment costs to estimated net realizable value and to cover operating lease commitments associated with these stores. The Company has no plans to open any new double drive-through stores. An additional $700,000 relates to future lease payments on double drive-through buildings subleased to franchisees. Also included in the total charge is a $1.0 million write-down of a facility that produces fried pies and honey buns. These products are not expected to be a core part of the Company's strategy going forward. Of the total charge, $5.6 million represents a charge for future cash outflows for lease payments on land and buildings while $3.6 million represents the write-down of land and the write-off of buildings and equipment. The remaining $250,000 represents the accrual of costs to remove double drive-through buildings from their leased locations. Land held for sale is carried at the estimated net realizable value determined through review of current prices for comparable retail locations. After an income tax benefit of $3,786,000, this action reduced fiscal 1999 earnings by $5,680,000 or $13.77 per share on a historical basis.

The above paragraph provides a detailed accounting of the $9.6 million restructuring charge. One might interpret this to mean that the company

KRISPY KREME DOUGHNUT CORPORATION

CONSOLIDATED STATEMENTS OF OPERATIONS
(IN THOUSANDS, EXCEPT PER SHARE AMOUNTS)

	YEAR ENDED		
	FEBRUARY 1, 1998	JANUARY 31 1999	JANUARY 30, 2000
Total revenues	$158,743	$180,880	$220,243
Operating expenses	140,207	159,941	190,003
General and administrative expenses	9,530	10,897	14,856
Depreciation and amortization expenses	3,586	4,278	4,546
Provision for restructuring	—	9,466	—
Income (loss) from operations	5,420	(3,702)	0,838
Interest income	179	181	293
Interest expense	1,603	1,507	1,525
(Gain) loss on sale of property and equipment	(529)	251	—

Income (loss) before income taxes	4,525	(5,279)	9,606
Provision (benefit) for income taxes	1,811	(2,112)	3,650
Net income (loss)	$ 2,714	$ (3,167)	$ 5,956
Basic earnings (loss) per share	$ 7.45	$ (7.68)	$ 12.75
Diluted earnings (loss) per share	$ 7.45	$ (7.68)	$ 12.13
Pro forma (Unaudited — Note 7):			
Basic earnings (loss) per share	$ .37	$ (.38)	$ .64
Diluted earnings (loss) per share	$ .37	$ (.38)	$ .61
Supplemental (Unaudited — Note 7):			
Basic earnings per share			$ .61
Diluted earnings per share			$ .58

NOTES TO CONSOLIDATED FINANCIAL STATEMENTS — (CONTINUED)

Segment operating income is income before general corporate expenses and income taxes.

	YEAR ENDED		
	FEBRUARY 1, 1998	JANUARY 31, 1999	JANUARY 30, 2000
	(IN THOUSANDS)		
REVENUES:			
Company Store Operations..............	$132,826	$145,251	$164,230
Franchise Operations..............	2,285	3,236	5,529
Support Operations..............	90,821	107,431	142,215
Intercompany sales eliminations..............	(67,189)	(75,038)	(91,731)
Total revenues..............	$158,743	$180,880	$220,243

OPERATING INCOME (LOSS):

Company Store Operations	$ 13,244	$ 13,029	$ 18,246
Franchise Operations	(183)	448	1,445
Support Operations	2,835	4,307	7,182
Unallocated general and administrative expenses	(10,476)	(12,020)	(16,035)
Provision for restructuring	—	(9,466)	—
Total operating income	$ 5,420	$ (3,702)	$ 10,838

DEPRECIATION AND AMORTIZATION EXPENSES:

Company Store Operations	$ 2,339	$ 2,873	$ 3,059
Franchise Operations	100	57	72
Support Operations	201	225	236
Corporate administration	946	1,123	1,179
Total depreciation and amortization expenses	$ 3,586	$ 4,278	$ 4,546

wanted to get all of its loss leaders off the books well ahead of this IPO. So it closed several stores and a bakery that specialized in fried pies and honey buns that apparently had no place in the company's future. After taking the big hit in 1999, the company was able to show a very strong 2000—just in time for the IPO. This would not necessarily be considered a red flag, but it is a concern for interested investors.

FINDING ADDITIONAL INFORMATION

What else might be of interest to investors? The report contains page after page of information on the business and its operations. Here is an example of the type of detail that you can learn about a company in the prospectus:

UNIT ECONOMICS

We estimate that the investment for a new store, excluding land and pre-opening costs, is $500,000 for a building of approximately 3,600 square feet and $500,000 for equipment, furniture and fixtures.

The following table provides certain financial information relating to company-owned and franchised stores. Average weekly sales per store are calculated by dividing store revenues by the actual number of sales weeks included in each period. Company-owned stores' operating cash flow is store revenues less all direct store expenses other than depreciation expenses.

	YEAR ENDED		
	FEBRUARY 1, 1998	JANUARY 31, 1999	JANUARY 30, 2000
In thousands			
Average weekly sales per store:			
Company-owned.........................	$ 42	$ 47	$ 54
Franchised.................................	23	28	38
Company-owned stores' operating cash flow as a percentage of store revenues......	19.3%	20.3%	23.2%

Average weekly sales for company-owned stores are higher than for franchised stores due to the lower average weekly sales volumes of older associate stores that are included in the franchised stores' calculations. However, franchised stores' average weekly sales have been increasing as higher-volume area developer stores become a larger proportion of the franchised store base. Additionally, new area developer stores' sales are principally on-premises sales, which have higher operating margins than off-premises sales. Company-owned and associate stores generate a significant percentage of revenues from lower-margin off-premises sales.

STORE OPERATIONS. Our new stores are approximately 3,600 square feet. They are equipped with automated doughnut-making equipment capable of making approximately 240 dozen doughnuts per hour. This capacity can support sales in excess of $100,000 per week.

We learn a little bit here about the bakery business: $1 million will get you the store and equipment; the stores crank out up to 240 dozen donuts an hour; and each store is capable of turning out more than $100,000 worth of donuts per week. We also learned that, on average, company stores generate about $58,000 a week in revenue, while the older franchised stores turn out about $38,000 worth of donuts a week.

Will any of that information help you make a better decision on Krispy Kreme stock? Not necessarily, but it's nice to know everything you can about the companies you're investing in. And you can find a tremendous amount of information in the prospectus and registration statement—who runs the company, how they are compensated, what the company's plans for growth and marketing are, and what risk factors the company will face.

There may be one other test you'll want to do for Krispy Kreme, however—the taste test. Bite into a Krispy Kreme before you invest. I recommend the *Original Glazed*.

COMBING THE 10-Q FOR THE LATEST QUARTERLY DEVELOPMENTS

INVESTORS AND ANALYSTS often wait with baited breath for the upcoming release of corporate 10-Q reports. Those quarterly earnings reports—and the comments that sometimes accompany them from company executives—can make a stock soar, stumble, or stay the course. They offer an insight into how the company has been performing in recent months, and perhaps a preview of how it may do in the months ahead.

The 10-Q is an unaudited financial report that provides a snapshot of the company's financial position during the year. The 10-Q must be filed for each of the company's first three fiscal quarters within 45 days of the close of the quarter. No 10-Q is due after the fourth quarter because that's when the 10-K and annual reports are filed.

In this chapter, we review recent 10-Q reports from Wal-Mart and Kmart (compare and contrast) to illustrate the type of information available to investors willing to dig deeply into these corporate quarterlies.

We hope to answer several important questions in the financial section of the report:

- Is the company profitable?

- Are its quarterly earnings and revenue up from the same quarter of the previous year?

- Is its cash flow solid?

- Are there other developments that could affect the stock price?

The 10-Q is kind of an abbreviated version of the 10-K. It offers a variety of financial tables, such as income statements, balance sheets, and statements of cash flow, as well as some commentary on the company's performance and operations. The following table of contents from the Kmart 10-Q report provides an idea of the type of information available in a quarterly report:

INDEX

REVIEWING KMART'S INCOME STATEMENT

The first thing you see in most 10-Q reports is the income statement. Kmart's statement of operations (pages 208 and 209) provides information on the company's income for the past three months and the past six months. It's not a pretty picture.

What are we looking for in this statement? Is the company making money? Are its quarterly sales and earnings up from a year earlier? This table also gives returns for the first six months. What are the six-month comparisons?

In Kmart's case, it's a bleak picture of a company going in the wrong direction:

•   Revenues are down for both the three-month period and the six-month period.

•   Gross margins have slipped dramatically, and it has no income—only losses.

•   Its net loss (before a gain for discontinued operations) had also broadened a little for the quarter and a lot for the six-month period.

•   Its per-share loss was about the same as the loss a year earlier, and the loss for the six-month period has grown dramatically.

COMPARING KMART WITH WAL-MART

Let's compare Kmart's figures to Wal-Mart's. You'll see that the two discount giants are going in opposite directions:

WAL-MART STORES, INC. AND SUBSIDIARIES
CONDENSED CONSOLIDATED STATEMENTS OF INCOME
(Unaudited)
(Amounts in millions except per share data)

	Three Months Ended July 31		Six Months Ended July 31,	
	2002	2001	2002	2001
Revenues:				
Net Sales	$ 59,694	$ 52,799	$114,654	$100,851
Other income—net	561	470	1,019	983
	60,255	53,269	115,673	101,834
Costs and expenses:				
Cost of sales	46,639	41,412	89,697	79,262
Operating, selling and general and administrative expenses	10,147	8,893	19,601	17,036
Interest costs:				
Debt	199	284	415	569
Capital leases	63	67	128	135

	57,048	50,656	109,841	97,002
Income before income taxes and minority interest	3,207	2,613	5,832	4,832
Provision for income taxes	1,124	954	2,056	1,764
Income before minority interest	2,083	1,659	3,776	3,068
Minority interest	(45)	(37)	(86)	(67)
Net income	**$ 2,038**	**$ 1,622**	**$ 3,690**	**$ 3,001**

Net income per common share:

Basic net income per common share;

Net income per common share	$ 0.46	$ 0.36	$ 0.83	$ 0.67
Average number of common shares	4,438	4,470	4,445	4,472

Diluted net income per common share;

Net income per common share	$ 0.46	$ 0.36	$ 0.83	$ 0.67
Average number of common shares	4,452	4,486	4,460	4,488

Unlike Kmart, Wal-Mart's numbers are moving in a positive direction:

- Revenues are up for the three-month and six-month periods.

- Net income is up for the three-month and six-month periods.

- Earnings per share were up more than 20 percent for both the three-month and six-month periods.

BREAKING DOWN THE CASH FLOW

Now let's look at the cash flow statement for both retailers to see what else we can learn about their growth momentum. Here is the Kmart report:

CONDENSED CONSOLIDATED STATEMENTS OF CASH FLOWS
(DOLLARS IN MILLIONS)
(UNAUDITED)

	26 WEEKS ENDED	
	JULY 31, 2002	AUGUST 1, 2001
CASH FLOWS FROM OPERATING ACTIVITIES		
Net loss	$(1,826)	$ (610)
Adjustments to reconcile net loss to net cash provided by (used for) operating activities:		

ITEM 1. FINANCIAL STATEMENTS

CONDENSED CONSOLIDATED STATEMENTS OF OPERATIONS

(DOLLARS IN MILLIONS, EXCEPT PER SHARE DATA)

(UNAUDITED)

	13 WEEKS ENDED		26 WEEKS ENDED	
	JULY 31, 2002	AUGUST 1, 2001	JULY 31, 2002	AUGUST 1, 2001
Sales	$ 7,519	$ 8,917	$ 15,158	$ 17,254
Cost of sales, buying and occupancy	6,226	7,253	13,242	14,087
Gross margin	1,293	1,664	1,916	3,167
Selling, general and administrative expenses	1,644	2,004	3,435	3,716
Equity income (loss) in unconsolidated subsidiaries	14	(8)	19	(24)
Charges for BlueLight.com and other	15	92	15	115
Loss before interest, income taxes, reorganization items and dividends on convertible preferred securities of subsidiary trust	(352)	(440)	(1,515)	(688)

208

Interest expense, net (contractual interest for 13 and 26 weeks ended July 31, 2002 was $100 and $202, respectively)	32	88	65	171
Income tax benefit	—	(163)	(12)	(272)
Reorganization items, net	13	—	278	—
Dividends on convertible preferred securities of subsidiary trust, net of income taxes of $0, $6, $0 and $12, respectively (contractual dividend for 13 and 26 weeks ended July 31, 2002 was $18 and $35 net of tax, respectively)	—	12	—	23
Net loss from continuing operations	(397)	(377)	(1,846)	(610)
Gain from discontinued operations	20	—	20	—
Net loss	$ (377)	$ (377)	$ (1,826)	$ (610)
Basic/Diluted loss per common share from continuing operations	$ (0.79)	$ (0.77)	$ (3.67)	$ (1.25)
Basic/Diluted gain per common share from discontinued operations	0.04	—	0.04	—
Basic/Diluted loss per common share	$ (0.75)	$ (0.77)	$ (3.63)	$ (1.25)
Basic/Diluted weighted average shares (millions)	502.7	490.6	502.8	489.6

Cash Flows Kmart (cont'd)

Gain from discontinued operations	(20)	—
Restructuring, impairments and other charges	827	115
Reorganization items, net	278	—
Depreciation and amortization	375	413
Equity (income) loss in unconsolidated subsidiaries	(19)	24
Dividends received from Meldisco	45	51
Changes in Operating Assets and Liabilities:		
Increase in inventories	(127)	(452)
Increase in accounts payable	716	292
Deferred income taxes and taxes payable	(10)	(225)
Other assets	104	158
Other liabilities	107	185
Cash used for store closings and other charges	(131)	(105)
NET CASH PROVIDED BY (USED FOR) OPERATING ACTIVITIES	319	(154)
NET CASH USED FOR REORGANIZATION ITEMS	(50)	—
CASH FLOWS FROM INVESTING ACTIVITIES		
Capital expenditures	(126)	(651)
Investment in BlueLight.com	—	(45)
NET CASH USED FOR INVESTING ACTIVITIES	(126)	(696)
CASH FLOWS FROM FINANCING ACTIVITIES		
Proceeds from issuance of debt	—	1,194
Debt issuance costs	—	(3)
Issuance of common shares	—	28
Payments on debt	(349)	(273)
Payments on capital lease obligations	(36)	(41)
Payments of dividends on preferred securities of subsidiary trust	—	(36)
NET CASH (USED FOR) PROVIDED BY FINANCING ACTIVITIES	(385)	869
NET CHANGE IN CASH AND CASH EQUIVALENTS	(242)	19
CASH AND CASH EQUIVALENTS, BEGINNING OF YEAR	1,245	401
CASH AND CASH EQUIVALENTS, END OF PERIOD	$ 1,003	$ 420

Everything seems to be heading south for Kmart. In addition to its huge net loss for the quarter ($1.826 billion), its cash flows from investing and financing activities also took a dive—and so did its cash and cash equivalents. Once again, we see a company in serious financial trouble.

Now let's look at Wal-Mart's cash flow statement and see how that company weathered the quarter:

WAL-MART STORES, INC. AND SUBSIDIARIES
CONDENSED CONSOLIDATED STATEMENTS OF CASH FLOWS
(Unaudited)
(Amounts in millions)

	Six Months Ended July 31,	
	2002	2001
Cash flows from operating activities:		
Net income	$ 3,690	$ 3,001
Adjustments to reconcile net income to net cash provided by operating activities:		
Depreciation and amortization	1,599	1,481
Increase in inventories	(1,679)	(1,631)
Increase in accounts payable	1,378	539
Other	(14)	(444)
Net cash provided by operating activities	4,974	2,946
Cash flows from investing activities:		
Payments for property, plant & equipment	(4,458)	(3,874)
Other investing activities	276	(53)
Net cash used in investing activities	(4,182)	(3,927)
Cash flows from financing activities:		
Increase (decrease) in commercial paper	713	(1,197)
Proceeds from issuance of long-term debt	1,526	4,141
Dividends paid	(666)	(625)
Payment of long-term debt	(649)	(1,222)
Purchase of Company stock	(1,672)	(254)
Other financing activities	(125)	(115)
Net cash provided by (used in) financing activities	(873)	728
Effect of exchange rates on cash	208	33
Net increase (decrease) in cash and cash equivalents	127	(220)
Cash and cash equivalents at beginning of year	2,161	2,054
Cash and cash equivalents at end of period	**$ 2,288**	**$ 1,834**

Supplemental disclosure of cash flow information:

Income taxes paid	$ 2,618	$ 1,786
Interest paid	553	732
Capital lease obligations incurred	9	29

It was a bit of a different story for Wal-Mart. Unlike Kmart, the company showed solid growth of net income, net cash provided by operations, and cash and cash equivalents for the period. That's exactly what you want to see in a company—particularly one in which you own stock or plan to buy stock.

ONTO THE FOOTNOTES FOR MORE DETAILS

While Wal-Mart seems to be on the right track, there is definitely some negative factors at Kmart. The footnotes in Kmart's 10-Q offer volumes on the company's troubles:

> 3. PROCEEDINGS UNDER CHAPTER 11 OF THE BANKRUPTCY CODE
>
> On January 22, 2002 ("Petition Date"), Kmart and 37 of its U.S. subsidiaries (collectively, the "Debtors") filed voluntary petitions for reorganization under Chapter 11 of the federal bankruptcy laws ("Bankruptcy Code" or "Chapter 11") in the United States Bankruptcy Court for the Northern District of Illinois ("Court").
>
> We decided to seek judicial reorganization based upon a rapid decline in our liquidity resulting from our below-plan sales and earnings performance in the fourth quarter of the 2001 fiscal year, the evaporation of the surety bond market and erosion of supplier confidence. Other factors included intense competition in the discount retailing industry, unsuccessful sales and marketing initiatives, the continuing recession, and recent capital market volatility. As a debtor-in-possession, Kmart is authorized to continue to operate as an ongoing business, but may not engage in transactions outside the ordinary course of business without the approval of the Court, after notice and an opportunity for a hearing.

Here we learn that Kmart has entered into Chapter 11 bankruptcy due to a variety of factors, including:

- "Below-plan sales and earnings performance"

- Evaporation of the surety bond market

- Erosion of supplier confidence

- Intense competition in the discount retailing industry

- Unsuccessful sales and marketing initiatives

- The continuing recession

- Capital market volatility

In other words, nothing has been going right for Kmart. But how does the company plan to right the ship? The company reveals its plans in another section of the 10Q:

2002 COST REDUCTION INITIATIVE

On August 19, 2002, we announced a cost reduction initiative aimed at realigning our organization to reflect our current business needs following the completion of the 283 store closures. We eliminated approximately 400 positions at our corporate headquarters and approximately 50 positions nationally that provide corporate support. As a result of the job eliminations we recorded a charge of $15 in accordance with SFAS No. 112, "Employers' Accounting for Postemployment Benefits." The charge includes severance, outplacement services and continuation of healthcare benefits in accordance with the severance plan provisions of our Key Employee Retention Plan ("KERP"), which was approved by the Court in March 2002. This charge is included in Charges for BlueLight.com and other in our unaudited Condensed Consolidated Statements of Operations.

We learn the company has closed 283 stores and laid off 400 people at the home office and another 50 in the field. Will the moves keep Kmart from going out of business altogether—or just delay the doom for a few more months? The company is not ready to predict an outcome, but it does point out in the 10-Q that a number of factors are stacked against its recovery:

The ability of Kmart to continue as a going concern is predicated upon numerous issues, including our ability to achieve the following:

- developing a long-term strategy and/or market niche to revitalize our business and return Kmart to profitability;

- taking appropriate action to offset the negative effects that the Chapter 11 filing has had on our business, including the loss in customer traffic and the impairment of vendor relations;

- operating within the framework of our DIP Credit Facility, including its limitations on capital expenditures, our ability to generate cash flows from operations or seek other sources of financing and the availability of projected vendor credit terms;

- attracting, motivating and/or retaining key executives and associates; and

– developing and, thereafter, having confirmed by the Court, a plan of reorganization.

These challenges are in addition to those operational and competitive challenges faced by Kmart in connection with our business as a discount retailer.

A plan of reorganization could materially change the amounts reported in the financial statements, which do not give effect to all adjustments of the carrying value of assets or liabilities that might be necessary as a consequence of a plan of reorganization.

So Kmart has a plan, and it recognizes the difficulty of turning the business around. The future performance of its stock will depend on management's ability to make the right moves to revitalize the company. But with growing competition in the discount business, Kmart's prospects seem questionable at best. There is certainly the possibility that the company will recover and return to profitability—at which point shareholders who stuck with the company through the bad times would be rewarded for their loyalty. But for investors looking for a strong, growing company to invest in, Kmart would not seem to be a logical pick.

Wal-Mart, on the other hand, seems to be going the right direction, based on its growing earnings per share. But what else can we learn about Wal-Mart that might give us a little more insight into the financial strength of the company? A look at the company's business-segment breakdown could help:

Net sales by operating segment were as follows (in millions):

	Three Months Ended July 31,		Six Months Ended July 31,	
	2002	2001	2002	2001
Wal-Mart Stores	$ 38,641	$ 33,870	$ 74,058	$ 64,621
Sam's Club	7,939	7,270	15,234	13,805
International	9,691	8,362	18,683	15,998
Other	3,423	3,297	6,679	6,427
Total Net Sales	$ 59,694	$ 52,799	$ 114,654	$ 100,851

This table shows a very solid company. Sales for every segment of the company's business are up for both the three-month and the six-month periods. That's a strong sign. But how were profits across the segments? The following table expands on information we already saw in the income statement:

Operating profit and reconciliation to income before income taxes and minority interest are as follows (in millions):

	Three Months Ended July 31,		Six Months Ended July 31,	
	2002	2001	2002	2001
Wal-Mart Stores	$ 3,046	$ 2,600	$ 5,600	$ 4,799
Sam's Club	275	267	493	485
International	510	315	891	530
Other	(362)	(218)	(609)	(278)
Operating profit	$ 3,469	$ 2,964	$ 6,375	$ 5,536
Interest expense	262	351	543	704
Income before income taxes and minority interest	$ 3,207	$ 2,613	$ 5,832	$ 4,832

We see in this table that all three key segments, "Wal-Mart Stores," "Sam's Club," and "International" showed gains in operating profit for both the three-month and the six-month periods. The most dramatic gains came in the company's international operations, which were up more than 60 percent for both the three-month and six-month periods.

What can we learn in the footnotes about Wal-Mart's operations? The company tells us exactly what led to its sales and earnings increases in the previous quarter:

The increase in the Wal-Mart Stores segment's operating income for the second quarter of fiscal 2003 resulted primarily from gross margin improvements and a reduction in operating expenses as a percentage of sales.

The Sam's Clubs segment sales increase for the quarter ended July 31, 2002 resulted from the Sam's Clubs segment's continued expansion activities and sales increases in comparable clubs.

The International segment sales for the quarter ended July 31, 2002 when compared to segment sales in the same period in fiscal 2002 increased as a result of continued expansion activities within the segment and due to an expansion of the types of products and services offered. During the second quarter of fiscal 2003, expansion in the International segment consisted of the opening of 20 units. International sales as a percentage of total Company sales increased from 15.8% in the quarter ended July 31, 2001, to 16.2% for the quarter ended July 31, 2002. This increase stemmed largely from the results of the international expansion program, and was partially offset by a $50 million negative impact of currency conversion on segment sales.

With growth across the board in its three key segments—particularly the international operations, Wal-Mart would seem to be the logical choice over Kmart for any investor looking for a retail stock that's headed in the right direction.

FUTURE OUTLOOK

One section of the 10-Q that investors and analysts are particularly interested in is the future outlook. Not every 10-Q contains a section on future prospects, but those 10-Qs that do draw the close scrutiny of investors.

A sterling earnings report may do very little for a company's stock price if its future outlook calls for slowing sales ahead. On the other hand, a tepid earnings report accompanied by a very positive future outlook report could cause a dramatic jump in the stock price.

Neither Wal-Mart nor Kmart included a future outlook section in their 10-Qs. Instead, let's look at the future outlook section from another retailer, Best Buy:

> Looking forward to the second quarter, we are projecting earnings of $0.30 to $0.32 per diluted share compared with $0.26 per diluted share in the second quarter of fiscal 2002. An anticipated 23% to 24% increase in revenues, as a result of new stores and a comparable store sales gain of 4% to 5%, is expected to drive the earnings increase.

> We anticipate that our gross margin rate will decline by approximately 0.3% of revenues, reflecting sales mix changes at Musicland stores (principally increased revenues from lower margin DVD movies and video gaming) as well as continued softness in prerecorded music sales. We also expect revenues from lower-margin computers to increase as a percentage of our sales mix in the second quarter. We expect these changes will be somewhat offset by the continued strength in higher-margin digital products revenues. The SG&A rate, in the second quarter, is expected to remain flat compared with that of the prior fiscal year.

> Second quarter earnings are expected to be reduced by approximately $0.04 per diluted share as a result of our investments in the remerchandising of Sam Goody stores, launching Best Buy stores in Canada and our profit improvement initiatives at Future Shop stores.

This section gives a mixed message. Earnings were expected to continue to climb, but the company's gross margin rate was expected to take a small dip due to a variety of factors, such as softness in the prerecorded music sales. The usually high-flying Best Buy looks to be slowed a bit by the recession, but earnings are expected to keep climbing thanks both to new store openings and comparable store gains.

How is that likely to affect Best Buy's stock price? That depends on what analysts had expected from the company prior to the report. In the first paragraph, we see that earnings per share were expected to climb from 26 cents a share to between 30 and 32 cents—a gain of about 15 to 20 percent. If that was within the range that analysts expected, it wouldn't have a significant affect on the stock price. But if it was higher than expected, it could have pushed the stock price up, or if it was lower than previous projections it could cause the stock to drop.

In reality, Best Buy's 10-Q had little effect on the stock price. But a Form 8-K current report the company issued about a month later had a significant effect on the stock price. Here is the key section from Best Buy's 8-K:

Best Buy Lowers Outlook
for Second Quarter Based on Sales

MINNEAPOLIS, Aug. 8, 2002—Best Buy Co., Inc. (NYSE: BBY) today lowered its earnings outlook for its fiscal second quarter, ending Aug. 31, 2002, to a range of 17 to 21 cents per diluted share, compared with the Company's prior guidance of 30 to 32 cents per diluted share. The First Call second-quarter consensus estimate as of Aug. 7, 2002, was 32 cents per diluted share. The Company's earnings in the second quarter of fiscal 2002 were 26 cents per diluted share. The Company also said that it expects its comparable store sales comparison for the second quarter to be modestly positive, versus prior guidance of a 4- to 5-percent gain.

In revising its outlook, the Company cited declines in consumer confidence resulting in flat comparable store sales in the past four weeks, which reflected general softening across most product categories.

In the announcement, Best Buy lowered its earnings expectations from a range of 30 to 32 cents a share down to a range of 17 to 21 cents a share. That's a significant drop. How did it affect the stock price? On the day of the announcement, Best Buy stock plunged about 50 percent—from about $30 to about $20 a share. Obviously, a change in future guidance can have a significant impact on the stock price.

The 10-Q quarterly report can provide an excellent glimpse of a company's ongoing financial performance. Although it does not offer quite the comprehensive coverage that the 10-K provides, it does present an important assessment of the company's progress over the course of the year. If you're considering investing in a company, checking out its latest 10-Q report is an essential step in the analysis process.

CHAPTER

10

THE 11-K: EMPLOYEE SAVINGS AND INVESTMENTS

THE 11-K FORM IS AN ANNUAL REPORT for employee stock purchase plans and similar savings and investment plans. All publicly
traded companies are required to file an 11-K annually with the
SEC.

The 11-K may not hold a lot of interest for investors. The
information it contains is fairly routine. But if you have a general interest in
the company, or if you're interested in working for the company, you may find
the 11-K particularly helpful.

In this chapter, we take a close look at the 11-K report from the Procter &
Gamble Company. In fact, many companies like P&G file several 11-K
reports—one for the main company and others for its subsidiaries and other
groups. In all, P&G filed five different 11-K reports in 2002, including one for
its Richardson-Vicks subsidiary, one for its Procter & Gamble Pharmaceuticals division, one for its Commercial Company Employees' Savings Plan, one
for its "Subsidiaries Savings and Investment Plan," and one for its "Subsidiaries Savings Plan." For our example, we'll review the company's "Subsidiaries Savings and Investment Plan."

Most 11-Ks start with a heading and table of contents:

THE PROCTER & GAMBLE
SUBSIDIARIES SAVINGS AND
INVESTMENT PLAN

FINANCIAL STATEMENTS FOR THE YEARS ENDED
DECEMBER 31, 2001 AND 2000 AND SUPPLEMENTAL
SCHEDULE AS OF DECEMBER 31, 2001
AND INDEPENDENT AUDITORS' REPORT

THE PROCTER & GAMBLE SUBSIDIARIES SAVINGS AND
INVESTMENT PLAN

TABLE OF CONTENTS

SUPPLEMENTAL SCHEDULES OMITTED—The follow-
ing schedules were omitted because of the absence of conditions under which they are required or due to their inclusion
in information filed by The Procter & Gamble

Master Savings Trust:

Reportable Transactions

Assets Acquired and Disposed of Within the Plan Year

Party-in-Interest Transactions

Obligations in Default

Leases in Default

The table of contents gives you a quick take on the information available
in the report. Generally, however, the reports are fairly short, so you can easily
skim through the reports to find and read the key elements.

AUDITOR'S LETTER

A letter from an auditing company provides an assessment of the savings and investment plan, and generally offers a tacit approval of the plan and the financial information reported by the company. Here is the auditor's letter for the P&G report:

INDEPENDENT AUDITORS' REPORT

To The Procter & Gamble Master Savings Plan Committee:

We have audited the accompanying statements of net assets available for benefits of The Procter & Gamble Subsidiaries Savings and Investment Plan (the "Plan") as of December 31, 2001 and 2000, and the related statements of changes in net assets available for benefits for the years then ended. These financial statements are the responsibility of the Plan's management. Our responsibility is to express an opinion on these financial statements based on our audits.

We conducted our audits in accordance with auditing standards generally accepted in the United States of America. Those standards require that we plan and perform the audit to obtain reasonable assurance about whether the financial statements are free of material misstatement. An audit includes examining, on a test basis, evidence supporting the amounts and disclosures in the financial statements. An audit also includes assessing the accounting principles used and significant estimates made by management, as well as evaluating the overall financial statement presentation. We believe that our audits provide areasonable basis for our opinion.

In our opinion, such financial statements present fairly, in all material respects, the net assets available for benefits of the Plan as of December 31, 2001 and 2000 and the changes in net assets available for benefits for the years then ended in conformity with accounting principles generally accepted in the United States of America.

Our audits were conducted for the purpose of forming an opinion on the basic financial statements taken as a whole. The supplemental schedule listed in the Table of Contents is presented for the purpose of additional analysis and is not a required part of the basic financial statements, but is supplementary information required by the Department of Labor's Rules and Regulations for Reporting and Disclosure under the Employee Retirement Income Security Act of 1974. The schedule is the responsibility of the Plan's management. Such schedule has been subjected to the auditing procedures applied in our audit of the basic 2001 financial statements, and, in our opinion, is fairly stated in all material respects in relation to the basic financial statements taken as a whole.

DELOITTE & TOUCHE LLP
June 10, 2002

As expected, the letter gives a passing grade to the company's plan. The key paragraph was the third paragraph, in which the auditor said "In our opinion, such financial statements present fairly, in all material respects, the net assets available for benefits of the Plan..."

In the vast majority of cases, that's all you need to see to be assured that the information is in compliance with standard regulations. If the auditor has a problem with the numbers or other aspects of the plan, it would be mentioned prominently in the letter, and that is something that should definitely be of concern—particularly if you're interested in working for the company or in investing in the stock.

NET ASSETS

After the letter from the auditor, the next thing you'll see is usually the "Statements of Net Assets Available for Benefits." It reports total assets and liabilities for the past two years, as well as net assets available for benefits, as the following example from P&G illustrates:

STATEMENTS OF NET ASSETS AVAILABLE FOR BENEFITS
AS OF DECEMBER 31, 2001 AND 2000

	2001	2000
ASSETS:		
Investment in The Procter & Gamble Master		
Savings Trust, at fair value	$ 28,986,204	$ 5,609,933
Loans to participants	869,392	56,681
Investment income receivable	33,288	892
Total assets	29,888,884	5,667,506
LIABILITIES—Accrued administrative expenses	21,192	4,946
NET ASSETS AVAILABLE FOR BENEFITS	$ 29,867,692	$ 5,662,560

See notes to financial statements.

CHANGES IN NET ASSETS

If there have been any changes in net assets for benefits, that would be reported next. Here is a change-in-net-assets table from the P&G 11-K report:

STATEMENTS OF CHANGES IN NET ASSETS AVAILABLE FOR BENEFITS
FOR THE YEARS ENDED DECEMBER 31, 2001 AND 2000

	2001	2000
ADDITIONS:		
Investment income (loss):		
Equity in net earnings (losses) of		
The Procter & Gamble Master Savings Trust	$ 779,661	$ (482,315)
Interest	77,313	5,789
Total changes	856,974	(476,526)
DEDUCTIONS:		
Distributions and withdrawals to participants	2,247,317	724,897
Administrative expenses	67,409	20,370
Total deductions	2,314,726	745,267
NET DECREASE PRIOR TO TRANSFER	(1,457,752)	(1,221,793)
TRANSFER FROM AFFILIATED PLANS	25,662,884	
NET ASSETS AVAILABLE FOR BENEFITS:		
Beginning of year	5,662,560	6,884,353
End of year	$ 29,867,692	$ 5,662,560

See notes to financial statements.

The 11-K report also includes a detailed description of the plan, including contributions and withdrawals, distribution, loans, and administration. The following plan summary comes from the P&G 11-K report:

1.   DESCRIPTION OF THE PLAN

The following brief description of The Procter & Gamble Subsidiaries Savings and Investment Plan (the "Plan") is provided for general information purposes only. Participants should refer to the Plan agreement for more complete information.

GENERAL—The Plan was established effective April 1, 1989 and is subject to the provisions of the Employee Retirement Income Security Act of 1974 (ERISA). The Plan is a defined contribution plan covering substantially all employees of Maryland Club Foods, Inc., all eligible employees of Shulton, Inc., former employees of Fisher Nut Company who were members of the Twin Cities Bakery and Confectionery Workers Union, Local No. 22, and all eligible employees of Dover Baby Wipes Company and Giorgio Beverly

GENERAL (cont'd)—Hills, Inc. Maryland Club Foods, Inc. was sold in May 1994 and Fisher Nut Company was dissolved in July 1998. Effective March 14, 1996, the Shulton Savings Plan and Fisher Nut Savings Plan were merged into the Maryland Club Foods, Inc. Retirement Savings Plan and The Procter & Gamble Company ("Company"), plan sponsor, changed the Plan name to The Procter & Gamble Subsidiaries Savings and Investment Plan. Effective May 1, 2001, the Dover Savings and Investment Plan ("Dover") and the Giorgio Employee Savings Plan ("Giorgio") were merged into the Plan.

CONTRIBUTIONS AND VESTING—Effective April 1996, all contributions to the Plan were suspended and all participants became fully vested. Dover and Giorgio contributions were suspended prior to merging with the Plan.

DISTRIBUTIONS—The Plan provides for benefits to be paid upon retirement, disability, death, or separation other than retirement as defined by the Plan document. Plan benefits may be made in a lump sum of cash or shares of common stock or in installment payments over a period not to exceed 120 months. Retired or terminated employees shall commence benefit payments upon attainment of age 70-1/2.

WITHDRAWALS—A participant may withdraw any portion of after-tax contributions once in any six-month period. Participants who have attained age 59-1/2 or have demonstrated financial hardship may withdraw all or any portion of their before-tax contributions once in any six-month period.

PLAN TERMINATION—Subsequent to December 31, 2001, the Company terminated the Plan subject to the provisions of ERISA (Note 6).

ADMINISTRATION—The Plan is administered by the Master Savings Plan Committee consisting of four members appointed by the Board of Directors of the Company, except for duties specifically vested in the trustee, PNC Bank, Ohio, N.A. ("PNC Bank"), who is also appointed by the Board of Directors of the Company.

TRANSFER FROM AFFILIATED PLANS—Amounts represent account balances of Dover and Giorgio Company employees transferred into the Plan.

LOANS—The Plan allows participants to borrow funds from their accounts in certain circumstances up to maximum amounts specified in the Plan agreement. Loans are repayable in at least monthly installments of principal and interest over a maximum term of five years (fifteen years if the loan is used to purchase a primary residence).

Principal and interest paid is credited to applicable funds in the borrower's account. Upon termination or retirement, the outstanding loan balance will be treated as a distribution to the participant.

PARTICIPANT ACCOUNTS AND INVESTMENT OPTIONS— Each participant account is credited with an allocation of Plan earnings. The benefit to which a participant is entitled is the vested benefit that can be provided from the participant's account. Participants may allocate their accounts in one or all of the following investment options offered by the Plan (Note 4):

ENHANCED CASH FUND—The prospectus indicates that this fund invests in short to medium length maturity, interest-bearing instruments.

COMPANY STOCK FUND—A fund that invests in shares of The Procter & Gamble Company common stock.

ACTIVE FIXED-INCOME CORE FUND—The prospectus indicates that this fund invests in a diversified portfolio of publicly and privately traded corporate, government, international, and mortgage backed bonds.

DISCIPLINED EQUITY FUND—The prospectus indicates that this fund invests in equity securities of approximately 300 domestic, large company stocks.

DIVERSIFIED FUND—The prospectus indicates that this fund invests in a balanced portfolio consisting of both equity and fixed securities.

INTERNATIONAL EQUITY FUND—The prospectus indicates that this fund invests in a diversified portfolio of equity securities of foreign corporations.

SMALL COMPANY EQUITY II FUND—The prospectus indicates that this fund invests in a portfolio of equity securities issued by small companies.

The 11-K also provides information on the accounting polices of the plan. The following example comes from the P&G 11-K report:

2. SUMMARY OF SIGNIFICANT ACCOUNTING POLICIES

BASIS OF ACCOUNTING—The accompanying financial statements have been prepared on the accrual basis of accounting and the Plan's net assets and transactions are recorded at fair value. The Plan's investment in Company common stock is valued at the closing price on an established security exchange. The Plan's investment

BASIS OF ACCOUNTING (cont'd)—funds (funds) are valued by the fund manager, JP Morgan Investment Management, Inc., based upon the fair value of the funds' underlying investments. Income from investments is recognized when earned and is allocated to each plan participating in The Procter & Gamble Master Savings Trust (Master Trust) by PNC Bank and to each participant's account by the Plan's recordkeeper.

EXPENSES OF THE PLAN—Investment management expenses were paid by the Plan in 2001 and 2000. All other fees were paid by the Company.

USE OF ESTIMATES—The preparation of financial statements in conformity with accounting principles generally accepted in the United States of America requires management to make estimates and assumptions that affect the amounts reported in the financial statements and accompanying notes. Actual results could differ from those estimates.

The Plan invests in Company common stock and in various mutual funds which include investments in U.S. Government securities, corporate debt instruments, and corporate stocks. Investment securities, in general, are exposed to various risks, such as interest rate, credit, and overall market volatility. Due to the level of risk associated with certain investment securities, it is reasonably possible that changes in the values of investment securities will occur in the near term and that such changes could materially affect the amounts reported in the statements of net assets available for plan benefits.

ACCOUNTING POLICIES—On January 1, 2001, the Plan adopted Statement of Financial Accounting Standards (SFAS) No. 133, Accounting for Derivative Instruments and Hedging Activities, as amended by SFAS No. 138, Accounting for Certain Derivative Instruments and Certain Hedging Activities. SFAS No. 133 establishes accounting and reporting standards for derivative instruments and for hedging activities. It requires that all derivatives, including those embedded in other contracts, be recognized as either assets or liabilities and that those financial instruments be measured at fair value. The accounting for changes in the fair value of derivatives depends on their intended use and designation. The adoption of this standard did not have a material effect on the Plan's financial statements.

Finally, the 11-K report gives you a breakdown of the investments in the plan, as illustrated in Figures 10-1 through 10-4, which include tables from the P&G 11-K report.

FIGURE 10-1

Investments, at fair value, held by the Master Trust at
December 31, 2001 are summarized as follows:

	COMPANY STOCK FUND	JP MORGAN FUNDS	TOTAL
<S>	<C>	<C>	<C>
The Procter & Gamble Company common stock	$ 64,337,834		$ 64,337,834
Mutual funds		$123,901,015	123,901,015
Short-term investments	4,291	8,264	12,555
Accrued interest and dividends		39,992	39,992
Total investments at fair value	$ 64,342,125	$123,949,271	$188,291,396
Plan's investment in Master Trust	$ 7,567,250	$ 21,418,954	$ 28,986,204
Plan's percentage ownership interest in Master Trust	12 %	17 %	15 %

FIGURE 10-2

Investment income (loss) from the Master Trust for the
year ended December 31, 2001 is summarized as follows:

	COMPANY STOCK FUND	JP MORGAN FUNDS	TOTAL
<S>	<C>	<C>	<C>
Net appreciation (depreciation) in fair value of investments	$ 221,329	$ (9,489,678)	$ (9,268,349)
Dividends	1,258,927		1,258,927
Interest	2,848	110,122	112,970
Total	$ 1,483,104	$ (9,379,556)	$ (7,896,452)
Plan's equity in net earnings (losses) of Master Trust	$ 1,840,113	$ (1,060,452)	$ 779,661

FIGURE 10-3

Investments, at fair value, held by the Master Trust
at December 31, 2000 are summarized as follows:

	COMPANY STOCK FUND	JP MORGAN FUNDS	TOTAL
<S>	<C>	<C>	<C>
The Procter & Gamble Company common stock	$ 70,010,072		$ 70,010,072
Mutual funds		$147,674,640	147,674,640
Short-term investments	1,799	3,796	5,595
Accrued interest and dividends	139	1,912	2,051
Total investments at fair value	$ 70,012,010	$147,680,348	$217,692,358
Plan's investment in Master Trust	$ 625,519	$ 4,984,414	$ 5,609,933
Plan's percentage ownership interest in Master Trust	1 %	3 %	3 %

FIGURE 10-4

```
Investment loss from the Master Trust for the year
  ended December 31, 2000 is summarized as follows:
```

	COMPANY STOCK FUND	JP MORGAN FUNDS	TOTAL
<S>	<C>	<C>	<C>
Net depreciation in fair value of investments	$(25,585,173)	$(8,079,528)	$(33,664,701)
Dividends	1,183,956		1,183,956
Interest	4,967	10,478	15,445
Total	$(24,396,250)	$(8,069,050)	$(32,465,300)
Plan's equity in net losses of Master Trust	$ (235,451)	$ (246,864)	$ (482,315)

The preceding tables show investment and gains and losses for the past two years. In full, the 11-K report can give you a detailed view of a company's employee investment and savings plan. It may not help you decide whether the company's stock is worth buying, but the 11-K is well worth keeping an eye on if you work for a company—or plan to—or do business with that company.

11

THE 8-K: REPORTING SIGNIFICANT CHANGES AND DEVELOPMENTS

A NYTIME A COMPANY TAKES SIGNIFICANT ACTION of importance to shareholders, the company has to report that information publicly. Often, they will do it in the annual 10-K report or the quarterly 10-Q report. But if the action takes place after the 10-Q or 10-K are issued, the company needs to file a Form 8-K to provide details of the changes.

The 8-K would typically provide more details on specific corporate action than either the 10-K or the 10-Q. The SEC describes the 8-K as a *"current report* that is used to report the occurrence of any material events or corporate changes which are of importance to investors or security holders and previously have not been reported by the registrant. It provides more current information on certain specified events than would Forms 10-Q or 10-K."

It's not unusual for a company to issue several 8-K reports over the course of a year. For instance, IBM issued half a dozen 8-Ks in 2001 and more than a dozen in 2002. So if you're following a stock you own or are interested in buying, it may be worth the effort to follow the 8-K reports to keep up on the company's latest developments.

The 8-K is filed for several important purposes:

- Announcement of an acquisition or sale

- Changes in control of registrant

- Bankruptcy or receivership

- Changes in the company's certifying accountant

- Resignations of the company's directors

- Financial statements and exhibits

- Change in fiscal year

- Other materially important events

Let's look at some of IBM's recent 8-K reports to see the type of actions that might be covered in an 8-K report. (Later, we look at some 8-Ks from Enron.) In the following Form 8-K, IBM announces the sale of its disk drive operation to Hitachi, Ltd.:

Item 5. Other Events

The company announced on June 4, 2002, the decision to sell its disk drive operations to Hitachi, Ltd. which under generally accepted accounting principles will be accounted for as a discontinued operation.

The quarterly consolidated financial results for 2001 and the first quarter of 2002 were previously filed on Form 8-K on July 9, 2002 to conform with this accounting treatment. The company is publishing consolidated financial earnings results for 2001 through 1997 in order to facilitate an analysis by users of the company's financial statements under this format. The financial results reported as discontinued operations include the external original equipment manufacturer (OEM) hard disk drive business and charges related to hard disk drives used in the company's e-server and e-storage products that were recorded in the Technology segment. The discontinued operations results do not reflect hard disk drive shipments to IBM internal customers which are eliminated in the company's consolidated financial results. These results are included in Exhibit 99.1 of this Form 8-K. In addition, the Computation of Ratio of Income from Continuing Operations to Fixed Charges is also presented for the years 2001 through 1997 in Exhibit 99.2 of this Form 8-K.

Along with the (preceding) announcement of the sale of the disk drive operation (above), the 8-K also included the financial results of its disk drive operation over the previous five years.

Here's another 8-K filing from IBM, this time to announce the purchase of PricewaterhouseCoopers' global business consulting and technology services unit. But unlike our first 8-K sample, which reads like a legal filing written by an attorney, this 8-K filing was submitted in the form of a press release. We've included just a portion of the full release:

IBM TO ACQUIRE PwC CONSULTING
Combining Business Insight and Technology to Help Clients
Drive Greater Business Returns

ARMONK, N.Y. AND NEW YORK, N.Y., July 30, 2002 . . . IBM and PricewaterhouseCoopers today announced that IBM would acquire PricewaterhouseCoopers' global business consulting and technology services unit, PwC Consulting. The combination of IBM and PwC Consulting will create a powerful, unmatched capability to help clients solve their business issues, exploiting world-class technology for improved business performance.

The two companies have signed a definitive agreement approved by IBM's board of directors and PricewaterhouseCoopers' leadership board. Under the terms, IBM will pay PricewaterhouseCoopers an estimated purchase price of $3.5 billion in cash and stock. The transaction is subject to regulatory approvals and approval of local PwC firms through votes of their partners, and is expected to be concluded around the end of the third quarter. PwC Consulting will no longer pursue its planned initial public offering.

"The client is the driving force behind today's announcement with PwC," said Samuel J. Palmisano, IBM president and chief executive officer. "Clients are not only looking for innovative ideas to improve their businesses, they are seeking a partner with deep business expertise and the ability to exploit leading, open standards-based technology to turn these ideas into bottom-line business benefits. This acquisition underscores our commitment to this strategy.

"Our consulting and services professionals will provide a powerful capability, beginning with business innovation and extending through implementation, to help clients improve their competitiveness and drive sustained growth and profitability," Palmisano said. "Together with the world-class innovations of IBM Research and our business partner offerings, this new business unit will deliver comprehensive end-to-end business and technology solutions."

Samuel A. DiPiazza, Jr., chief executive officer of Pricewaterhouse-Coopers, said, "This transaction fulfills our commitment to fully separate PwC Consulting from PwC. It will unleash the consulting unit from the regulatory restraints of our industry, and will allow the business to reach its full potential. Combining PwC Consulting with IBM not only fully achieves the goals we set for the separation, it provides clients and our professionals with greater opportunities and access to innovative solutions."

(Continued)

PwC Consulting, with estimated fiscal-year 2002 consulting revenues of approximately $4.9 billion, excluding client reimbursables, and some 30,000 employees, will be combined with the Business Innovation Services unit of IBM Global Services, creating a new global unit. Ginni Rometty, currently general manager of IBM Global Services—Americas, will become general manager of the new unit, reporting to Doug Elix, senior vice president and group executive, IBM Global Services.

This new global business unit will pull from the extensive portfolio of IBM capabilities to offer clients innovative, integrated solutions through business and technology consulting, industry insight and business process expertise together with the comprehensive services capabilities of the rest of IBM Global Services. . .

The article included additional information on both companies, and some other quotes from company executives. Also included in the same filing was the transcript from the press conference announcing the acquisition hosted by IBM. Here's an excerpt from that release:

Thank you, Mandy. Good afternoon. This is Hervey Parke, Vice President of Investor Relations for IBM, and thank you all for joining us. . .

At this time, let me turn the call over to John Joyce, IBM's Senior Vice President and Chief Financial Officer.

Thanks, Hervey. Good afternoon, and welcome to our conference call announcing the acquisition of PwC Consulting.

Back at our November and May Security Analysts meetings in New York City, Sam Palmisano spoke about an underlying change in the IT industry.

To remain competitive in their own markets, and to invest in Information Technology wisely, our customers are looking for more than just hardware and software products. They want to know how an integrated technology plan can leverage their business plan, driving efficiencies through the transformation of their own business processes.

And this is the focus of IBM's strategy, to deliver superior business value to clients through the integration of technology and business process insight.

Today's announcement of the acquisition of PwC Consulting underscores IBM's commitment to this strategy—accelerates it—and uniquely positions IBM with capabilities to deliver superior business value and winning IT infrastructure solutions to our customers. . .

The briefing, directed to IBM shareholders and analysts, continued with more details on the significance of the acquisition and the potential of the business IBM was buying from PriceWaterhouseCooper.

ENRON'S 8-KS

Let's look at the type of 8-K reports that Enron filed during its financial collapse in 2001.

The company filed two 8-Ks in the first half of 2001. The first was a press release, which announced the company's plans to issue convertible bonds.

The second was a 63-page report on its operations similar to a 10-K, with detailed descriptions of its business segments and a wealth of financial data. It even included a letter from its auditor, Arthur Anderson.

As professional and objective as the letter appeared, it was one of the documents that ultimately put Arthur Anderson out of business. By endorsing Enron's financial statements—which later proved to be false—Arthur Anderson helped sully its own reputation and seal its own fate. Here is the letter (one of many that Arthur Anderson wrote approving of Enron's accounting policies over a span of several years):

REPORT OF INDEPENDENT PUBLIC ACCOUNTANTS
To the Shareholders and Board of Directors of Enron Corp.:

We have audited the accompanying consolidated balance sheet of Enron Corp. (an Oregon corporation) and subsidiaries as of December 31, 2000 and 1999, and the related consolidated statements of income, comprehensive income, cash flows and changes in shareholders' equity for each of the three years in the period ended December 31, 2000. These financial statements are the responsibility of Enron Corp.'s management. Our responsibility is to express an opinion on these financial statements based on our audits.

We conducted our audits in accordance with auditing standards generally accepted in the United States. Those standards require that we plan and perform the audit to obtain reasonable assurance about whether the financial statements are free of material misstatement. An audit includes examining, on a test basis, evidence supporting the amounts and disclosures in the financial statements. An audit also includes assessing the accounting principles used and significant estimates made by management, as well as evaluating the overall financial statement presentation. We believe that our audits provide a reasonable basis for our opinion.

In our opinion, the financial statements referred to above present fairly, in all material respects, the financial position of Enron Corp. and subsidiaries as of December 31, 2000 and 1999, and the results of their operations, cash flows and changes in shareholders' equity for each of the three years in the period ended December 31, 2000, in conformity with accounting principles generally accepted in the United States.

As discussed in Note 18 to the consolidated financial statements, Enron Corp. and subsidiaries changed its method of accounting for costs of start-up activities and its method of accounting for certain contracts involved in energy trading and risk management activities in the first quarter of 1999.

Arthur Andersen LLP

Enron did not issue another 8-K until late in the year—well after the company's stock took a precipitous tumble. And that 8-K had nothing to do with the company's troubles. It announced a revolving credit line for one of its subsidiaries. Another 8-K, issued several days later, announced a merger agreement between Enron and Dynergy.

The company's final 8-K of the year, issued in December of 2001, was a bombshell—an announcement that the company had filed for bankruptcy. Here is that announcement:

ITEM 3. Bankruptcy or Receivership.

(a) On December 2, 2001, Enron Corp. (the "Company") and certain other subsidiaries of the Company (collectively, the "Debtors") each filed voluntary petitions for relief under chapter 11 of title 11 of the United States Code (the "Bankruptcy Code") in the United States Bankruptcy Court for the Southern District of New York (the "Bankruptcy Court") (Case Nos. 01-16033, 01-16034, 01-16035, 01-16036, 01-16037, 01-16038, 01-16039, 01-16040, 01-16041, 01-16042, 01-16043, 01-16044, 01-16045 and 01-16046). Between December 3, 2001 and December 6, 2001, additional subsidiaries of the Company each filed voluntary petitions for relief under chapter 11 of the Bankruptcy Code in the Bankruptcy Court (Case Nos. 01-16048, 01-16076, 01-16078, 01-16080, 01-16109, 01-16110 and 01-16111). As of midnight, Eastern Standard time, on December 13, 2001, no additional subsidiaries of the Company had filed voluntary petitions for relief under chapter 11 of the Bankruptcy Code in the Bankruptcy Court. The Debtors manage, and will continue to manage, their properties and operate their businesses as "debtors-in-possession" under the jurisdiction of the Bankruptcy Court and in accordance with the applicable provisions of the Bankruptcy Code.

On December 2, 2001, the Company issued a press release relating to the foregoing, a copy of which is attached hereto as Exhibit 99.1 and incorporated herein by reference.

On December 3, 2001, the Company and certain of its subsidiaries received binding commitments for a $1.5 billion debtor-in-possession revolving crecit facility (the "DIP Facility"), subject to the satisfaction of certain conditions precedent. The DIP Facility is being provided by JPMorgan Chase Bank and Citicorp USA, Inc.

On December 3, 2001, the Bankruptcy Court entered an interim order approving, among other things, a loan of up to $250 million of the commitments under the DIP Facility to the Company and certain of its subsidiaries. On December 3, 2001, the Company issued a press release relating to the DIP Facility, a copy of which is attached hereto as Exhibit 99.2 and incorporated herein by reference.

Unfortunately, Enron's prior trail of 8-Ks gave little indication that the bankruptcy was coming. But as we were later to learn, the main reason there was no warning of the company's pending financial demise was blatant dishonesty by the company's officers as well as its accountants at Arthur Anderson. Enron was simply hiding the truth.

In most cases, however, companies will be honest in their filings, and their 8-K reports could provide some honest insight into their significant actions and developments.

EARNINGS GUIDANCE

Analysts are particularly interested in 8-K reports that deal with a company's projected earnings. If a company determines that its earnings or revenue may not meet previous projections, it has an obligation to issue an 8-K report (which typically also doubles as a press release) to revise their projected numbers. That can have a dramatic affect on the stock price. We see an example of this in Chapter 9 with an 8-K report from Best Buy that lowered the company's projected earnings estimate and caused the stock price to drop about 50 percent in one day.

Let's look at another example—an excerpt of an 8-K report from Maytag in September of 1999 that caused the stock to drop about 40 percent in one day:

Maytag 3Q 1999 Results to Approximate 3Q 1998

NEWTON, Iowa—(September 10, 1999)—Maytag Corporation announced it expects results for the third quarter 1999 to approximate its record earnings per share (EPS) performance in the third quarter 1998, but will not meet the consensus earnings estimate of $.99 published by First Call. For the quarter, Maytag sees a modest increase in sales revenue with earnings per share approximating the normalized $.84 that was reported in the third quarter 1998.

Maytag indicated third quarter results, compared to the prior year, will be influenced primarily by lower unit volume at the mid to lower price points in home appliances, where the corporation has yet to fully develop and implement its innovation strategy. For the quarter, the overall strength in premium brand appliances likely will not be sufficient to offset continued share erosion at the mid to low price points. Inventory adjustments, due to lower than expected unit volume in home appliances, are expected to result in higher operating costs and inefficiencies compared to the prior year.

Additionally, the corporation's sales, general, and administrative expenses will approximate the levels experienced in the first and second quarters of 1999, but will be higher compared to last year's third quarter. The higher year over year SG&A is related primarily to initiatives aimed at extracting more growth from the current product line-up and initiatives to deliver future growth by driving innovation more rapidly, especially in premium brands.

In this 8-K, Maytag lays out several bits of bad news:

- Earnings per share were not expected to meet previous projections.

- The company faces lower unit sales volume for its mid- and lower-priced appliances.

- Sales, general, and administrative expenses were expected to be higher than the previous year.

Investors reacted immediately to the announcement by selling off Maytag stock in huge volume. On that day, trading volume was about five times the normal level and the share price dropped from a high of $56 to a low of $35 before bouncing back a little to close at $41.

If you want to stay abreast of the latest developments involving your stocks of interest, it pays to keep a close eye on the 8-K filings. But you'd better be prepared to act quickly. An 8-K with significant news can be a bombshell in the market.

C H A P T E R

12

GEMS ON THE WEB: OTHER SITES TO SEE FOR VITAL STOCK RESEARCH

EDGAR **IS NOT THE ONLY SPOT ON THE W**EB to find valuable, in-depth information on thousands of stocks. There are hundreds, if not thousands, of great commercial sites you can use, absolutely *free,* to augment the research available at EDGAR. There are so many investment sites, in fact, that you need a road map to find the ones with the best information.

Investment Web sites can assist you in a number of ways. They can help you track your portfolio and keep up with the latest news and developments on the stocks that are of interest to you. They can offer detailed information on business, the stock market, and the economy. They provide a multitude of performance charts, graphs, and tables on every stock, as well as a vast range of ratios, growth rates, analysts ratings, earnings estimates, and other current data on who's buying, who's selling, and who's holding. In fact, some sites even offer very specific stock ratings with pros, cons, and detailed analysis.

This chapter shows you which sites might be best to explore, and what to look for in analyzing stocks online. First, let's look at some of the features that you can take advantage of at many of the top online research sites:

- **Stock screening.** Looking for stocks that will meet your very specific criteria? Do you want low-P/E stocks, high-growth stocks, small-cap stocks, high-dividend stocks, or stocks with great return on equity? Are you looking for tech stocks that have posted at least 15-percent revenue growth the past few years, or retail stocks that have posted 20-percent earnings growth the past three years? Or would you prefer a high-dividend stock with a low P/E that has had earnings and revenue growth of at least 15 percent per year? Whatever it is that you're looking for in a stock, you can find it by using the stock-screening tools offered by many of the top investment sites.

- **Track history.** Many online sites offer financial histories, including quarterly earnings and revenue figures that go back several years. It's helpful to look through a company's financial history to see if it posts steady increases in earnings and revenue and other key financial items.

- **Stock price history.** How has the stock price done from year to year, month to month, week to week, or day to day? Many sites provide stock histories, some with graphs, others with the actual numbers. A company's stock price history can give you a good idea of its long-term stability and short-term momentum.

- **Financial ratios and other measures.** Find out a stock's P/E, price-to-sales, return on equity, return on investment, debt-to-equity, current ratio, quick ratio, book value, dividend yield, and other key measures of success. Then compare it to other stocks and to its industry average. Some sites (such as *multexinvestor.com*) provide a broad range of specialized measures designed to reveal the stock's true value.

- **Quarterly and annual balance sheets.** Check out every detail of the company's most recent fiscal returns, both for recent quarters and years, at many online financial sites. You can look at revenue, cash flow, net income, and a variety of other key factors on the balance sheet.

- **News reports.** Learn the latest news on any company by searching through its press reports available at dozens of financial sites. You can also learn about upcoming earnings announcements and industry news that could affect the price of your stocks.

- **Analysts' recommendations and projected earnings.** View analysts' recommendations and earnings projections on thousands of stocks at most of the leading investment sites. But buyer beware! As sorry investors learned during the Internet crash, even if a unanimous consensus of analysts offer a stock the highest possible recommendation, that may mean nothing. Many a $200-a-share Internet stock with a "strong buy" consensus among analysts covering the stock are now trading for pennies a share—or are out of business altogether. Not to paint all analysts with the same brush—because there are excellent ones who generally know what they're doing—but many analysts are sheep who follow the crowd. Others are too intimidated by the companies they're covering to give a bad stock the low rating it deserves. That's why it is best to do your own thorough analysis first, and use the analysts' recommendations only as one small factor in deciding whether or not to buy (or sell) a stock.

- **Stock ratings.** Some sites offer free stock ratings, with detailed analysis of the company and its potential for growth. If you're on the fence on a particular stock that you are considering buying or selling, these stock-rating features may help influence your decision one way or the other. These ratings tend to be more detailed and more revealing than the analyst reports, maybe even more accurate. But again, do your own analysis first, and use the stock-rating features as yet another factor to consider in making your final decision.

- **Annual and 10k reports.** Although the easiest place to find 10-K reports is EDGAR, many sites do offer convenient links to 10-K and annual reports. You can also find annual reports and links to 10-Ks and other financial reports in the Web sites of most publicly-traded companies.

WHERE TO FIND IT

With so many financial sites on the Web, you could search for hours to find a site with the specific type of stock information you need. To make your search a little easier, here is a road map to some vital-yet-hard-to-find research information and tools on the Web.

Six-year financial tables. Look back six years for earnings, revenue, net income and a variety of other financial items for thousands of stocks. Go to *www.businessweek.com.*

Four-year financials with quarterly numbers. For more details on a company's growth, you can find earnings and revenue numbers for each quarter over the past four years. Go to *www.multexinvestor.com.*

Company snapshot. Get a full glimpse of a stock's current status, including stock price, 52-week highs and lows, dividend information, current ratio, quick ratio, return on equity, return on assets, return on investment, book value, price-earnings ratio, price-to-sales ratio, and other key measures. Go to *www.multexinvestor.com* and *money.cnn.com.*

In-depth company profiles. Find long, informative corporate profiles on thousands of stocks. Go to *www.businessweek.com.*

Earnings reports calendar. Which corporate earnings reports are coming up? Find out at *www.bloomberg.com.*

Earnings news and profit warnings. See which companies recently came out with earnings reports or profit warnings. You have many choices, including *www.bloomberg.com*, *cbs.marketwatch.com*, and *money.cnn.com.*

Stock ratings. Looking for another opinion on a stock? There are a couple of good sites to visit for free stock analysis—*Quicken* and *CNBC.*

The *Quicken* site has a "One click scorecard" and "Stock Evaluator," which provide detailed analysis of each stock, including ratings for revenue growth, income growth, cash flow, return on equity, price-earnings ratios, and other measures, as well as analysis of growth trends, financial health, management performance, and intrinsic value. It also has a chart that shows if the stock's current price is in the recommended "buy" range.

The *CNBC* site offers rating summaries for hundreds of stocks, including, a pro and con breakdown, a rating and analysis section, and a short-term outlook for each stock. Go to *www.quicken.com* and *moneycentral.msn.com.*

Historical stock quotes. Get daily, weekly, or monthly stock prices going back many years, including high, low, open, close, and volume. Go to *www.businessweek.com* and *www.wallstreetcity.com.*

TOP FREE SITES FOR INVESTORS

Which sites offer the best investment information on the Web? Because there are so many sites from which to choose, I've tried to narrow the field to the very best free financial sites based on their depth of current and historic information on stocks, the market, the economy, and general business. Many of the sites profiled here provide some unique features not available anywhere else on the Web. Almost every financial site—including the ones listed here—offers stock quotes and some basic information about individual stocks and their recent performance. Most also have a portfolio tracker, stock-screening features, other investment tools and calculators, company news and earnings

FIGURE 12-1

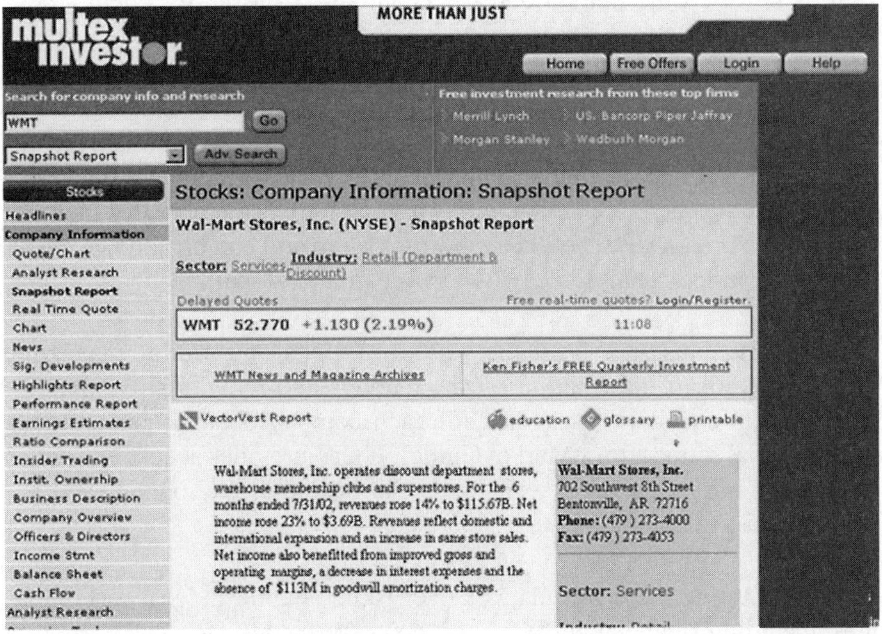

Perhaps the best free site on the Web for stock market investors interested in in-depth research, MultexInvestor offers a wealth of financial information on every stock.

reports, and stories on investing and the markets. But some sites are definitely better than others.

Here are some of the leading free investment sites.

Bloomberg.com. Operated by the financial news and media services company founded by New York City Mayor Michael Bloomberg, this site contains a wealth of information on business, market news, market trends, stocks, bonds, mutual funds, and economics, as well as original columns by *Bloomberg* writers. Its coverage of individual stocks is adequate but not exceptional, but the site does offer some excellent resources for serious investors. Go to *www.bloomberg.com.*

BusinessWeek Online. This site, produced by *Business Week* and Standard and Poor's, offers up-to-the-minute market information, tons of articles on business and the markets, and some great information on individual stocks for investors. The stock information includes current quotes, historical quotes, analysts' estimates, insider trading, in-depth profiles, six-year financial reports, and other stock data and graphs. Go to *www.businessweek.com.*

CBS MarketWatch. This site offers stock quotes and other information, as well as news on the market and the economy. It has an excellent stock-screening tool. Go to *cbs.marketwatch.com.*

CNBC online. CNBC's financial information is offered through Microsoft's *MSN.com.* You'll find plenty of information on stocks and the market, including the standard quotes, charts, financial histories, and earnings estimates. It also offers one other excellent feature—a stock-rating summary that includes a rating and brief analysis of the stock, with a pro and con breakdown, and a short-term outlook analysis. Go to *moneycentral.msn.com.*

CNNMoney. This site, from the editors of CNN and *Money* magazine, offers a wealth of information on the markets and individual companies, including an excellent "snapshot" of each company's stock performance and financial ratios (from Market Guide). It also provides access to articles in *Money*, and many other articles on the business, the market, and the economy. Go to *money.cnn.com.*

Hoover's Online. Extensive data on over 10,000 public and private companies, including financial performance, news, Web addresses, and corporate profiles. You can find a lot of good information on individual stocks at *Hoover's*, although much of the best information is available only to subscribers. Go to *www.hoovers.com.*

MultexInvestor. Perhaps the best free site on the Web for stock market investors interested in in-depth research, *MultexInvestor* offers a wealth of financial information on every stock. Its best offering is its snapshot report that includes current stock price, 52-week highs and lows, dividend information, current ratio, quick ratio, return on equity, return on assets, return on investment, book value, price-earnings ratio, price-to-sales ratio, and other key measures. The site also gives investors the option of ordering stock research reports from a range of brokerage houses and independent research firms over the Internet. Although some of the reports are free, most are offered on a pay-per-view basis. The only drawback to the site is that you get an annoying pop-up ad every time you click from one item to another. Go to *www.multexinvestor.com.* (See Figure 12-1.)

Quicken.com. Outstanding financial site with a wealth of information on individual stocks. One of its best attractions is its stock analysis section that includes a "One click scorecard" and a "Stock Evaluator" that provide a detailed analysis of each stock, including ratings for revenue growth, income growth, cash flow, return on equity, price-earnings ratios, and other measures. It also provides analysis of growth trends, financial health, management performance, and intrinsic value. In addition, it has a chart that shows if the stock's current price is in the recommended "buy" range. Go to *www.quicken.com.*

Reuters.com. The site offers excellent market and business news and some financial information on stocks. Go to *www.reuters.com.*

SmartMoney.com. This site provides a great depth of information on each stock, as well as many timely, original stories on business, the economy, and the stock market. Go to *www.smartmoney.com.*

Wall Street City. This site includes articles on business, the economy, and the market, and a great deal of information and tables on individual stocks. It also provides historical stock quotes. Go to *www.wallstreetcity.com.*

Yahoo!Finance.com. This is one of the most comprehensive sites on the Web for information on individual stocks. You can also read market news and research, scan the message boards for the latest rumors, or create a custom portfolio. Although the site is a little too helter-skelter, it may be worth the eyestrain—*Yahoo!Finance* contains a vast amount of information on every stock. Go to *finance.yahoo.com.*

For free research, those sites are among the best on the Web, but there are certainly many others worth exploring.

AND A FEW MORE

There are some sites on the Web that charge a subscription that are also popular with investors. *America Online* (which is a subscription site) has a huge section on stocks and investing, with some great screening tools, historic stock quotes, and detailed financial information on thousands of stocks. Other outstanding subscription sites that might aid your investment research include *TheStreet.com, ValueLine.com*, and *The Wall Street Journal Online* (*http://online.wsj.com/public/us*).

You also might want to check out a few other free sites that offer some unique features:

- *Allstarstocks.com*, which offers stock quotes, financial information, news, market updates, stock screening, educational articles, model portfolios, original articles by Gene Walden, and links to all of the top investment sites mentioned here (*allstarstocks.com*)

- *InvestorGuide* (*www.investorguide.com*), which includes a wide range of information on investing, and well-organized links to hundreds of other investment Web sites

- *Gazebo* (*www.gazebo.com*), a relatively new site that offers preselected portfolios geared to both bull and bear markets

- *WebFN*, which presents live, online television programming covering the market and investment issues with a steady lineup of top national experts (including regular appearances by Gene Walden) from 8 a.m. to 8 p.m. EST (*www.webfn.com*)

- *Fool.com*, the Internet home of investing's Motley Fool (*www.fool.com*)

- *Morningstar.com,* a very comprehensive research site for both stocks and mutual funds that offers some free information and some subscription services

- *MSCI.com* (operated by Morgan Stanley Dean Witter), which is the best site on the Web for information on the foreign stock markets—includes up-to-date performance data on all foreign markets, including both the major markets and the emerging markets (*www.msci.com*)

There is clearly no shortage of stock market information on the Internet. By exploring EDGAR and some of the Web sites featured here, you can uncover a veritable encyclopedia of information on nearly every stock on the market.

There's no guarantee that the numbers you uncover will always be honest—particularly until the SEC does a better job policing corporate accounting practices—nor that the trends you detect will continue to work in the company's favor. But if you're willing to take the time to navigate that complex maze of line items and footnotes—past the false leads, the wrong turns, and the dead ends that come with every corporate financial report—you should be able to assemble an outstanding portfolio of solid, blue chip stocks.

All the tools you need are at your fingertips—and they're all yours for *free*!

SEC OFFICES

The Securities and Exchange Commission has twelve offices across the country:

SEC Headquarters
450 Fifth Street, NW
Washington, DC 20549
Office of Investor Education and Assistance
(202) 942-7040
email: *help@sec.gov*

Northeast Regional Office
Wayne M. Carlin, Regional Director
233 Broadway
New York, NY 10279
(646) 428-1500
email: *newyork@sec.gov*

Boston District Office
Juan M. Marcelino, District Administrator
73 Tremont Street, Suite 600
Boston, MA 02108-3912
(617) 424-5900
email: *boston@sec.gov*

Philadelphia District Office
Ronald C. Long, District Administrator
The Curtis Center, Suite 1120E.
601 Walnut Street
Philadelphia, PA 19106-3322
(215) 597-3100
email: *philadelphia@sec.gov*

Southeast Regional Office
David Nelson, Regional Director
1401 Brickell Avenue, Suite 200
Miami, FL 33131
(305) 536-4700
email: *miami@sec.gov*

Atlanta District Office
Richard P. Wessel, District Administrator
3475 Lenox Road, N.E., Suite 1000
Atlanta, GA 30326-1232
(404) 842-7600
email: *atlanta@sec.gov*

Midwest Regional Office
Mary Keefe, Regional Director
175 W. Jackson Boulevard
Suite 900
Chicago, IL 60604
(312) 353-7390
email: *chicago@sec.gov*

Central Regional Office
Randall J. Fons, Regional Director
1801 California Street, Suite 4800
Denver, CO 80202-2648
(303) 844-1000
email: *denver@sec.gov*

Fort Worth District Office
Harold F. Degenhardt, District Administrator
801 Cherry Street, 19th Floor
Fort Worth, TX 76102
(817) 978-3821
email: *dfw@sec.gov*

Salt Lake District Office
Kenneth D. Israel, Jr., District Administrator
500 Key Bank Tower, Suite 500
50 South Main Street
Salt Lake City, UT 84144-0402
(801) 524-5796
email: *saltlake@sec.gov*

Pacific Regional Office
Randall R. Lee, Regional Director
5670 Wilshire Boulevard, 11th Floor
Los Angeles, CA 90036-3648
(323) 965-3998
email: *losangeles@sec.gov*

San Francisco District Office
Helane Morrison, District Administrator
44 Montgomery Street, Suite 1100
San Francisco, CA 94104
(415) 705-2500
email: *sanfrancisco@sec.gov*

USEFUL TELEPHONE NUMBERS AT THE SEC

SEC Toll-Free Investor Information Service:
1-800-SEC-0330
To obtain free publications and investor alerts, learn how to file a complaint, and contact the SEC.

Information Line (General SEC Information):
(202) 942-8088
TTY: (202) 942-7114

Personnel Locator:
(202) 942-4150
TTY: (202) 942-4095

Public Affairs:
(202) 942-0020
For press inquiries.

Public Reference:
(202) 942-8090
TTY: (202) 942-8092
For obtaining copies of public Commission records such as corporate filings and notices of Commission action.

Division of Corporation Finance, Office of Chief Counsel:
(202) 942-2900

Division of Investment Management:
See *Division of Investment Management: Directory of Telephone Numbers and E-Mail Addresses.*

Division of Market Regulation, Office of Interpretation and Guidance:
(202) 942-0069

EDGAR Filer Support (Office of Filings and Information Services):
(202) 942-8900

EDGAR Filing Fee Information (Office of Filings and Information Services):
(202) 942-8989

Filing Desk for Paper Filings (Office of Filings and Information Services):
(202) 942-8050

Investor Assistance and Complaints:
(202) 942-7040
TTY: (202) 942-7065

Office of Municipal Securities:
(202) 942-7300

Publications Unit:
(202) 942-4040
For obtaining blank copies of SEC forms (BD, 144, etc.) and other SEC publications.

Regional and District Offices:
See *SEC Addresses: HQ, Regional, and District Offices.*

Branch of Registrations and Examinations (Office of Filings and Information Services):
(202) 942-8980

Office of the Secretary:
(202) 942-7070

Office of Small Business - Small Business Ombudsman; Division of Corporation Finance:
(202) 942-2950
http://www.sec.gov/contact/2phones.htm

SEC DIRECTORY

Toll-Free Consumer Information No.   1-800-SEC-0330
Investor Information and Complaints   (202) 942-7240
Filings by Registered Companies   (202) 942-8090
Forms and Publications   (202) 942-4040
Instant Information Recording   (202) 942-8088
Personnel Locator   (202) 942-4150
SEC Web site   *http://www.sec.gov*
For deaf/hard-of-hearing persons, please use relay service at 711 to make calls
to any of the numbers listed above.

COMMISSIONERS	TERMS EXPIRE JUNE 5
Harvey L. Pitt, Chairman	
942-0100	2007
Isaac C. Hunt, Jr.	
942-0500 (Recess appointment)	2005
Cynthia A. Glassman	
942-0600 (Recess appointment)	2006

PRINCIPAL OFFICES

Division of Corporation Finance
Alan L. Beller, Director
942-2800

Division of Enforcement
Stephen M. Cutler, Director
942-4500

Division of Investment Management
Paul F. Roye, Director
942-0720

Division of Market Regulation
Annette L. Nazareth, Director
942-0090

Office of Administrative Law Judges
Brenda P. Murray, Chief Administrative Law Judge
942-0399

Office of Administrative and Personnel Management
Jayne L. Seidman, Associate Executive Director
(Administration/Personnel)
942-4000

Office of the Chief Accountant
Robert K. Herdman, Chief Accountant
942-4400

Office of Compliance Inspections and Examinations
Lori A. Richards, Director
942-7400

Office of Economic Analysis
Lawrence E. Harris, Chief Economist
942-8020

Office of Equal Employment Opportunity
Deborah K. Balducchi, Director
942-0040

Office of the Executive Director
James M. McConnell, Executive Director
942-4300

Office of Filings and Information Services
Kenneth A. Fogash, Associate Executive Director
942-8938

Office of Financial Management
Margaret J. Carpenter, Associate Executive Director
(Finance)
942-0340

Office of Freedom of Information and Privacy Act Operations
Barry D. Walters, FOIA Officer
942-4320

Office of the General Counsel
Giovanni P. Prezioso, General Counsel
942-0900

Office of Information Technology
Michael E. Bartell, Associate Executive Director, Chief
Information Officer
942-8800

Office of the Inspector General
Walter J. Stachnik, Inspector General
942-4461

Office of International Affairs
Felice Friedman, Acting Director
942-2770

Office of Investor Education and Assistance
Susan Ferris Wyderko, Director
942-7040

Office of Legislative Affairs
Jane O. Cobb, Director
942-0010

Office of Public Affairs
Christi Harlan, Director
942-0020

Office of the Secretary
Jonathan G. Katz, Secretary
942-7070

Director of Communications
Brian J. Gross
942-0010

COMPLETE ALPHABETICAL LIST OF SEC PUBLICATIONS

About Settling Trades in Three Days: Introducing T+3 (also in print)

About the SEC's Office of Investor Education and Assistance

Affinity Fraud: How to Avoid Investment Scams That Target Groups

After-Hours Trading: Understanding the Risks

All About Auditors

Analyzing Analyst Recommendations

Arbitration Procedures

Ask Questions (also in print)

Bankruptcy: What Happens When Public Companies Go Bankrupt (also in print)

Broken Promises: Promissory Note Fraud

Certificates of Deposit: Tips for Investors

Cold Calling: Unsolicited Calls from Brokers (also in print)

Compliance Guide to the Registration and Regulation of Brokers and Dealers (also in print)

Complaints and Inquiries (also in print)

Day Trading Margin Requirements: Know the Rules (tips from NASD)

Day Trading: Your Dollars at Risk

Facts on Saving and Investing: 1999 Report on Financial Literacy (also in print)

The Fleecing of Foreign Investors: Avoid Getting Burned by "Hot" U.S. Stocks

Financial Facts Tool Kit

Form for Taking Notes (also in print)

Get Info About Companies

Get the Facts on Saving and Investing

"High Yields" and Hot Air

Holding Your Securities—Get the Facts UPDATED!

International Investing: Get the Facts

Internet Fraud: How to Avoid Internet Investment Scams

Invest Wisely

INDEX

About the Author

Gene Walden is the author of more than 20 books on investing, including such classics as *The 100 Best Stocks to Own in America* and *The 100 Best Mutual Funds to Own in America.* Walden has been a contributor to *The Wall Street Journal, Investor's Business Daily,* and other influential publications and has also been a columnist for *Your Money, OnMoney.com,* and other magazines and Web sites. He has been a frequent guest on CNBC's *Power Lunch* and has appeared on every major television network as well as hundreds of local and regional programs. He operates a popular investment Web site at www.allstarstocks.com.